THE COFFEE TASTING HANDBOOK

TIM RIDLEY

MITCHELL
BEAZLEY

Contents

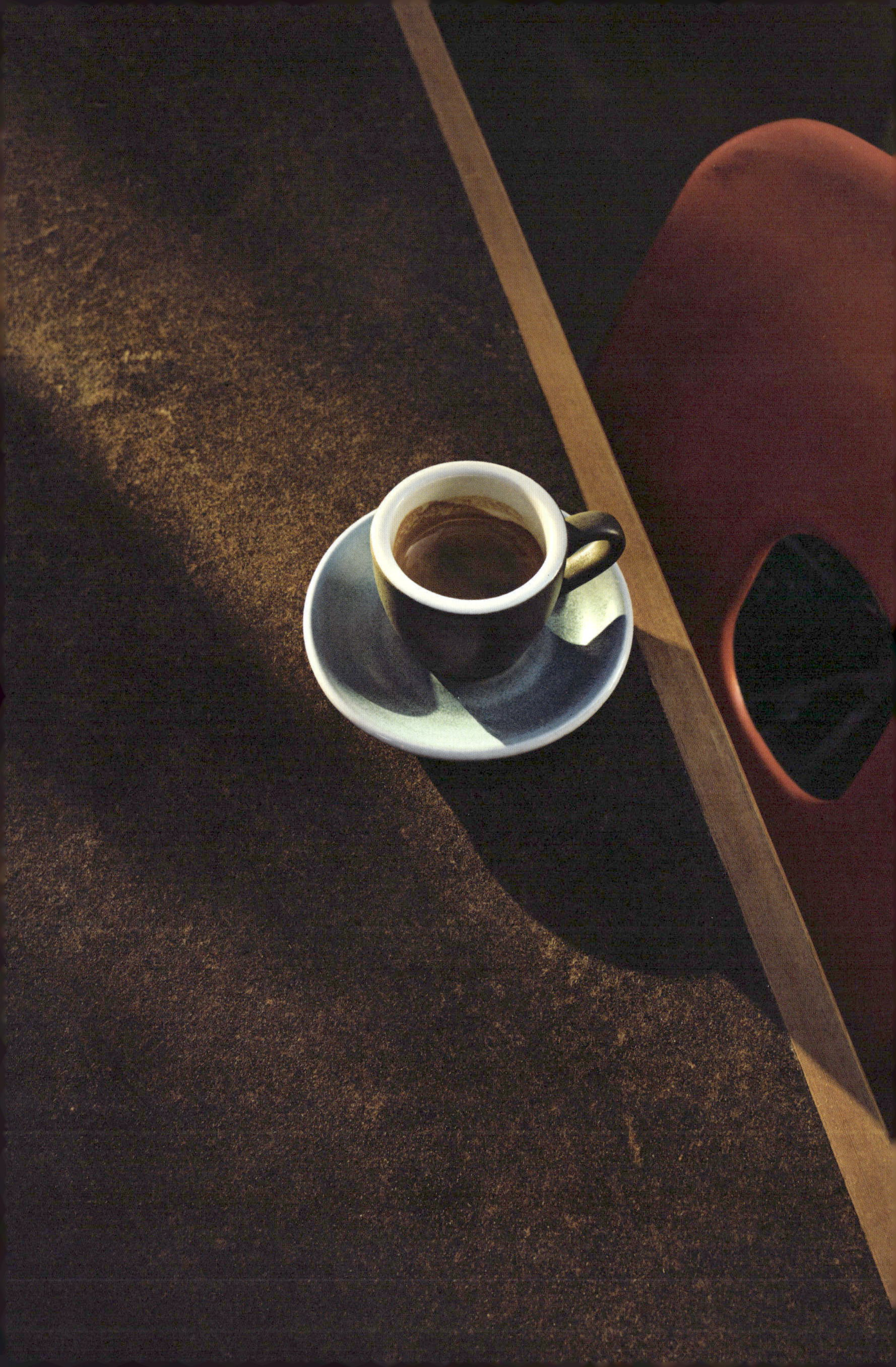

Getting Started Tasting Coffee

In the pursuit of the best coffees for you, let's focus on something that is of great importance: identifying the coffees that give you the greatest pleasure. The simple hedonistic joy of drinking coffee is often overlooked and taken too little into account when considering the purpose of tasting coffee. Quality is important, but we're going to put tastiness front and centre. As we will discover, there is often little correlation between a cup score and the capacity a coffee has to give you that unique blend of satisfaction and delight.

This handbook equips you to identify each coffee's defining characteristics. The subsequent chapters address specific elements of tasting. To parse coffee's tasting notes and identify suitable coffees requires a knowledge of the primary tastes, an appreciation of the spectrum of possible flavours and aromas, and an understanding of the key concepts of balance and alignment.

But as well as developing a good understanding of coffee, it's also important to appreciate your own coffee-drinking habits and predilections. By the end of this chapter, and before we even pick up a cup, you'll be able to identify your own coffee-drinking expectations.

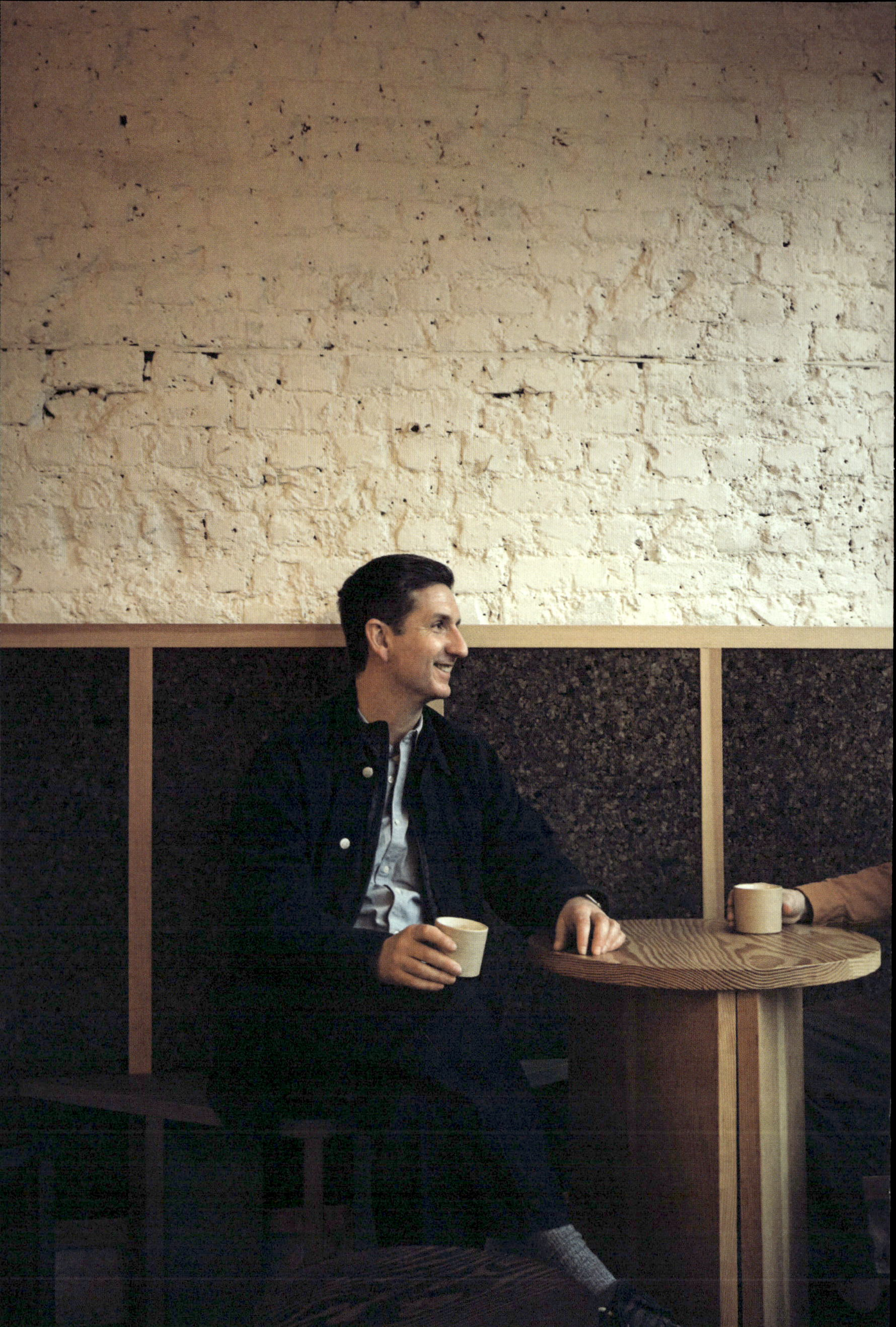

The World's Favourite Drink

A QUICK HISTORY OF COFFEE

People love drinking coffee. With hundreds of possible aromatic compounds, each cup of coffee is packed full of distinctive flavours. It's the most complex drink that many people consume.

The array of flavours can be overwhelming, but delicious coffees have an orderly structure. Understanding its characteristics will help you navigate each coffee, regardless of its origin, variety or process. It will then be much easier to choose coffee that you enjoy. With millions of different coffees available each year, there's a coffee for everyone.

One of the best ways to start an exploration of coffee's flavours is to take a quick tour through coffee's history. We start in the highlands of Ethiopia, twist and turn as coffee drinking spreads across the globe, and then arrive at the forebears of today's coffee shops. This journey helps us put coffee tasting in context and explains why coffee has become the world's favourite beverage.

THE WORLD'S FIRST BARISTA

Coffee's founding myth starts in the ninth century with a twenty-something named Kaldi. He endured a day job that he found boring and unrewarding but was destined to become the world's first barista.

Kaldi was tasked with tending his family's goats but, by all accounts, he was not a natural farmer. Idealistic and given to flights of fancy, he found the work lonely and isolating. His father thought Kaldi was guiding the herd through the forest-covered hills above the village. But most days he would decamp to a remote glade, let the goats wander freely and pass the hours daydreaming, keen to rejoin the conviviality of the village at dusk.

As the villagers returned from work and gathered around the evening fire, a different aspect of Kaldi stirred. He was by nature an entertainer and delighted in the dramatic. After everyone had eaten, he would perform gripping tales of how he had led his flock to previously unvisited valleys, protected the goats from wild beasts or cavorted with beautiful women from neighbouring villages.

These stories were too fanciful for the other goatherds. They were practical men with little need for dreams. Jealous at his ability to capture the villagers' attention, they would roll their eyes and mock his jokes. But they were also charmed. Aware they had to awake before dawn, the goatherds would turn in while the night was young, but never before Kaldi's first performance.

It was Kaldi's lack of sleep that led his goats to discover the life-enhancing properties of the coffee cherry. The story goes that Kaldi drifted off one afternoon leaving the goats unattended. He woke to find his herd dancing on their hindquarters and having a jolly good time. Instead of assuming he was dreaming again, he got up to find out what was going on. Having roamed deeper into the forest than the other herds, his goats had discovered a rare shrub. While its dark-green leaves did not make good eating, the bright-red cherries made the goats giddy with energy.

Today's Ethiopian coffee ceremony is the strongest link we have to the earliest days of coffee

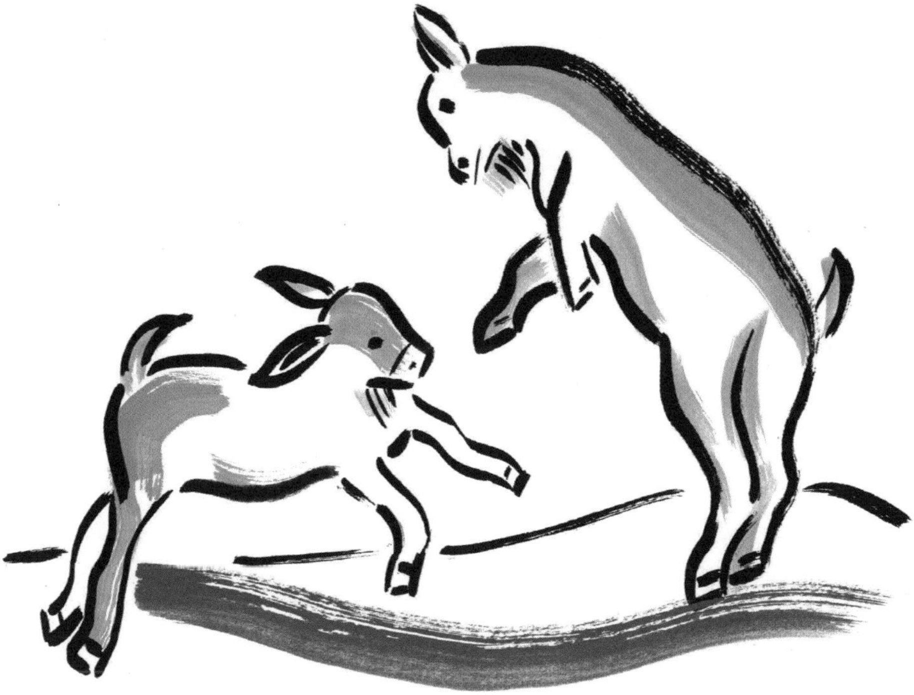

Kaldi has earned his place in coffee's origin story because he was self-composed enough to be unperturbed by the goats' peculiar behaviour, curious enough to want to know what was happening and open-minded enough to join in. In eating the red cherries, he was the first person to experience coffee's caffeine kick. Most tales leave Kaldi dancing with his goats. I think it's better to imagine this warm-hearted young man picking as many cherries as he could before returning to the village to share his experience. The atmosphere in the village as he told this tale, and shared the cherries, must have been magical.

Today's Ethiopian coffee ceremony is the strongest link we have to the earliest days of coffee. The ceremony takes place around an open fire. Freshly cut grass is spread over the ground. The seeds from coffee cherries are roasted in a cast-iron pan before being ground with stone tools. The ground coffee is placed into water, which simmers in a clay pot.

The brew is dark and thick. While the coffee is prepared, people gather around the fire to chat, gossip and share ideas. It is traditional to add ghee and salt to the bitter brew. If you joined a coffee ceremony in Ethiopia today, you would also likely be served salty popcorn or peanuts.

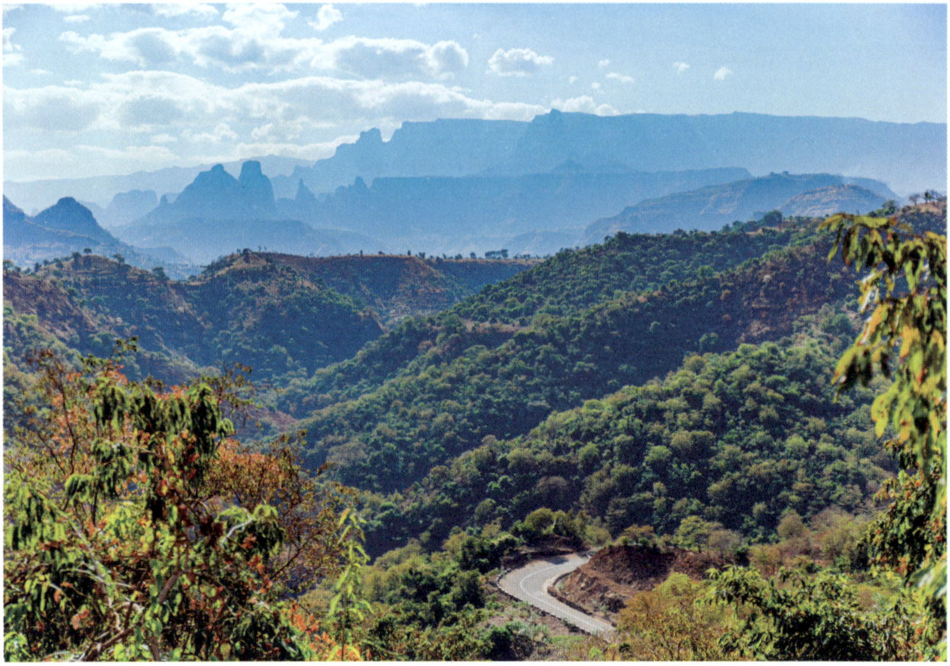

THE RISE OF THE COFFEE MERCHANTS

Coffee conquered the world slowly. The Ethiopian Highlands are the only place in the world where *Coffea arabica* is indigenous. Every arabica plant ever grown is a descendant of the shrubs found there.

Awareness of coffee spread faster than its cultivation. Each coffee 'bean' is the seed of a coffee cherry. Once the cherry is harvested, its flesh is removed and the seed is dried. At this stage the seed is a pale-green colour. Today coffee is exported from origin in this 'green' state. Dried seeds are sufficiently stable to be packed into large sacks and shipped by sea to coffee drinkers around the world.

The Solomonic emperors who governed Ethiopia in the 14th century were frequently at war with their immediate neighbours, so their main export market for coffee was across the Red Sea on the Arabian Peninsula. Demand in Yemen quickly outstripped Ethiopian supply, largely because cherries were still foraged from the wild-growing shrubs in the highlands.

It didn't take the enterprising Yemeni merchants long to identify the source of the beans and subsequently initiate coffee cultivation at home. No longer was coffee grown wild; commercial farms were established to meet the rising local demand.

The archetypical expression of this initial stage of coffee's global expansion was the Sufi mystics, who consumed coffee to both stay awake during night prayers and to enter a state that was a little closer to the divine. But within decades of first arriving in Yemen, coffee gained popular appeal and transitioned from the sacred to the secular to the mercantile. For the first time, coffee became affordable and was established as an everyday staple. No longer drunk solely on ceremonial occasions, new coffee-drinking habits arose. A popular option was to consume dark bitter coffee with sweet dates and salty nuts.

The transformation of the green seed into a roasted bean was kept a closely held trade secret by the Yemeni merchants. They successfully incorporated the lesson of their intellectual property theft from the Ethiopians and introduced strict export controls, requiring all green coffee seeds be roasted or boiled before shipping. This deception is the reason why we still refer to coffee seeds as 'beans'.

For the next two hundred years Yemeni merchants dominated international coffee production. Their strategy allowed them to corner the market and vertically integrate coffee growing, processing, roasting and export. The profits rolled in as global sales surged. It is a textbook example of cornering a market that remains the envy of today's multinational coffee corporations.

The Yemeni merchants' market dominance was eventually broken by Baba Budan, a 16th-century Sufi pilgrim returning home to India through Yemen who turned his hand to smuggling when he hid seven coffee seeds inside the hem on his jacket. This was a tremendous risk as it was a crime punishable by death. But he succeeded, and from this point onwards coffee production would fan out across the tropics.

Very little coffee is grown in Yemen today, but this period echoes into the present. The port the Yemeni merchants exported from was Mokha. Every morning people throughout the world prepare coffee on a hob using a moka pot. An equal number order a mocha – a shot of espresso sweetened with chocolate and topped with steamed milk – from their coffee shop.

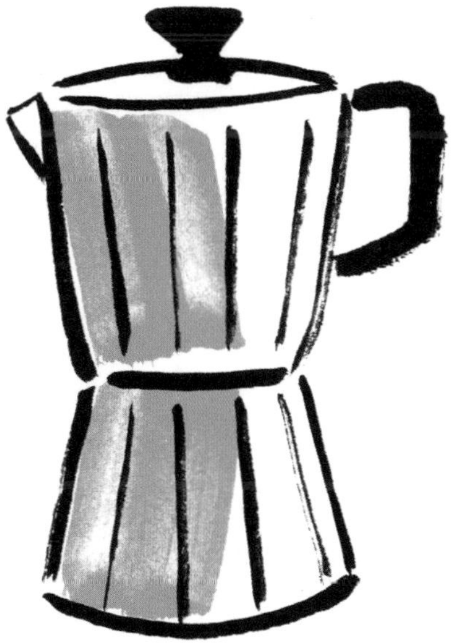

THE FIRST COFFEEHOUSES

By the middle of the 17th century coffee was gaining a foothold in Europe's capitals. Pasqua Rosée, an Ottoman Greek, opened the first coffeehouse in the City of London in 1652. He was a servant to Daniel Edwards, an English merchant at the Levant Company. They had returned together the previous year from the coastal city of Smyrna (now İzmir) in the Ottoman Empire.

While abroad, Edwards developed a coffee habit that matched his work ethic. Back in London, he started receiving friends and business contacts at home for coffee to conduct gossip and catch up on their business affairs. By today's standards two or three cups a day isn't remarkable, but this was during the Interregnum – the period between the execution of Charles in 1649 and the restoration of the monarchy in 1660. Coffee was novel and expensive. So popular were Edwards' coffee meetings that he quickly realized their commercial value and formed a business plan to profit from his hospitality.

Unable to own a coffee business because of his conditions of employment with the Levant Company, Edwards provided the capital to Rosée to run the coffeehouse. It would be both strangely familiar and completely unrecognizable to a present-day customer. Unable to afford prime rents, the establishment was tucked down an alleyway in a shed, just a minute or two from the Royal Exchange and Bank of England.

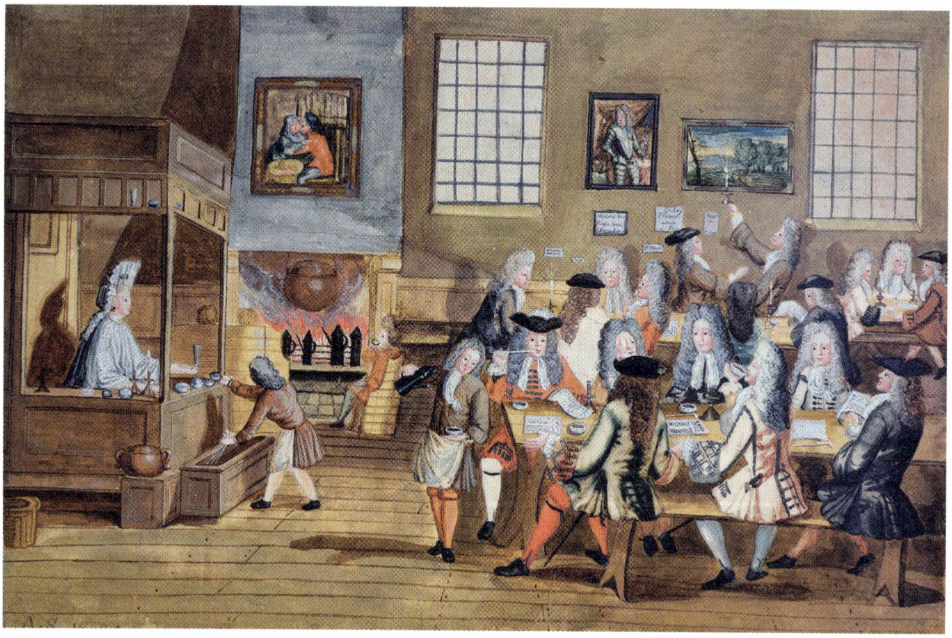

The coffeehouse quickly became packed with workers, not the type who labour with their hands, but those who trade ideas, futures and commodities. Rosée's genius was to localize the coffeehouse for English tastes. The men who frequented this establishment became more productive than their desk-bound colleagues. The caffeine increased their mental capacity, and the coffeehouse brought together and sped up their various social and information networks. It proved so popular that hundreds of other coffeehouses would open in the neighbourhood over the coming decades.

Licensing prohibited the cooking and selling of food, so, like London's espresso bars today, these coffeehouses specialized in coffee, tea and hot chocolate. Little was available to eat: coffee was most commonly consumed with dry biscuits or toast. The coffee drunk in London at this time was grown in Yemen, exported through Constantinople, the Ottoman capital, and traded via the merchants of Venice and sometimes the Dutch. Sugar was rare and a luxury, so bitter coffee was augmented with spices such as clove, cinnamon and cardamom.

By 1659 Rosée was out of the business, but those short years were transformational for London and the world. During the time of Rosée's proprietorship the Lord Protector Oliver Cromwell commenced a strategy to acquire new colonies in the Americas. The English captured Spanish-colonized Jamaica in 1655, which was already shifting agricultural production from tobacco to sugarcane.

The fundraising, underwriting and trading in the City of London, almost certainly by the men frequenting the coffeehouses, would provide the financial architecture to support sugar plantation expansion and the creation of a new triangular trading route. Finished goods were exported from Europe to Africa and sugar was brought back from the Caribbean to Europe. Completing the circuit was the transatlantic slave trade. People were captured, enslaved and transported from the West African coast across the Atlantic to the Americas to work the land in servitude. Coffee has had a complicated relationship with sugar from the very beginning.

A EUROPEAN AWAKENING

A pivotal moment in European history also marks an inflection point for coffee. Less than a decade after the London coffeehouse boom, the Ottomans embarked on their conquest of Europe. By the summer of 1683 they were making good progress, having made it as far as Vienna to which they now lay siege. The city was the gateway to Western Europe, and the continent's fate hung in the balance.

It's said that an army marches on its stomach. The Ottoman forces were making rapid progress, maybe because they were fuelled by caffeine. The empire had developed a profitable business re-exporting Yemeni coffee and the Ottoman Turks had developed a taste for it. Even with stretched supply lines, they prioritized hauling sacks of green coffee ready for roasting. The beans were roasted in a pan, finely ground and boiled with water in a small copper pot with a long handle. The technique, and the *cezve* pot, remain largely unchanged to this day.

A coalition of armies from the Holy Roman Empire, the Polish–Lithuanian Commonwealth and various German states were walled up behind Vienna's extensive fortifications. Today residents of these nations are among the largest consumers of coffee anywhere in the world, but that September their situation was increasingly desperate.

The hero of our story is an unknown baker who, rising early to prepare bread for the city's citizens, heard the faint sound of the Ottomans tunnelling beneath the city's walls. A report was sent, forces were marshalled and a counterattack was launched. The European coalition forces successfully broke the Ottoman line. Routed, the Ottoman army withdrew, and as the victorious coalition forces looted the abandoned camps they discovered sacks of green seeds. In the most entertaining version of this story, the soldiers initially overlooked this bounty thinking that the seeds were elephant feed, but they were, of course, unroasted coffee.

In another story that's probably too good to be true, the bakers of Vienna, to celebrate, created a special bread made with a laminated, salty dough folded into the shape of the Ottoman crescent. The bread is known as *kipferl* and is regarded as the progenitor of the croissant, part of the family of enriched yeast pastries collectively known as *viennoiserie*.

A distinct Viennese coffee culture emerged soon after the siege. Unlike the small, rowdy coffeehouses in London, Vienna's coffeehouses would become as grand as banks and theatres. They are showcases of urban sophistication, cosmopolitan in outlook and places for intellectual and multilingual discourse, as well as low-level tittle-tattle.

The Viennese had a sweeter tooth than the Ottomans and were richer than the English, and sugar was becoming more plentiful. The city's opulent coffeehouses came

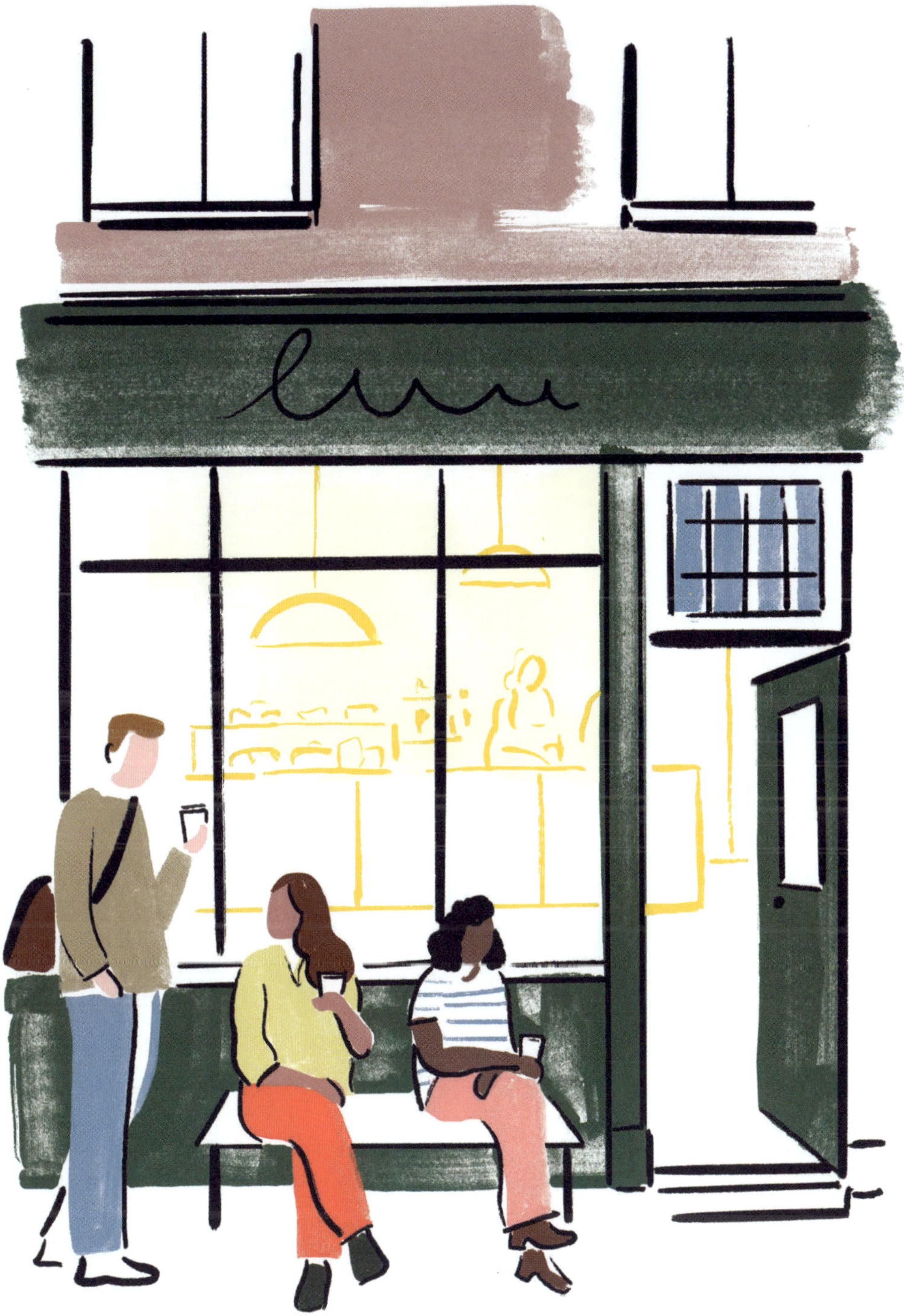

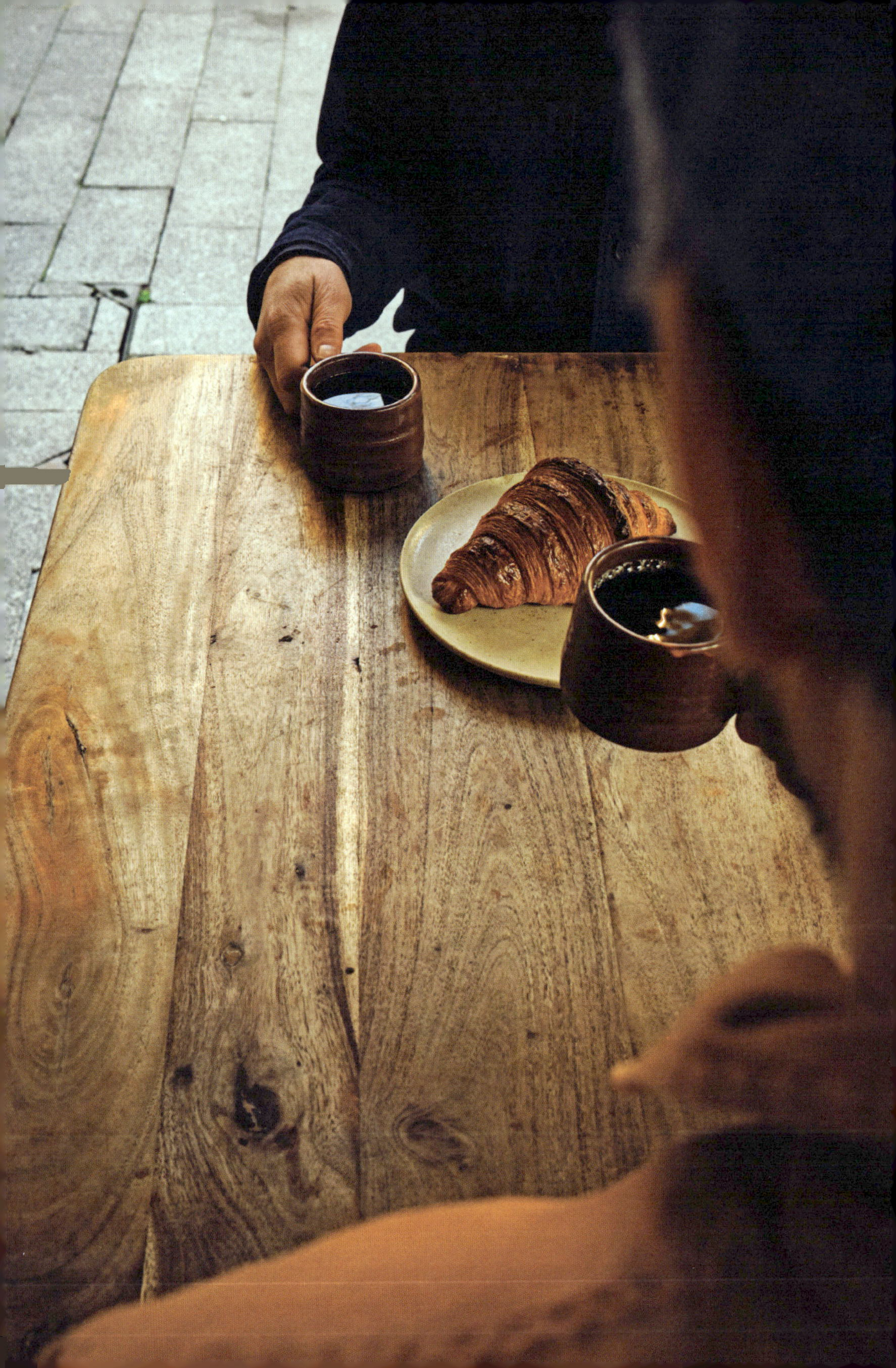

of age as both coffee and baking became increasingly luxurious. At first, milk was added to soften the bitterness, then hot milk, then cream. Sugar, once carefully rationed by the staff, became so abundant that customers were free to add as much as they wished. Sugar was used liberally in baking, to create new sweet cakes that complemented bitter coffee. The zenith of Viennese coffee culture is marked as much by the national treasures of strudel and Sachertorte as by the city's vibrant literary, artistic, musical and scientific output.

These trends endure into the present. Should you order a Viennese-style coffee today, it will arrive in a tall glass to highlight its layers. The base is a shot of espresso mixed with sweet melted chocolate; next comes a layer of hot milk, and finally a topping of sweetened whipped cream. Plus, there will probably be bittersweet chocolate grated on top. The style has many imitations and is the forerunner to the family of seasonal and signature coffee drinks, the most famous of which is the Pumpkin Spice Latte.

More generally, the combination of coffee and baking has become the global standard for coffee shops. The two fit together as though they have always coexisted. Many popular combinations started by drawing on local traditions and flavours before finding international appeal. But whatever their genesis, the pairings are almost always sweet, with a touch of bitterness and a dash of acidity.

A HISTORY OF GOOD TASTE

The templates laid down through coffee's expansion continue to shape the world today. Merchants buy coffee from producers to export to global markets. Businesses throughout the supply chain obscure coffee producers or rebrand coffee to capture a greater portion of a cup's value. The greatest mark-up still occurs when coffee is transformed. Once upon a time it was sufficient to mask a coffee's origins by roasting it; now international brands repackage ground coffee into sachets, capsules and granules.

Out of the home, coffee is inherently a social drink. Baristas enjoy working in teams, coffee drinkers appreciate the social buzz of a coffee shop, and cafés are places that blend work and pleasure.

Coffee continues to both encroach on the divine and satisfy the mercantile impulse. It is the drink we turn to when we want to be the best version of ourselves or when we need to do our best work. Coffee has always been drunk as much for its caffeine as for its flavour.

As we think about tasting coffee, it's important to recognize that, like Kaldi, coffee helps us escape the tedium of work. Like the mystic, it helps us to plot our course through the universe. Like the Ottoman warrior, it enables us to power on. It fuels the enterprising energy of the coffeehouse that brings people, ideas and capital together. And coffee continues to be a small indulgence and an everyday luxury. I hope you've had the good fortune to experience that coffee is always best shared with friends and enjoyed over good conversation.

This select edit of coffee's lore and history also reveals to us a greater, universal truth: across generations and cultures, people have enjoyed coffee by balancing the basic tastes of bitter, sour, salty and sweet. It is with this understanding of taste that our exploration of coffee's distinct and vibrant flavours begins.

Coffee continues to both encroach on the divine and satisfy the mercantile impulse

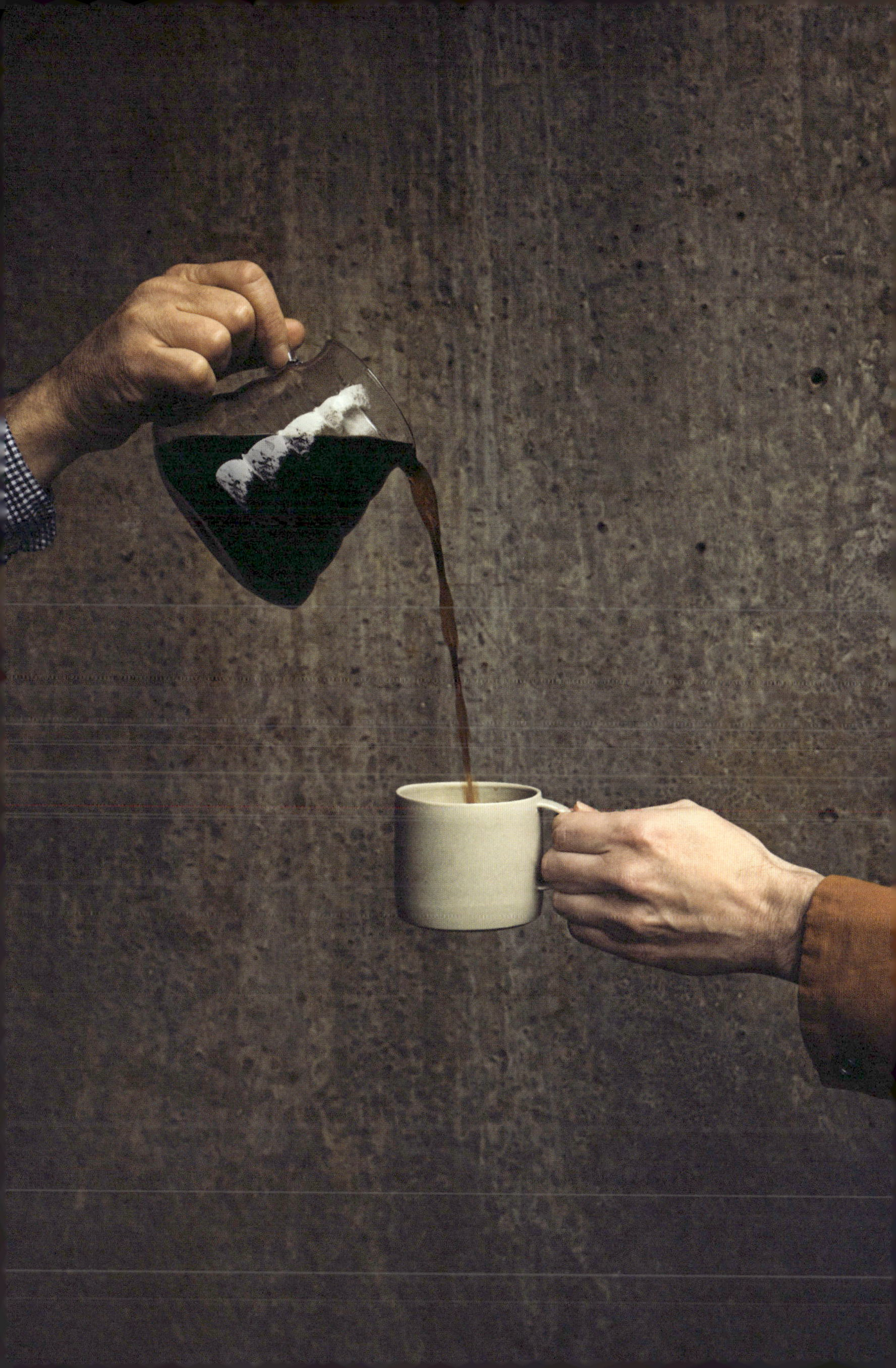

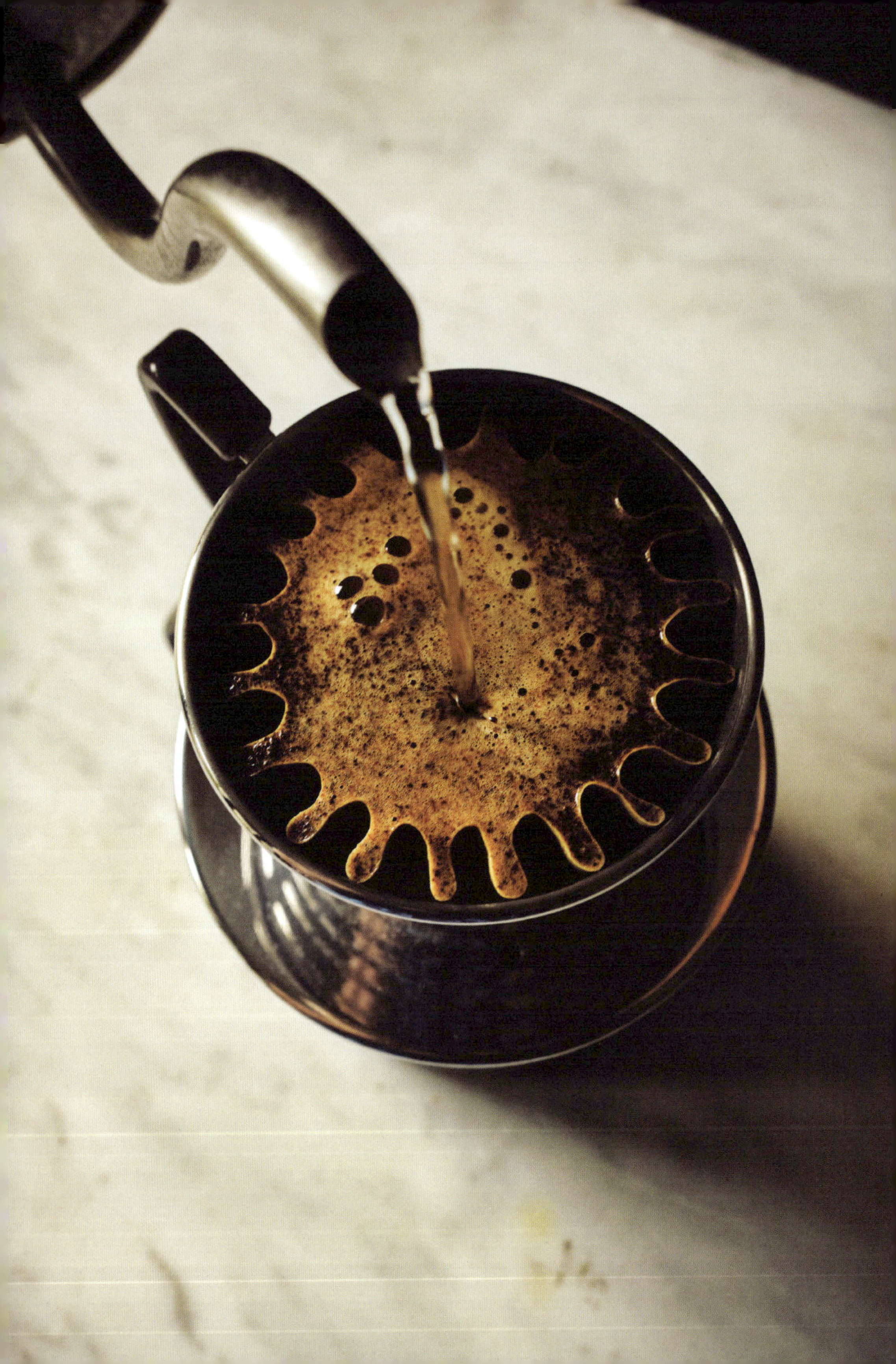

Why Some Coffees Are Tastier Than Others

APPRECIATING YOUR EXPECTATIONS

An understanding of your own expectations, as well as of coffee's defining characteristics, is necessary when selecting coffee. The ability to taste coffee has many benefits. It opens whole worlds of flavour, community and understanding. But often your motivation may be no more complicated than being able to pick a coffee that you will enjoy. Tasting notes can be word salads of unfamiliar placenames, esoteric terms and bold promises. Selecting a suitably tasty bag of beans, or a brew in a coffee shop, can be surprisingly, and unnecessarily, difficult.

Everyone has their own approach to drinking coffee. Some people opt to savour it; others gulp. Many people use coffee to kickstart the day, but this could be a pot at home, a takeout flat white or an espresso taken while standing at a bar. In some cultures, drinking coffee in the evening causes fear of a poor night's sleep; elsewhere it's a popular way to socialize. And almost all coffee drinkers have strong ideas about the origins they like and how their coffee should be prepared. Coffee choices are deeply personal, and each of us has ideas about what's best. This handbook contains the insights, techniques and tips you need to appreciate why you like some coffees more than others.

Tasting coffee

Essential to choosing coffees you find pleasurable is the know-how to match a coffee's profile with your expectations, or vice versa. As you use the tasting techniques offered here, it will become increasingly apparent that it is the structure of each coffee's characteristics that shapes your appreciation of it.

There are four key coffee profiles, each of which meets a different set of expectations. For now, don't worry about the tasting terminology if it is unfamiliar to you. Rather, consider what your own coffee-drinking expectations might be.

Flavour Profiles
Classic

Classic coffees skew towards bitterness; you might instinctively describe coffees with a classic profile as 'heavier', 'darker' or 'deeper'. The more pleasant versions have sufficient sweetness to create a balance of tastes. A good number of these coffees are astringent, which is a drying sensation in the mouth. The better versions benefit from an alignment between the mouthfeel and flavour. They might have tasting notes such as cocoa, tobacco, leather, spice or nuts. The lower-quality versions lack either balance or alignment and can be rough on the palate.

The highest-quality Classic coffees typically have a foundation of bitterness combined with adequate sweetness and a hint of fruit. Coffees with these traits are often described as 'chocolatey'.

TIM'S TASTING TIP
We explore pairing coffee and food in Magical Moments (see page 201) and when discussing Alignment (see page 111).

> An average Classic coffee doesn't score highly in grading or competition, but many coffee drinkers really like this profile

Because this note is attractive, the term appears frequently and is also used to cover a multitude of sins. Consequently, approach a 'chocolate' descriptor with suspicion. When used accurately, it identifies the bitterness of dark chocolate as well as its associated cocoa-like astringency. Classic coffees are also defined by their low levels of acidity, but the best versions have just enough sourness to offer a balance of tastes.

An average Classic coffee doesn't score highly in grading or competition, but many coffee drinkers really like this profile and there are many high-quality Classic coffees available. You may appreciate

A TYPICAL RANGE OF AROMA AND FLAVOUR

Cocoa

Walnut

Clove

Tobacco

Leather

the 'heavy' mouthfeel of a Classic coffee, and the 'strong' flavours might appeal, particularly if you associate the intensity of these tastes and flavours with caffeine. If you don't like Classic coffees you might instinctively describe then as 'dirty' or 'dark', or professionals might criticize their 'lack of clarity'. Other people find Classic coffees too straightforward, too simple and, if there isn't sufficient sweetness, unbalanced.

Classic coffees are also useful when pairing coffee with food. A coffee that might be a little too bitter for pleasant drinking by itself can be a tasty counterweight to sweet baking, such as a tart or cake. When used in a serve containing sugar, cream or chocolate (such as a sweet signature drink) or in a dessert (tiramisu is the best example), these coffees add a hint of bitterness, which enhances balance and pleasantly provokes the senses.

Flavour Profiles
Comfort

Comfort coffees are very popular, and many coffee drinkers will solely seek out these coffees

People typically enjoy these coffees because they offer a sense that all is right with the world – everything is 'balanced'. Comfort coffees are 'sweeter' than Classic coffees. You may have opted for a coffee of this profile at breakfast this morning.

Comfort coffees can be readily identified by their harmonious balance of tastes. If Classic coffees are typically predominantly bitter, Comfort coffees are predominantly sweet but have sufficient bitterness to create their signature balance.

Comfort coffees feature alignment between taste and flavour. To match the sweet taste, there are more, heavier esters (see the Aroma Map, page 66–7) in Comfort coffees than in Classic coffees, which give notes of dried fruits or aged spirits. Many have noticeable furans, giving the impression of vanilla or caramelized sugars. And almost all have greater quantities of pyrazines, which manifest as toast or nuts.

Many of the tastiest Comfort coffees benefit from a dash of acidity to enhance the balance and add liveliness. If so, there are typically corresponding flavours of berry or drupe, such as raspberry, apple and pear. And many Comfort coffees have a streak of earthy, boozy or spicy flavours to match the bitterness.

This is a good example of how structure plays a critical role in tastiness. Some Comfort coffees are 'darker' and 'heavier' and closer to Classic coffees; others are 'lighter'. The highest-quality Comfort coffees often have a full stack of flavours from the top, middle and bottom of the Flavour Wheel (see page 101).

TIM'S TASTING TIP
Comfort coffees can be identified by their balance between sweet and bitter.

A WIDE RANGE OF AROMA AND FLAVOUR

- Vanilla
- Raspberry
- Green Apple
- Caramel
- Hazelnut

Comfort coffees are very popular, and many coffee drinkers will solely seek out these coffees, although some drinkers find them too predictable and safe to be highly enjoyable. However, almost everyone appreciates a high-quality Comfort coffee in the right setting. If you typically drink Classic coffees, a quality Comfort coffee may be surprisingly flavoursome and enjoyable but equally unfamiliar because of the low intensity of its bitterness. If you enjoy coffees from the next two profiles, high-quality Comfort coffees will be attractive because of their structure but may lack vibrancy.

Flavour Profiles
Clarity

Clarity coffees can have a wide range of flavours. The defining structural trait is that they offer a sense of momentum through the flavours because the tastes, while harmonious, are not of equal intensity. This single characteristic draws an immediate contrast with the stationary, reassuring quality of sweet Comfort coffees. A similarly sweet Clarity coffee will taste more vibrant, usually because it has more acidity.

In theory, Clarity coffees may have a similar range of aromas and flavours to Comfort coffees, but in practice the aromas and flavours are more towards the top of the Flavour Wheel (see page 101). That is, it's not uncommon for these coffees to have prominent notes of citrus, berries, tropical drupes and fleshy fruits.

Some Clarity coffees are basic while others are very sophisticated. Basic coffees are those that have just one or two readily identifiable flavours. Complex coffees can have five, or even many more, distinct flavours. For example, you may have drunk a coffee that has wafts of bergamot, a lemon citrusy flavour and an earthy note.

The balance of tastes may be achieved between any of sourness, sweetness and bitterness. Clarity coffees are often dominantly sour and sweet, but higher-quality Clarity coffees have all three of these basic tastes. Clarity coffees also have strong alignment between taste and flavour. So, drawing on the above example, you might be able to appreciate how bergamot, lemon and earthy flavours align with sourness, sweetness and bitterness.

Drinkers of Clarity coffees typically value their harmonious balance of tastes, strong alignment and, often, complexity. They may appreciate textbook examples of hallmark origins; equally, most archetypical coffees have evolved to be both harmoniously balance and well aligned.

TIM'S TASTING TIP
Clarity coffees have a balance between sweet, sour and/or bitter, but are typically more acidic than Comfort coffees.

A WIDE RANGE OF AROMA AND FLAVOUR

Lemon

Bergamot

Nectarine

Almond

Aged Spirits

Often, these coffees are vibrant to drink, and many are enjoyable by themselves. This means that some are difficult to pair with food because they don't offer a sufficient counterweight to a food's saltiness or sweetness to make for a satisfying pairing.

A challenge for the Clarity coffee drinker is that many of these coffees are from acclaimed origins and producers, have limited supply and high demand, and consequently command a price premium. Many Clarity coffee drinkers have bursts of enthusiasm for lesser-known and up-and-coming coffees with other profiles in the search for greater value. However, time and again they revert to buying coffees from esteemed producers because they find them delicious. The good news is that well-priced tasty Clarity coffees are available, if you know where to look.

Flavour Profiles
Curious

With multiple aromas and flavours, Curious coffees are complex, but are identifiable by their less-than-straightforward alignment between taste and flavour. This creates a tasting experience that can be exhilarating but is sometimes confounding or confusing.

Many Curious coffees feature lighter and vibrant flavours including drupe, tropical and citrus fruits. However, what identifies the majority of Curious coffees is that the intensity of the taste doesn't match the flavours. For example, it can be disconcerting to drink a coffee that is predominantly sour, but doesn't have aligned tropical or citrus flavours. Conversely, it's weird to perceive, say, pineapple flavour but not perceive adequate sourness and sweetness.

With many distinct aromas and flavours, these coffees can be awarded high-quality grades, but they are almost always the most divisive coffees. Some people are greatly excited by their novel flavour combinations while others are repelled by their lack of familiarity or put off by their lack of balance or alignment.

TIM'S TASTING TIP
Most Curious coffees commonly have citrus and tropical fruit flavours to align with any acidity.

Curious coffees frequently have at least two tastes, but they are often not harmoniously balanced. For example, with insufficient sweetness or bitterness to create balance, the brew may taste predominantly sour. Many coffee drinkers find acidity challenging, but pretty much everyone finds sourness that is unbalanced – and without aligned flavours – unpleasant. Occasionally, a coffee may have an umami or salty taste, which often pushes it into the Curious coffee profile because it is unusual.

There are an increasing number of Curious coffees available because coffee producers are progressively experimenting with innovative production methods and coffee professionals often appreciate their novelty. For some coffee drinkers,

A DIVERSE RANGE OF AROMA AND FLAVOUR

Lychee

Pistachio

Hibiscus

Cashew

Broth

an appreciation of Curious coffees is a signifier of their superior palate. Of course, this is just a specific set of expectations that may say more about the drinker than it does about the drink. Because Curious coffees lack often balance, they can create exciting pairings with food and drink.

As with all coffees, there are both higher-quality and lower-quality Curious coffees. A coffee's tastiness, in general, is a combination of its complexity, balance and alignment. You may have noted that complex, balanced and aligned coffees are usually categorized as Comfort or Clarity coffees, while a simple, unbalanced and poorly aligned coffee is largely undrinkable. The Curious coffee profile is required to identify the segment of coffees that are complex, neither well balanced nor aligned, but are nevertheless tasty.

THE BEST COFFEES FOR YOU

The borders between these profiles are porous, so it's better to conceptualize them as a spectrum of possibilities rather than as distinct categories. Often best-selling coffees meet the definitions of two profiles, which shouldn't be surprising since this represents appeal to a greater number of consumers.

Most people's coffee-drinking preferences are not fixed and shift based on occasion, context and mood. For example, you might prefer Comfort coffees in the morning, a Clarity coffee in the afternoon, drink Classic coffee in the office, and opt to gift a Curious coffee to a friend. It is almost always more important to match a coffee to your expectation and context than it is to commit to a specific cup score or flavour profile.

Understanding your default preferences has two key benefits. As we embark on tasting coffee, it helps to appreciate the expectations with which you currently judge coffee. The benefit of using a tasting methodology is that it enables us to assess each coffee in a more impartial manner. It helps us both to appreciate positive attributes that might not instinctively appeal to us and to identify the negative characteristics that we might otherwise be prone to overlooking. All good tasters strive to park their personal preferences when appraising coffee. Of course, even the best tasters revert to their preferences as soon as they leave the tasting room.

The other key benefit is that it allows us to see our preferences in a broader context and appreciate the preferences of others. Often, a debate over whether a coffee is good or not is simply two people attempting to ascribe quality through the prism of their differing expectations. A tasting methodology enables us to perceive each coffee's defining qualities and to talk about these characteristics in a meaningful way.

Later in the book you will learn how to select coffees that you enjoy. But next, let's equip you with a range of coffee-tasting skills and ensure you have an adequate grasp of key tasting concepts. So, with your personal preferences identified, I now encourage you to put them aside. Let's just focus on identifying the characteristics that make each coffee unique. Afterwards, we can then return to your expectations, unpack what they mean, and explore how to choose coffees based on your preferences, context and food pairings.

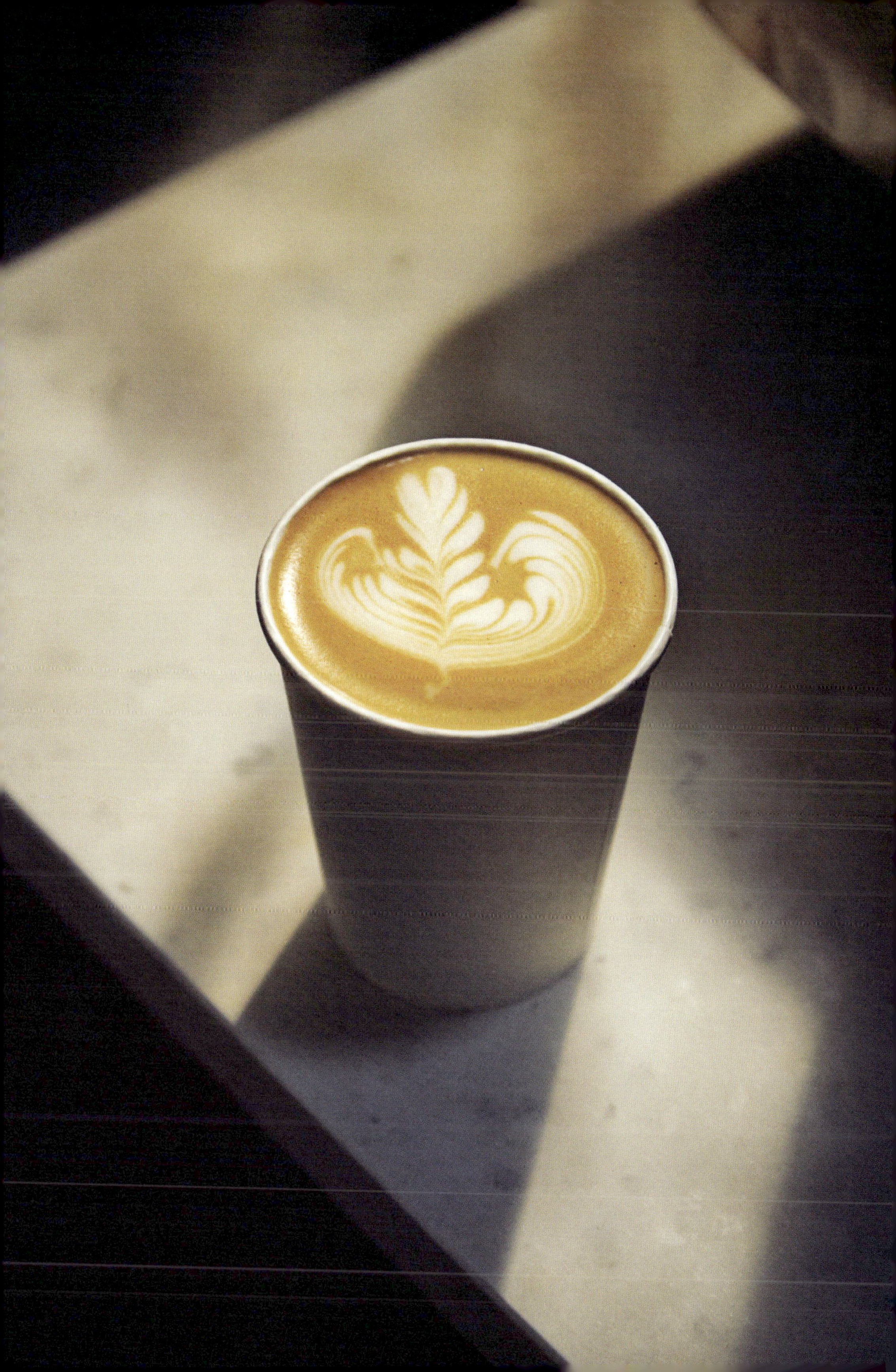

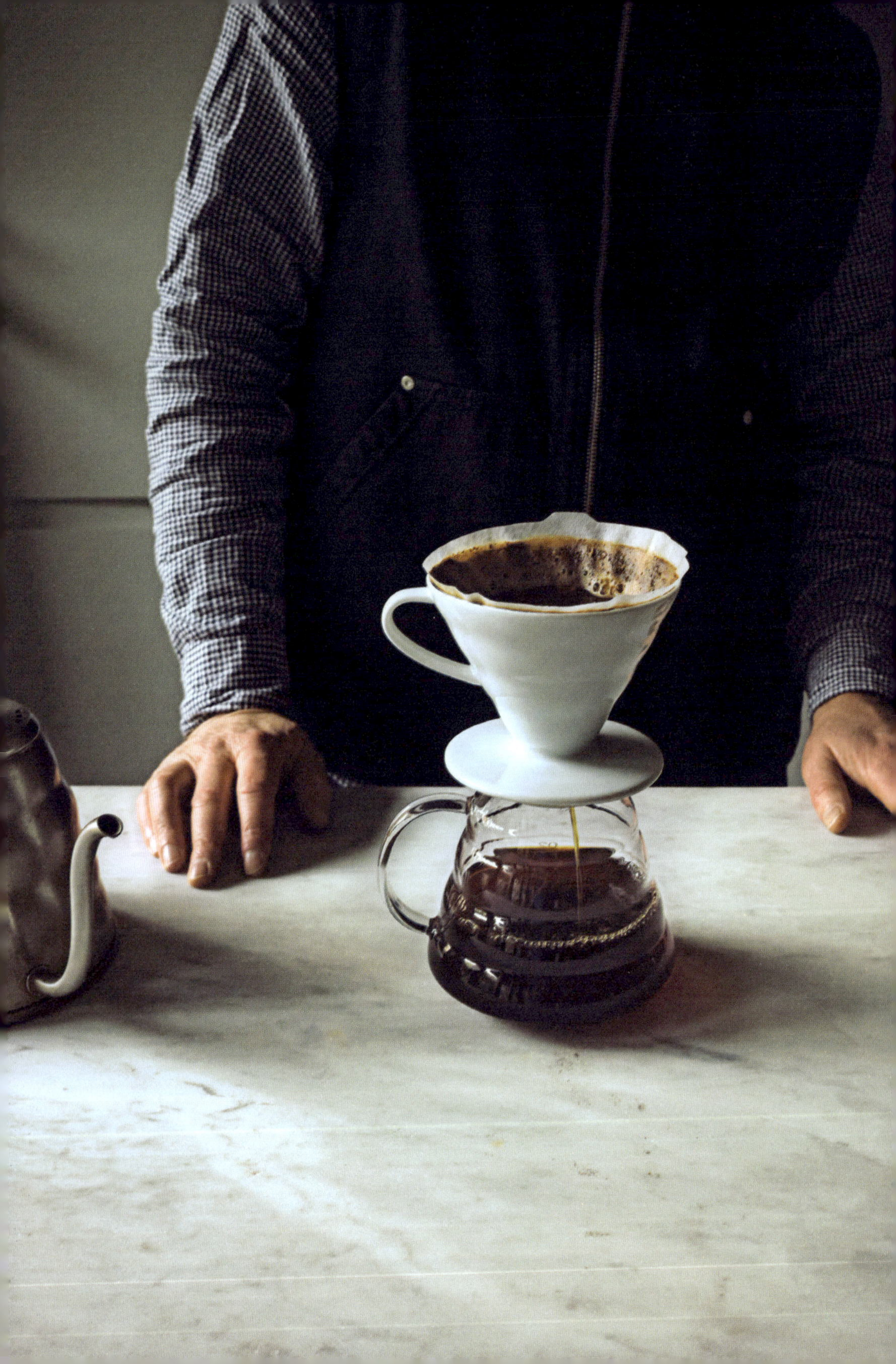

Brewing Coffee for Tasting

SET YOURSELF UP FOR SUCCESS

Start by hiding any tasting notes that came with the coffee. There's a chance that the tasting notes are wrong, misleading or misguided. Notes are often written to sell coffee at least as much as to describe it. You can expect unpleasant characteristics to be described euphemistically. The other possibility is that the tasting notes are spot on, in which case, it's all too easy to feel obliged to stick to them.

Ideally, brew two to four coffees from differing origins and processes so you can compare and contrast. You can, of course, taste coffee individually, but tasting as part of a group enriches the experience. It is the fastest way to learn where there is agreement as well as where people's preferences may diverge.

Once you've finished the assessment, you can reveal the tasting notes and compare your notes with the professionals'. If you rehearse this tasting method several times, then use it to mentally assess each of the coffees you drink, in no time at all your notes will be as least as good as the tasting notes you've just hidden.

DON'T BE INTIMIDATED

Trained coffee professionals do not have superior palates. Study after study has found nothing to physiologically distinguish professionals from amateurs. Professionals do not have better noses, more sophisticated taste buds or stronger memories. What they do have is a method, a conceptualization of what they should be assessing, and domain-specific knowledge.

Multiple researchers have found that just several hours' training is sufficient for a complete novice to start closing the gap with a professional. Forget the daunting 10,000 hours' practice thesis. As little as four hours is all that is required to master the basics.

Tasting requires several forms of knowledge that operate in concert. Fundamentally, all tasters require an understanding of what they are perceiving. They need to be able to distinguish sweet from sour or bitter; appreciate the distinctions between aromas and flavours; and be able to identify various mouthfeel textures. These experiences should be paired with the ability to correctly label what is perceived. For example, if a coffee is sour or bitter, or has a silky mouthfeel or is unbalanced, each of the terms needs to be used correctly to have meaning.

Good tasters also have a framework that enables consideration of how their perceptions amalgamate. If a coffee is bitter, rough and poorly aligned, how does that compare to a coffee that is balanced and complex and benefits from strong alignment? This conceptual understanding is necessary so you can locate your experience within the gamut of possibilities.

The combination of this perceptual and conceptual tasting knowledge is exceptionally powerful, despite being relatively quick and easy to acquire. General tasters are almost as good at tasting specific food or drink items as the relevant domain specialist. What domain specialists have is product expertise. Much of their knowledge and experience is focused on the process of making the product. For coffee, this type of knowledge includes an understanding of coffee growing and processing, the supply chain, roasting and brewing.

However, it's important to recognize at the outset that this knowledge doesn't necessarily make you a better taster. Domain knowledge is powerful when it is leveraged with relevant perceptual and conceptual knowledge. This equips tasters that have all three types of knowledge to draw correlations between perception and production, as well as vice versa, and identify common patterns.

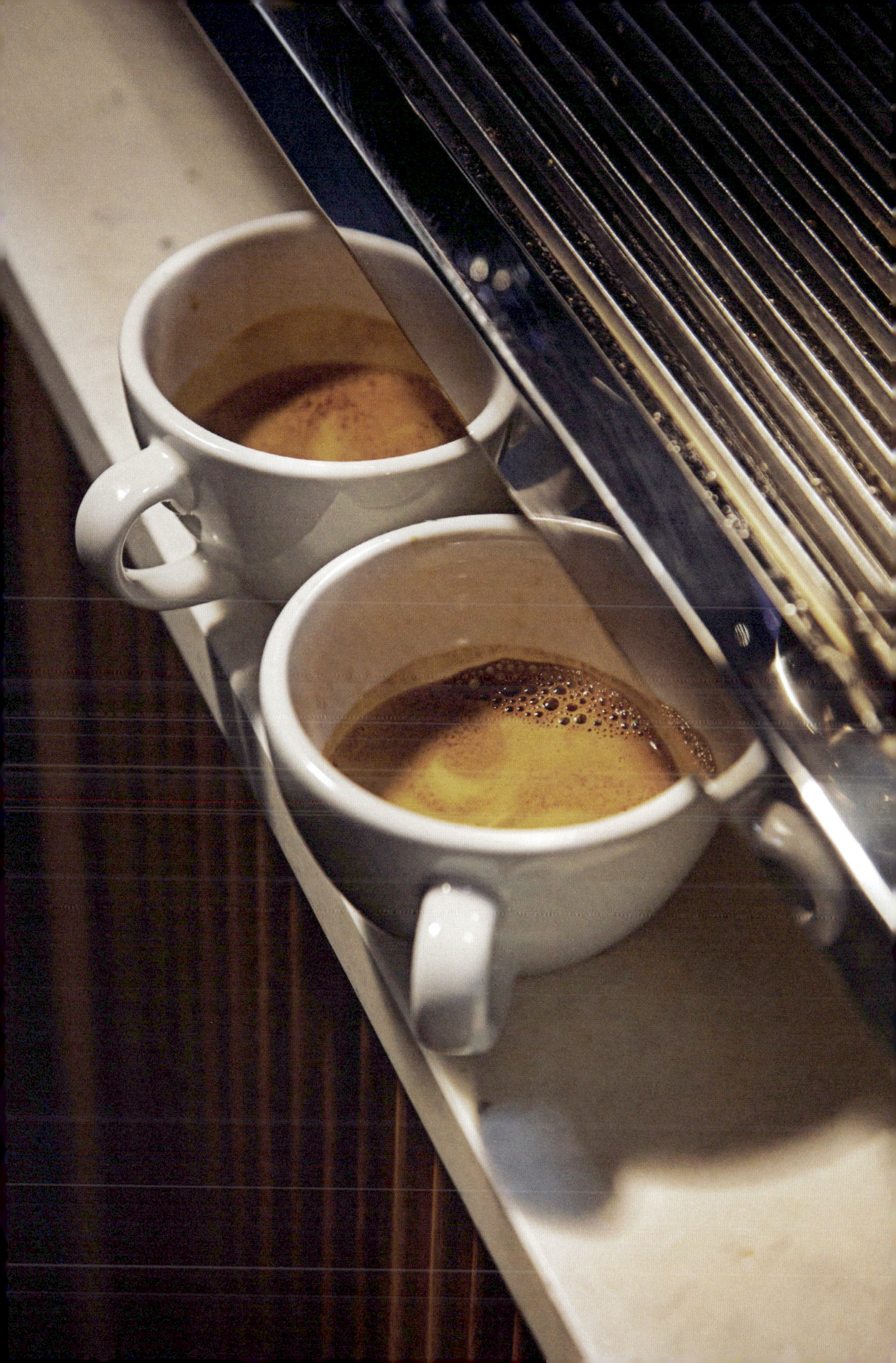

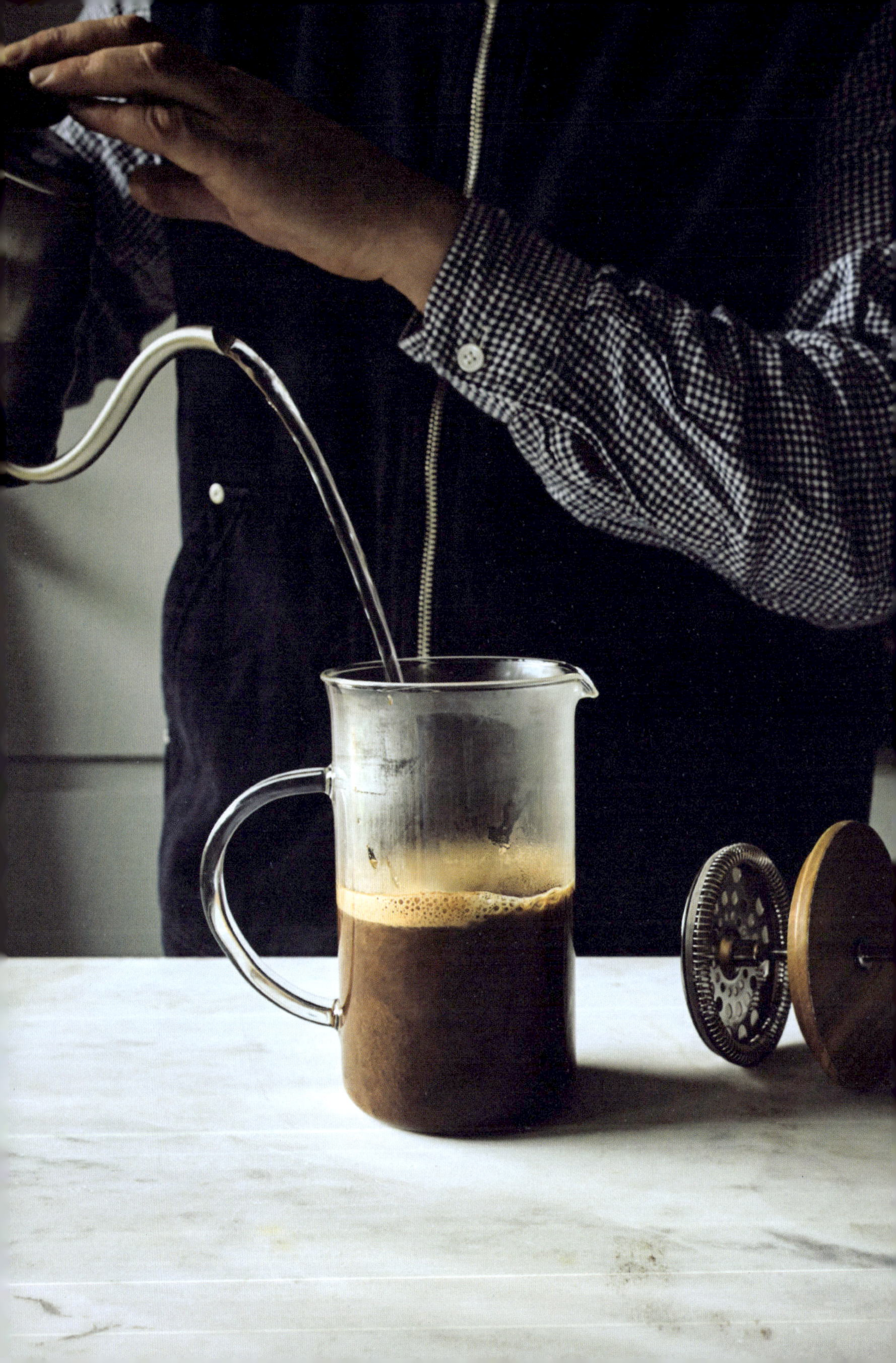

PREPARING THE COFFEES

You can taste coffee prepared any-which way, but I'm going to assume throughout that you are tasting black filter coffee. Filter offers the greatest clarity and transparency on a coffee's origin and flavours. There are many filter coffee-making methods that use a range of devices and appliances, including the brands of Hario, AeroPress, Chemex, Technivorm and Ratio. While you can brew coffee for tasting using a 'full immersion' method such as a cafetière (French press), flavours are easier to identify from 'drip filter' methods, which typically use a paper filter. (A simple method for brewing drip filter coffee for tasting is available on page 44.)

You could also prepare the coffee from a pod or espresso machine. Please start by using whichever method you are currently familiar with. Decide in advance whether you are going to drink each coffee or sample it. A typical serve of filter coffee is 200–250ml (about 7–8½fl oz). However, you don't require a full serve when tasting. In practice, 100ml (about 3½fl oz) of coffee is more than sufficient to sample it. Plus, most people will find three or four samples of 100ml more than enough caffeine.

The ideal number of coffees and group size depends on your objective. Sometimes, you might taste several coffees that piqued your interest. Other times, you might work through a flight that explores an origin, variety or process method. In general, people will enjoy consuming about 200–400ml (about 7–14fl oz) of coffee across the tasting. So, if tasting one coffee, I would brew a cup per person, and if tasting three or more coffees, I would prepare about 100ml per person. The smallest volume people can typically use is about 30–40ml (about 1–1½fl oz).

Sometimes, I attend tastings or award judging panels and we are expected to sample as many as 50 coffees in a day. It can be rather demanding and quite unpleasant. On these occasions I spit out as much sample coffee as I can so that I ingest as little caffeine as possible. If tasting a large number of coffees in a group, you should provide a spittoon. This could be as simple as an opaque mug for each person.

Finally, you need to decide whether to brew the coffees in advance or just before each round. I usually brew all the coffees in advance and serve them one at a time from thermal carafes. Tasting this way has a nice rapid pace. Conversely, there's nothing wrong with tasting a coffee, and then brewing the next; the advantage is that you sample each coffee at a similar temperature.

BREWING COFFEE

Coffee-brewing recipes are designed to extract a pleasant quantity of soluble compounds from the ground coffee. If the ground coffee should give too few soluble compounds, the resultant brew will be thin and sour. If too many soluble compounds are extracted, the resultant brew is typically thick and bitter.

All coffees have some sourness and bitterness. It's best to brew coffee for tasting in a neutral style as we want the tastes and flavours of the coffee to be clearly on display. We want the coffee to be showcased, not the brewing method.

The default recipe is 60g of coffee per litre (2oz per qt) of water. Let's say I am brewing using a cafetière and it has a capacity of 750ml (25fl oz), which is 3 cups. Using the default ratio, I can dose 45g (just over 1½oz) of coffee. Baristas seldom change the ratio; instead, they vary the grind size and the brewing time.

More finely ground coffee has a greater surface area, so more soluble compounds are available to infuse with the water. Furthering the cafetière example, if the resultant brew is too bitter, coarsen the grind or reduce the steeping time.

Most brewing-method recipes reduce the variables in play to solely the grind size and standardize the other variables:

Roast date

Freshly roasted coffee is more flavoursome than old, stale coffee. Prioritize buying coffee that was roasted within the last couple of days. I usually buy coffee in approximately 250g (9oz) bags and taste each coffee within two weeks of roasting.

Water

Most coffee guides recommend water with a total hardness of 50–150ppm (parts per million), a total alkalinity of 40mg/L (ppm), and a neutral pH, and that it should be free from foul odours, colours and particles. Some baristas make brewing water using minerals, many purchase bottled water from the supermarket, while others use a professional water filter. If your local water is inadequate, you can greatly improve your coffee quality by using a basic domestic water filter jug.

Grinding coffee

It is best to grind coffee just before preparation to maximize the quantity of aromatic compounds infused into the cup. Grinders with either flat or conical burrs grind coffee more evenly than blade grinders.

Heating water

It is typical to brew coffee with water that is heated to about 93°C (200°F). You can purchase electronic kettles that automatically switch off when the desired temperature is reached. I use a digital thermometer inserted into my pouring kettle. If you have a standard kettle, bring the water to the boil and then wait about five minutes for the water to cool before pouring.

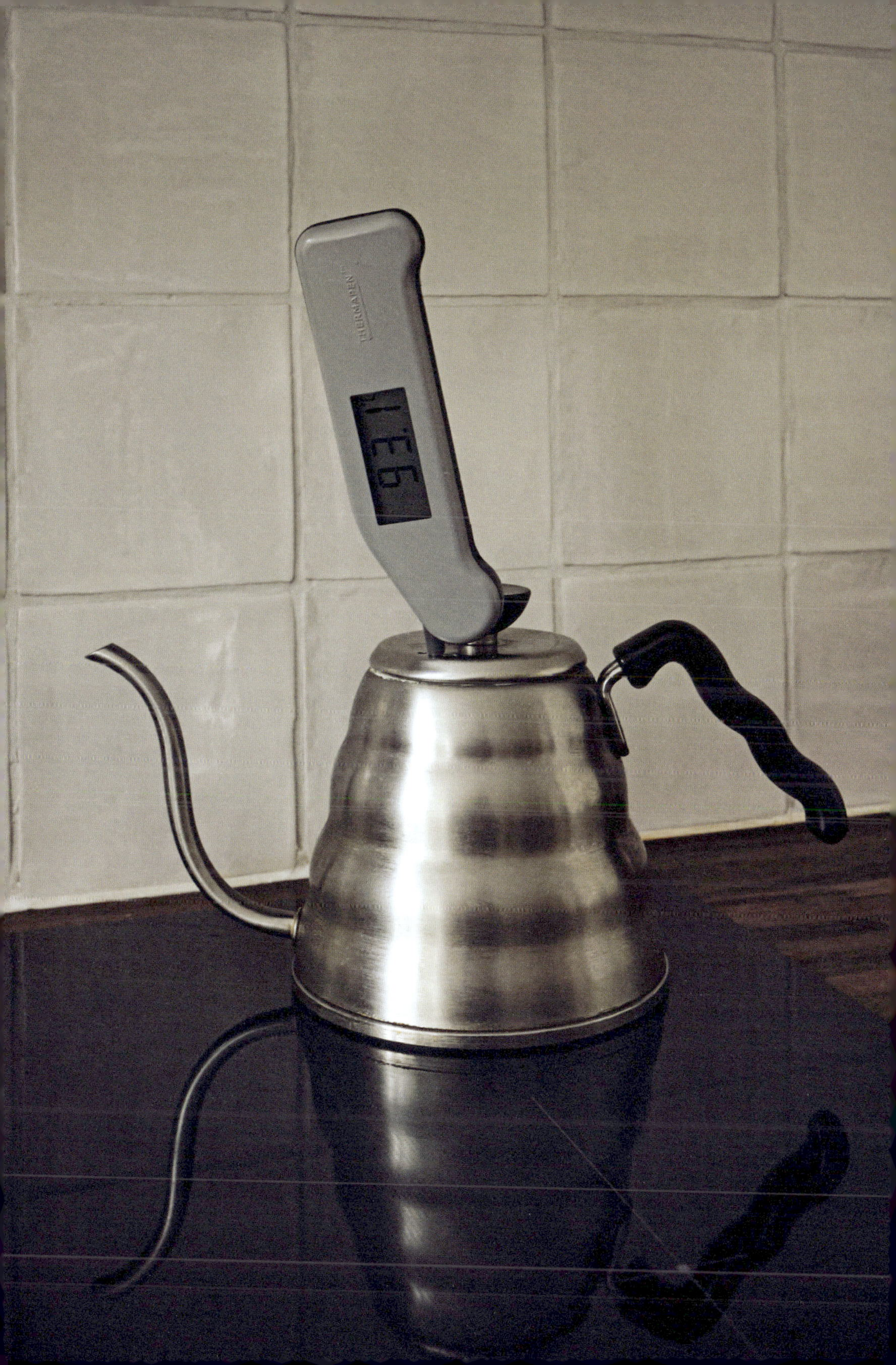
THERMAPEN

UNIVERSAL BREWING

I brew almost all coffees the same way. It's the same method I have used for years. It's about 28g (1oz) of freshly ground coffee placed in a Hario V60 two-cup ceramic brewer. Furthermore, I almost never change the grind size. This is because I am more interested in tasting each coffee than I am in optimizing the brew for each coffee. Having a consistent approach makes it easier to identify the differences between coffees and even the differences between various roast lots of the same coffee.

TASTE IS THE ULTIMATE CRITERION

Learning to taste coffee helps you avoid the tyrannical logic that dictates coffee brewed according to an established recipe from a reputable source must taste good. This confuses inputs with outputs. It is, of course, the other way around. Taste is the ultimate criterion.

Improvements to your coffee-making setup or refinements of your technique will consistently improve the balance of tastes, enhance the pleasantness of the mouthfeel and increase flavour clarity. Everything you do should be in pursuit of these characteristics. This approach empowers you to deploy utility with your coffee making. If the increased cost, hassle or time improve the pleasantness and your enjoyment of the coffee, then you might judge it as a worthwhile investment.

JUST GET STARTED

So before you buy new equipment, change your brewing method or source different coffees, I encourage you to just get started using the coffee, setup and method you already use.

You are already familiar with coffee brewed in this way, and it will be helpful for you to start tasting using these reference points. If you identify that you are consistently over- or under-extracting coffee, then tweak your brew ratio. Should you grow frustrated that a coffee's flavours are swinging from delicious to disgusting because of variations in dose or water temperature, consider investing in a digital scale or temperature-controlled kettle. You can expand your coffee-making equipment and refine your technique over time.

Otherwise the most important aspect of tasting coffee is to use your senses and brain to actively consider what you are perceiving. When first working through the methodology it will be easier if you are somewhere conducive to tasting. Ideally, use a space that is well lit, quiet and odour free. You will need a surface for tasting and writing. If you are at

TIM'S TASTING TIP

If you are willing to invest in just one item, I recommend purchasing a good electric grinder that has flat or conical burrs. Consistently grinding coffee just before preparation is the most significant step towards brewing tasty coffee.

home, the kitchen or dining table are often good locations so you have ready access to a coffee preparation space, drinking water and the sink.

All the subsequent tips for brewing coffee or setting up a tasting are designed to standardize and simplify the process, enhance flavour clarity and put yourself in the right mindset. If you can already do these things, then feel free to brew yourself a cup of coffee and skip to the next chapter.

If coffee making and tasting is new to you, let's get you set up for success. Coffee making need not be overly complicated or finicky. As we methodically consider each of a coffee's characteristics, let's never forget that you are drinking coffee because you like it.

With that said, let's hide the tasting notes, brew some coffee and get started tasting!

Filter
Hario V60 two-cup

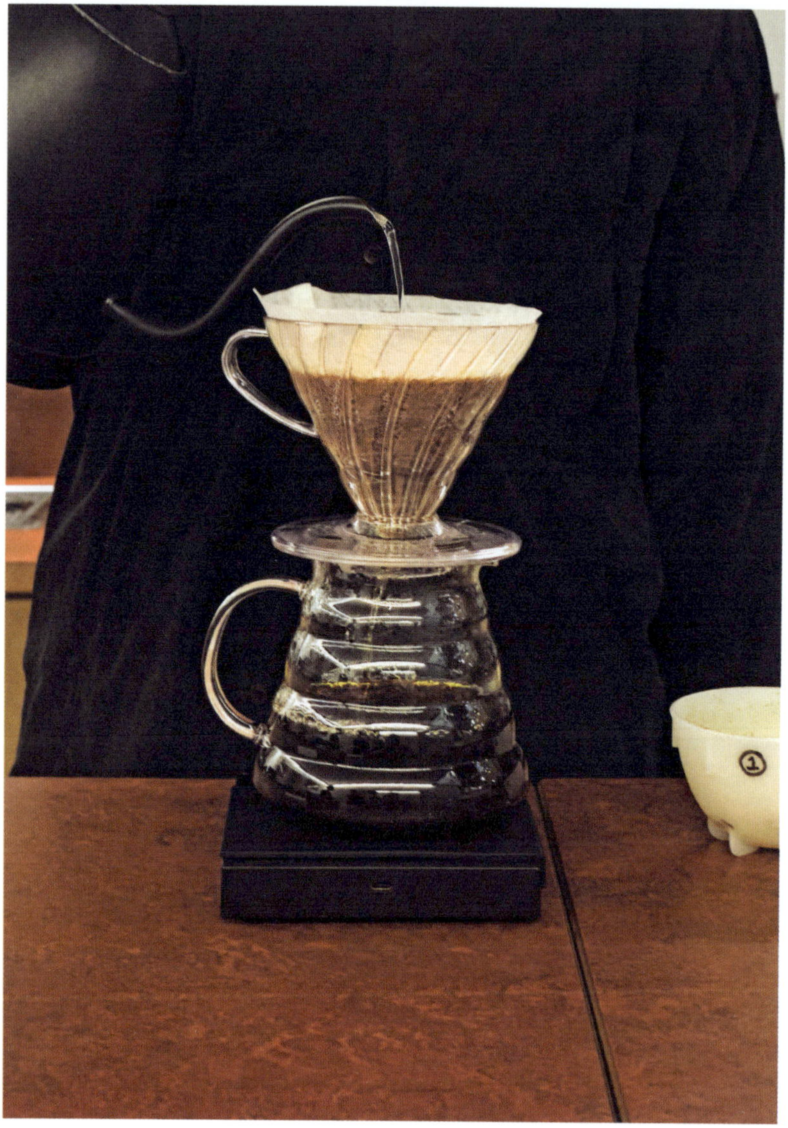

Drip filter brewing gives greater flavour clarity because the paper filter is finer than the metal filter in most cafetières. Use this recipe on a Hario V60, Chemex, Kalita Wave or pretty much any other drip brewer.

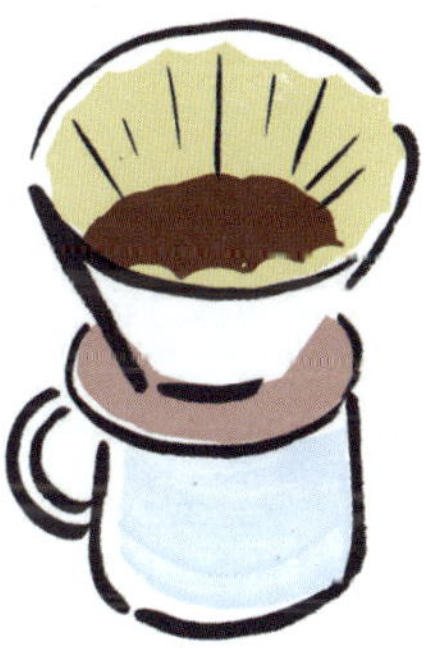

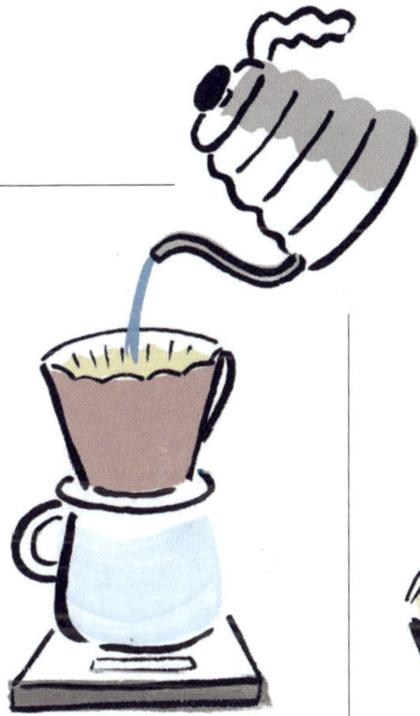

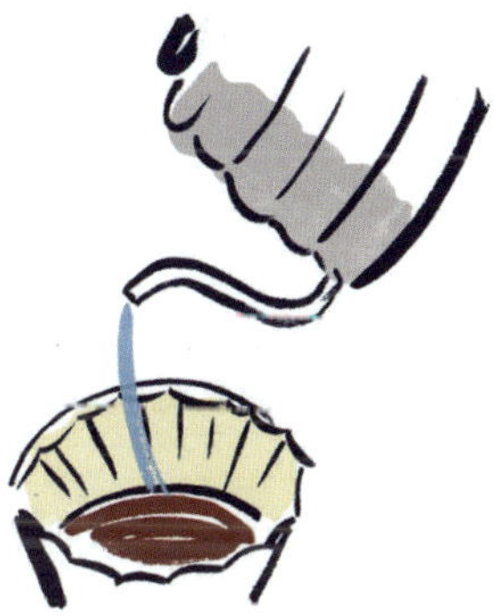

1. Add about 28g (1oz) of medium-ground coffee to the filter paper.

2. Pour 40–60ml (1½–2fl oz) of water over the bed of coffee and pause for about 30–40 seconds.

3. Evenly pour a total of about 450ml (15fl oz) of water into the dripper so it is all added by 2 minutes.

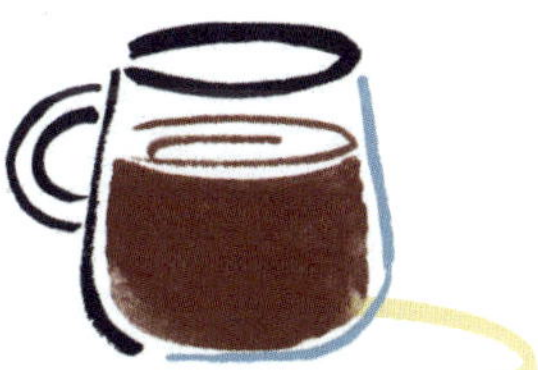

4. The total brew time should be about 2 minutes 30 seconds. If it is faster, then consider reducing the grind size for the next brew; if the brew is much longer, then you will need to coarsen the grind size for the next brew.

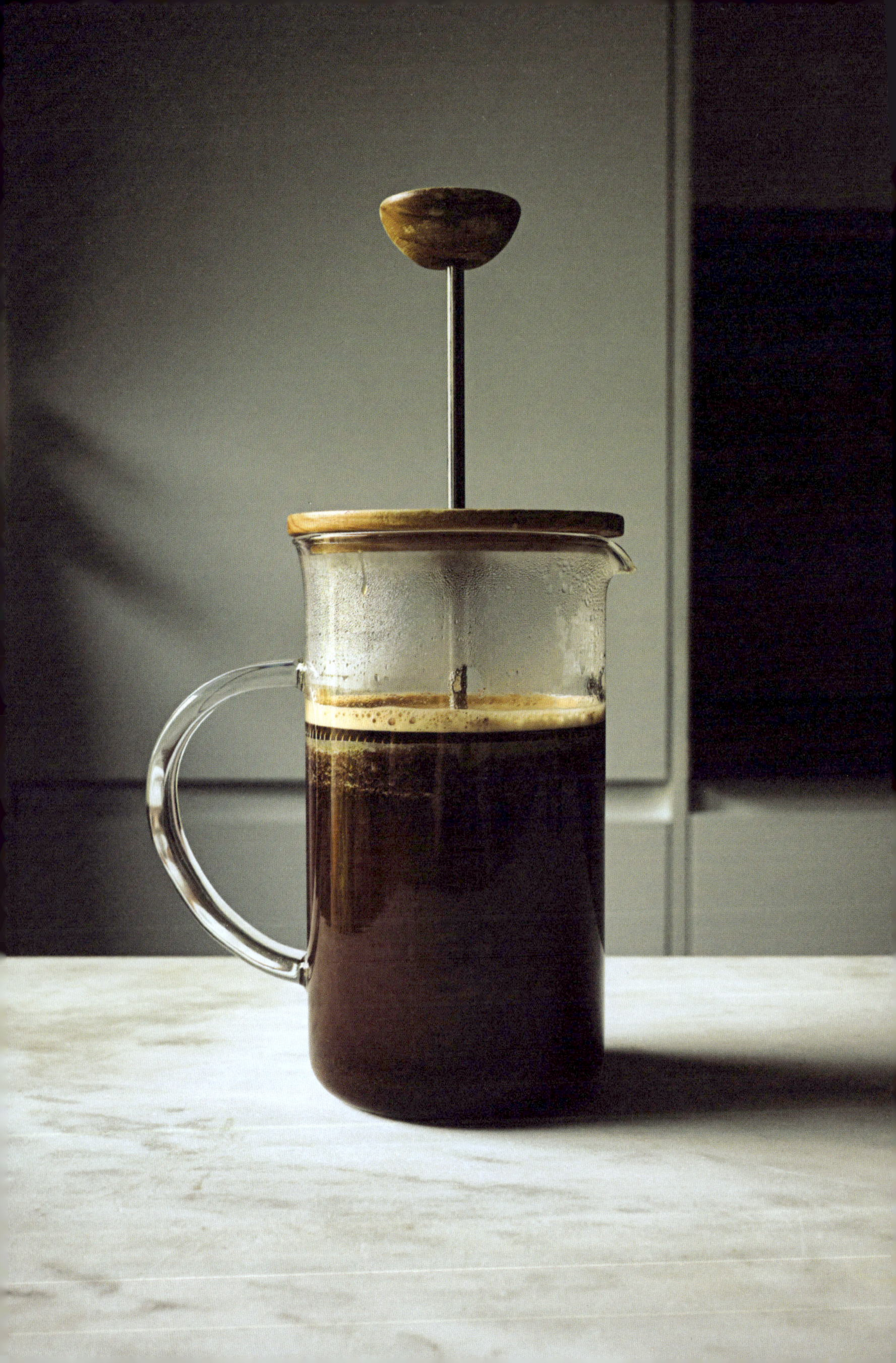

Cafetière

This is a common and easy way to prepare coffee for a group. You can use the 60g per litre (2oz per qt) ratio for most full-immersion brewing methods.

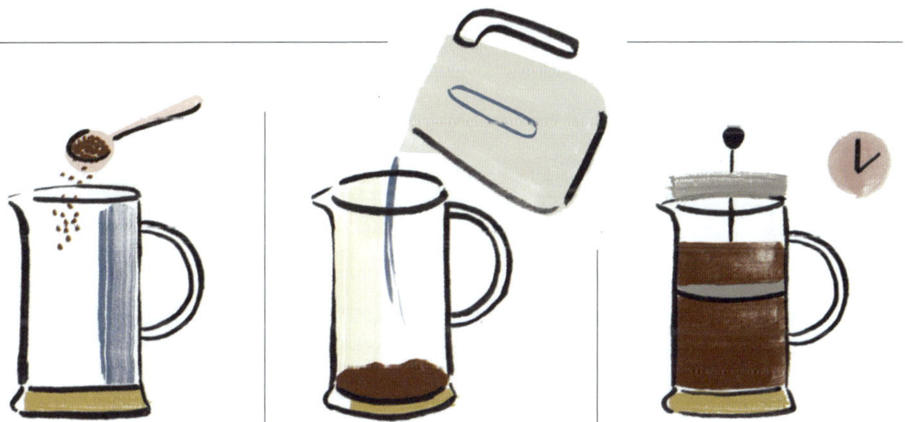

1. Add about 60g (2oz) of medium-ground coffee to the press per litre of water. If you are preparing 500ml (18fl oz), that's 30g (1oz), which is about 6 teaspoons.

2. Add the hot water to the press, stir the coffee, and place the lid on the press.

3. Depress the plunger so the ground coffee is submerged.

4. Wait about 3 minutes and then fully depress the plunger.

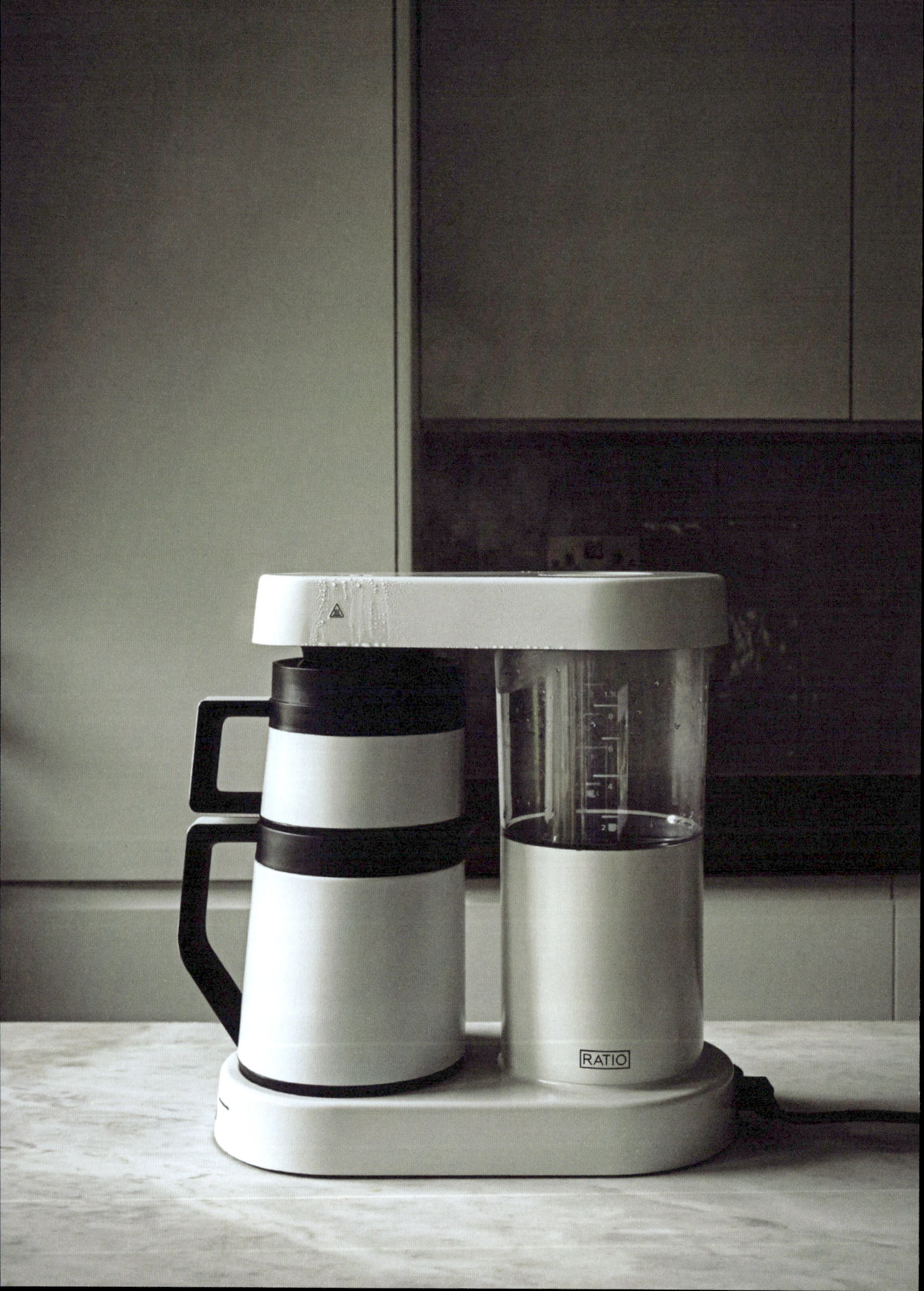
RATIO

Brewer
Ratio Six

It's often easier to brew for a group using an electric brewer, such as a Ratio or Technivorm. A paper filter is inserted into the brew basket and the machine heats and drips water over the bed of coffee. Brewers with flat-bottomed brew baskets typically make tastier coffee.

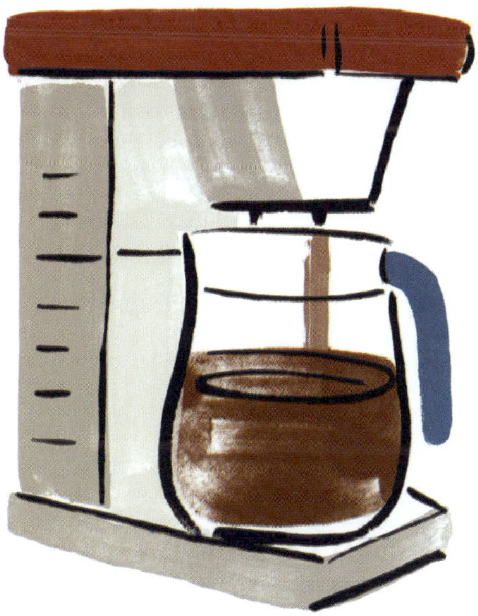

1. Insert the paper filter into the brew basket and add 60g (2oz) of medium-ground coffee.

---

2. Add 1 litre (36fl oz) of water to the reservoir. The machine will determine the brewing time.

---

3. You can change the extraction by adjusting the grind size of the coffee.

Pods
Opal One

Pods are a popular way to drink coffee. There are few variables as the coffee dose, grind size and water temperature are all preconfigured. I have an Opal One, which is suitable for Nespresso-compatible capsules.

1. Use the Lungo setting, if your pod machine has this setting. It is generally easier to detect the flavours when the brew is less intense.

2. You can also opt to brew a shot and then dilute the coffee with 50–100ml (2–3½fl oz) of hot water.

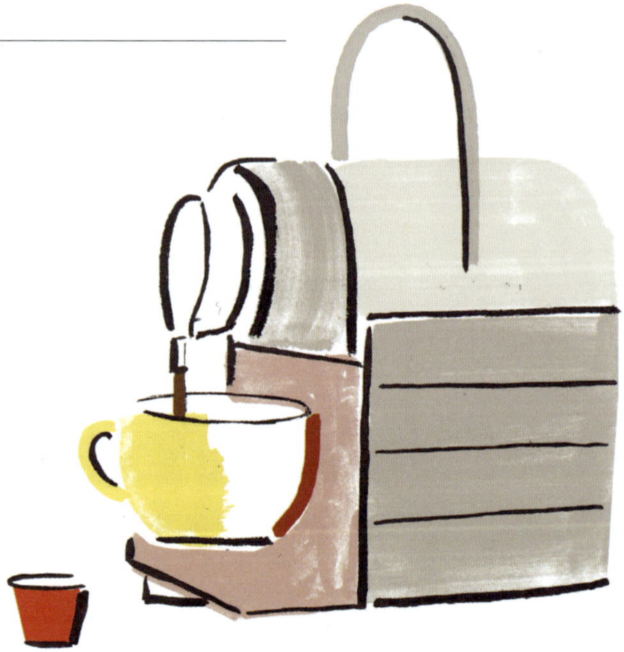

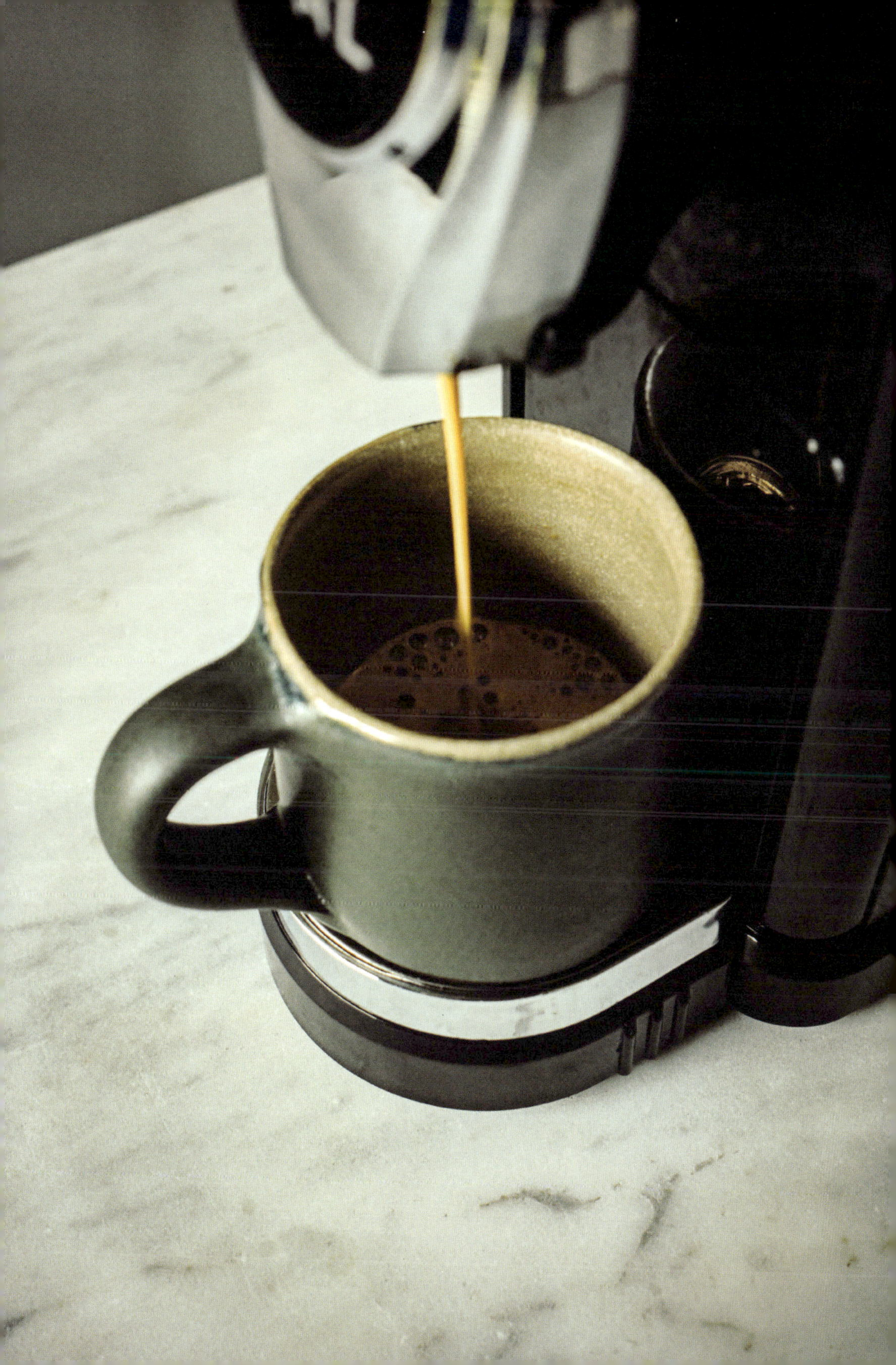

COFFEE ASSESSMENT SHEET

Name

Date

Coffee

Producer

Variety

Process

Roast Date

VISUAL

Transparency

Clear — Opaque

red-brown

green-brown

yellow-brown

AROMA

Intensity

Low — High

Notes

Top

Middle

Base

MOUTHFEEL

Body

Light — Heavy

Notes

TASTE

Sweetness

Dry — Sweet

Sourness

Low — High

Bitterness

Low — High

Notes

Saltiness

Low — High

Umami

Low — High

FLAVOUR

Finish

Short — Long

Notes

Top ....
Middle ....
Base ....

ALIGNMENT

Taste–Flavour

Poor — Strong

Mouthfeel–Taste

Poor — Strong

ASSESSMENT

Mouthfeel

Unpleasant — Pleasant

Balance

Poor — Harmonious

Alignment

Poor — Strong

Complexity

Low — High

Profile

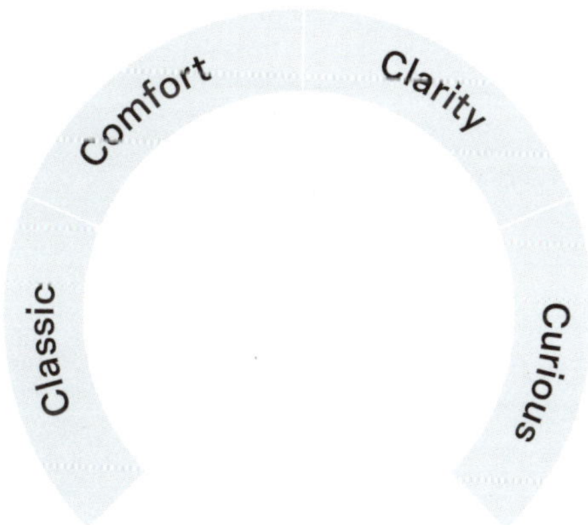

Quality

Good	Very Good	Excellent	Outstanding

Notes

....
....
....

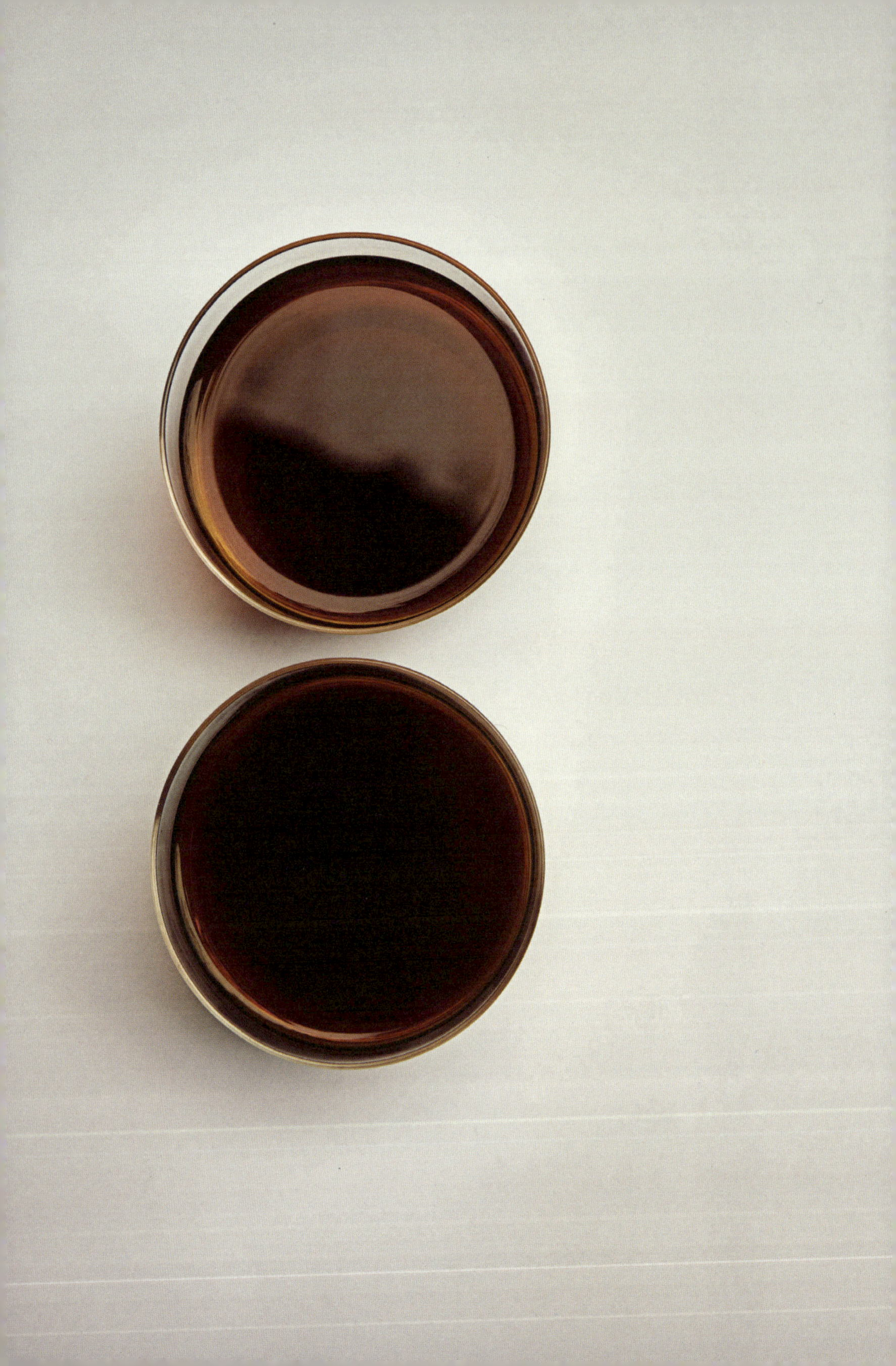

Visual: Look Before You Sip

CONSIDER EACH COMPONENT

Place several filter coffees side by side and you will notice that they have different hues and opacities. The first step of assessing coffee is to inspect it visually. This step takes just seconds, but it is a valuable moment to both document each coffee and appreciate how our sense of sight shapes our anticipation of the tastes and flavours to come.

Tasting methods need to achieve two competing outcomes. It's the step-by-step approach that helps us to appreciate how each of our senses perceives what we are eating or drinking. Breaking down your experience of a coffee into distinct assessments reveals each coffee's defining characteristics.

The second outcome is that it equips us to see correlations between each of the constituent parts. As you consider each characteristic in turn, predict what you expect to experience next. Over time you will start to see patterns and appreciate which characteristics commonly coexist, and understand the combinations of characteristics that are pleasant.

VISUAL ASSESSMENT: TRANSPARENCY

Start by assessing the transparency. Some coffees are completely opaque: as you look down through the liquid, it is impossible to see the bottom of the cup. At the other end of the spectrum, some coffees are transparent.

As you might expect, opaque coffees generally have a heavier body because they have more particles suspended in the water. And the converse is also true: the more transparent a coffee is, the more likely it is to have a lighter mouthfeel.

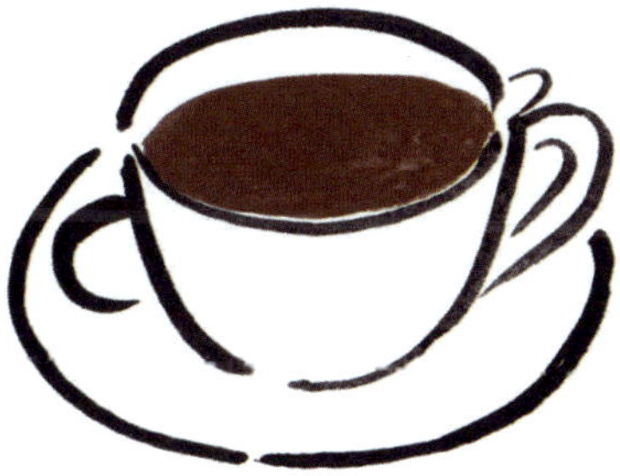

VISUAL ASSESSMENT: COLOUR

Some coffees are red-brown, some green-brown and others yellow-brown. Consider the hue of your brew and note how it sets your expectations. The correlation between colour and flavour in coffee is low, but the colour can nonetheless shape our sense of taste and flavour.

People participating in an experiment were found to be more alert to sweetness when a liquid was artificially coloured green compared to a colourless liquid of the same sweetness. But colouring a liquid either yellow or red made the participants less sensitive to sweetness.

Colour also impacts our perception of the other basic tastes, too. In the same experiment, both bitterness and sourness were more readily identified in a transparent liquid than in a coloured one. The green, red and yellow liquids all had to be more intense for the taste to be perceived.

Interestingly, the colour of the liquid had no impact on the perception of saltiness. What I take away from this study is that the basic tastes are more readily perceived when they confound our visual expectations. The element of surprise makes them noticeable.

Colour also impacts how we perceive flavour. In one of my favourite studies, participants were given green, red and yellow liquids to drink. The colour and flavour were added artificially so any of the liquids could be flavoured with cherry, lime, orange

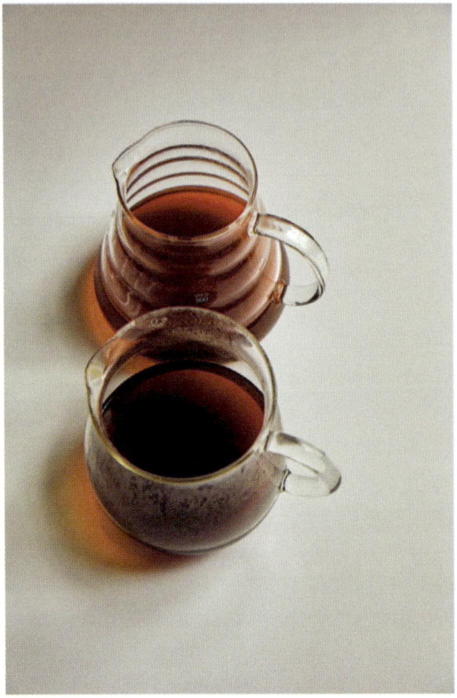

or lemon. There were also liquids that were colourless and flavourless.

People were twice as likely to correctly identify the flavour when the flavour aligned with the colour of the liquid, compared with the colourless control. For example, 37 per cent of people identified cherry flavour in the colourless liquid compared to 70 per cent when the liquid was coloured red. And, again, just 37 per cent of people identified orange flavour in the colourless liquid compared to 82 per cent when the sample was dyed orange. There was a less pronounced result for lime, but people still found the flavour easier to identify when the liquid was artificially coloured green.

As we progress through the tasting, it is important to remember

Visually inspecting coffee creates a moment to reset and focus

that we can all be easily misled. When we are, it's often because we are inadvertently conflating information from one sense with the implications of another. For example, half the participants incorrectly identified a flavour in a flavourless liquid when it was coloured. They were seeking to identify flavour with their eyes rather than their olfactory nerves.

It's in this context that I cautiously share with you that red-brown coffee may be sweeter, sometimes fruiter; yellow-brown coffees can be lighter on the palate and more acidic; and green-brown coffees may have greater bitterness and astringency, which can also be a sign of possible staleness. But there are so many exceptions that this doesn't even warrant being called a rule of thumb.

MAKE A PREDICTION

Visually inspecting coffee also creates a moment to reset and focus. Tasting coffee requires concentration and can be mentally demanding. Throughout a tasting I continually consider my thought process as well as what I am perceiving from the cup. It's necessary to question whether my snap judgements are based on an individual characteristic, the relationship of two characteristics that commonly coexist, or whether I've inadvertently conflated two things that are unconnected.

When hosting a tasting, I have often been busy setting the table, brewing coffee and greeting people. As I visually inspect the brew, I can finally turn my attention to the coffee and leave aside the other demands of the day. For the coming time I can just enjoy drinking coffee.

If you are holding a cup of coffee, now is an ideal moment to give it your undivided attention and predict how this coffee might smell and taste. The value of predictions is that they force you to articulate your assumptions. Having identified them, you will next systematically assess the coffee to see whether your initial impression was warranted...or completely unjustified.

Assessing the coffee's visual qualities

Look, really look, at the coffee. This may be the first time you've actually studied the aesthetics of coffee.

1.

Serve the coffee in a glass tumbler so you can easily assess colour and transparency. A white porcelain cup is also acceptable.

2.

If using a tumbler, place it on a light surface (such as a white tablecloth or a sheet of paper, if your tabletop is dark or textured).

3.

Fill each glass with an equal volume of liquid.

4.

Assess the opacity/transparency and the colour of the coffee:

- How transparent is the coffee? Some coffees are completely opaque, while others are sufficiently clear to be able to see the bottom of the glass.
- Does the coffee have a reddish, yellowish or greenish hue?
- How does the transparency and colour shape your expectations for the coffee's mouthfeel, taste and flavour?

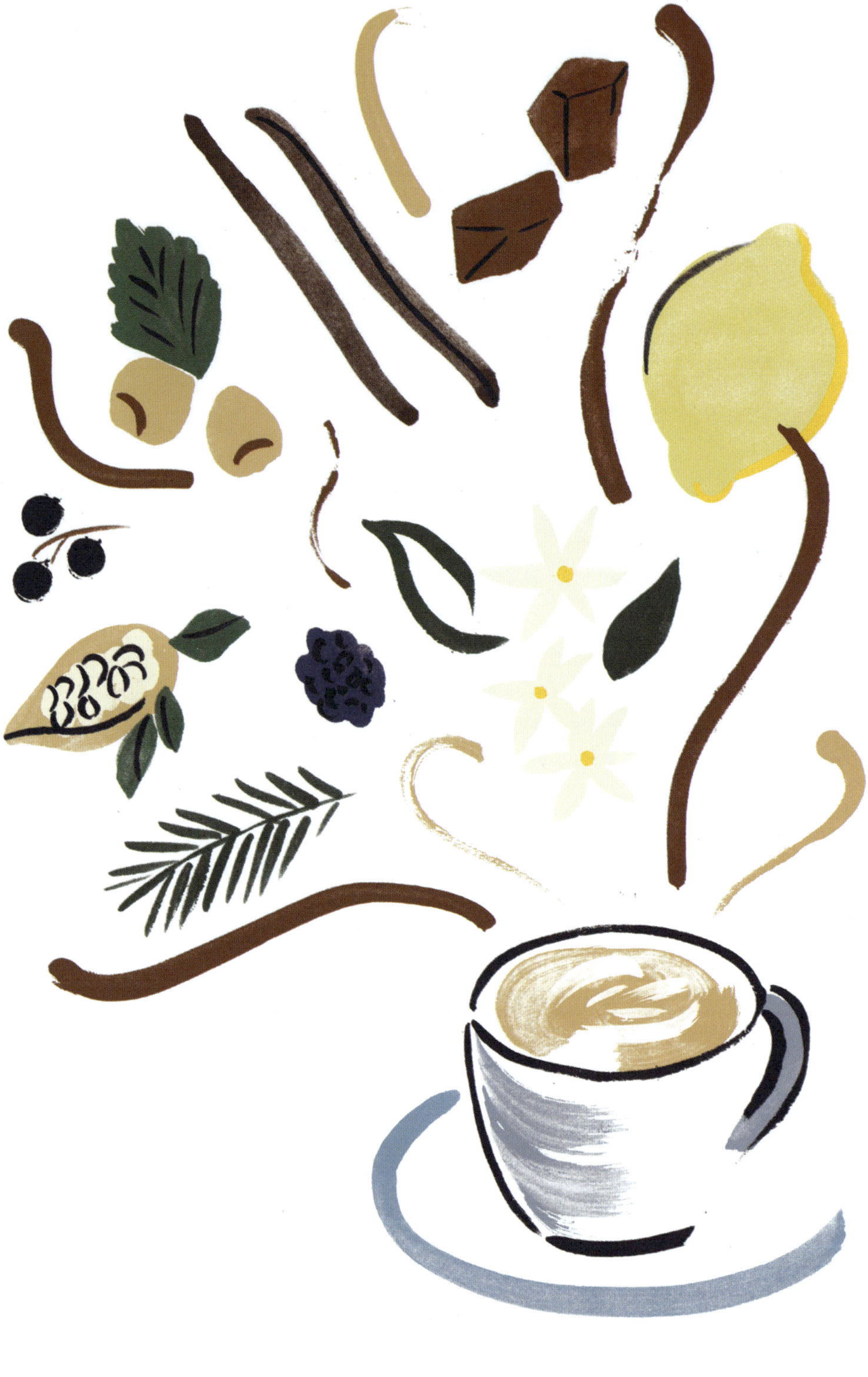

Understanding Aroma

THE DELICIOUS SMELL OF COFFEE

Coffee's aromas are complex, beguiling and evocative. Roasting triggers a series of chemical reactions that transform the pale-green seeds. Heat creates new aromatic compounds that are trapped within the molecular structure of the roasted coffee bean. When the beans are ground, these gases are released into the air and the brew. The compound responsible for much of coffee's 'freshly brewed' aroma is 2-furfurylthiol. Its smell can lift the spirits. But our sense of smell is peculiar. The same aromatic compound in different contexts and intensities can smell like rotting cabbage or even sewage.

So while coffee smells delicious, I have never been entirely sure that it is wholly pleasant. I am pretty sure that I have been conditioned, like one of Pavlov's dogs, to salivate at the smell of coffee being ground. It is the promise of things to come and a prompt that I am about to ingest caffeine.

The way humans detect aroma offers two important points for us to appreciate as we start tasting. We want both to harness the immense potential of our sense of smell and to guard against personal bias and a misreading of our body's physiological shortcuts.

TIM'S TASTING TIP
Whenever possible, use freshly ground coffee. It tastes demonstrably better and makes your work easier and more enjoyable.

AROMA AND FLAVOUR: A COMPLICATED RELATIONSHIP

Aroma and flavour are detected by the olfactory nerves in the nasal cavity, just below your brain (see opposite). Aroma and flavour share qualities, but are physiologically distinct.

Aroma comes from smelling. Aromatic compounds enter the nasal cavity without passing through the mouth. Smelling directly through the nose, which is technically called 'orthonasal olfaction', evolved to warn us off ingesting food or drink that could make us sick. The proximity of the olfactory nerves to the brain enables signals to travel straight into the amygdala – where pleasure as well as fight-or-flight responses are processed – and the hippocampus – where memories are catalogued for later retrieval. As a consequence, aromas can make your mouth water at the smell of food caramelizing and can prompt revulsion by the odour of rotting food.

These physical reactions are possible because your brain automatically logs everything you eat or drink. Much of the skill of the taster lies in the ability to categorize these memories into an orderly mental catalogue so they can recall relevant aromas, flavours and information.

Flavour is also detected by the olfactory nerves, but from aromatic compounds that have risen from the back of your mouth into the nasal cavity. Retronasal olfaction evolved to give us one last chance to spit out potentially harmful food before we swallow it.

Aromatic compounds that enter the nasal cavity through the nose are referred to as aromas, while aromatic compounds that arise from the mouth are called flavours. Coffee's aromas can be perceived without drinking. Flavours come from tasting a brew once ingested through the mouth.

Most languages hint at this distinction with categories of aromas that are not flavours. For example, something can smell 'floral' but it can't taste 'floral'. There are, however, other aromatic compounds that smell and taste alike. A coffee can both smell and taste of, say, strawberries.

To be proficient at identifying coffee's aromas it's useful to have both an appreciation of the array of coffee's aromas and, ideally, some basic coffee production knowledge (for more on this, see Terroir and Taste, page 131). This enables you to rapidly cross-link each distinctive aroma you encounter with a morsel of information. Skilled tasters have invested in building vast mental databases of aromas, each of which is tagged with various taxonomies: the aroma's category, its chemical compound and associated production processes.

But let's not let the ideal get in the way of the pragmatic. It's simply not necessary to complete this task to either enjoy drinking coffee or to develop a working understanding that enables you to navigate coffee's aromas and appreciate your preferences.

OLFACTORY SYSTEM

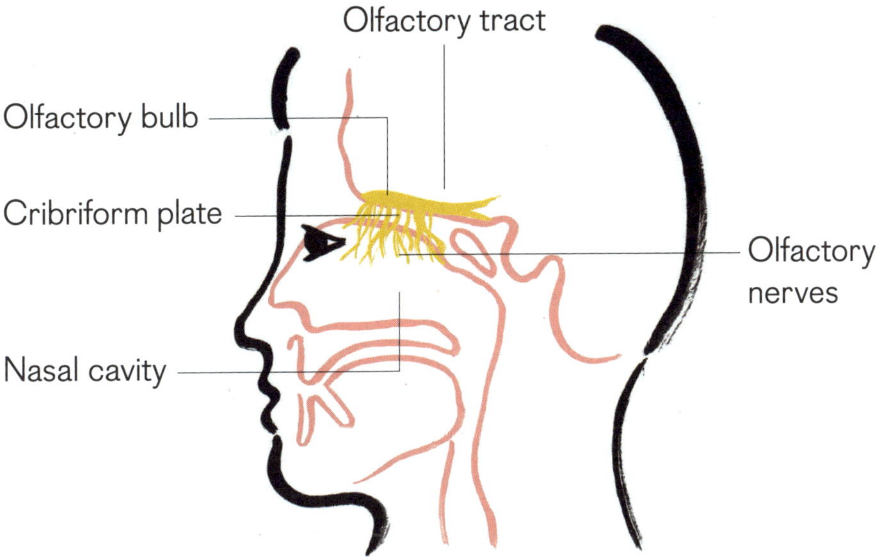

TRIGEMINAL NERVE

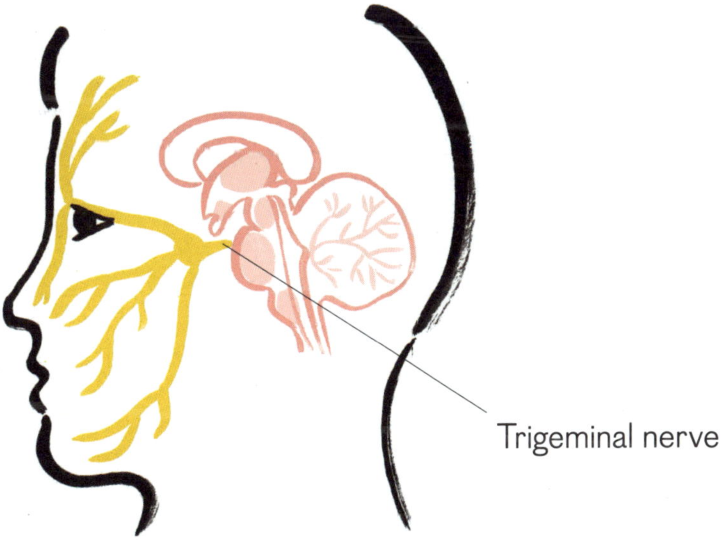

AROMA

THE EVOCATIVENESS OF AROMAS

Our foraging ancestors required mental maps detailing the best places to find ripe fruit, harvest mushrooms in season and locate fresh drinking water, as well as a strong memory of whether the food or drink was edible and nutritious.

Each time you eat or drink something, your brain notes the physical location. The underlying purpose of these memories is to enable you to safely eat and drink in the future, so your brain also stores how what you've consumed makes you feel, immediately and in the hours afterwards. The process requires no deliberate choice on your part. Signals are sent from the olfactory bulb directly to the hippocampus, bypassing the thalamus, which processes the information from your other senses.

The direct relationship between the olfactory nerves and the brain is why aromas can have the power to transport you to another time and place. The brain automatically scans its catalogue for places you once consumed food or drink that shared these aromas. The objective is to offer feedback on whether it's likely safe to be consumed, but often that information arrives with a flood of associated memories. The smell of strawberries still teleports me to my grandmother's strawberry patch in Christchurch, New Zealand.

Such memories can be powerful and deeply personal. They are powerful because aromas can trigger memories with little mental processing that feel very direct and profoundly true. And they are personal because no one else shares your reference point.

Skilled tasters bolt additional information onto these memories. When you smell something that evokes a personal memory, harness it to identify the aroma, make a mental note of the other aromas that are also present and try to understand what in the coffee's processing contributed to the creation of these aromatic compounds. This brings us to an important aspect of coffee tasting: identifying tasting notes for yourself and communicating them to others are two entirely different undertakings.

Coffee is an inherently social drink and is made to be shared. To talk or write about a coffee in a meaningful way demands that you use a common, shared language. Don't be fooled by the depth of your emotion. Harness the power of your memories, but then translate these into generalized terms before you share them with others. You can, of course, record personal tasting notes for your own benefit. When tasting a coffee by myself, I often use personal memories and references for speed. But these notes are a unique shorthand or a personal code. When I write tasting notes for the benefit of peers or the public, I first translate them into tasting notes that can be both readily appreciated and that accurately represent the experience.

IDENTIFYING AROMAS

The Aroma Map (see pages 66–7) is comprised of aromas commonly reported by baristas, buyers and quality graders. Each aroma is organized both by category and its dominant aromatic compound. For example, 'Dark Chocolate' is categorized in 'Cocoa' and 'Lactones'. To identify key aromas, identify the category and then browse the aromas in the category for a more specific descriptor.

Most tasty coffees will have at least one aroma from the top loop and one aroma from the bottom loop. Many coffees also have aromas associated with the heavier esters, which are in the area where the two circles overlap.

Some coffees will have aromas not included in the Aroma Map. There are more than 600 aromatic compounds potentially present in coffee – the Map includes just 101 of the most common aromas.

Don't overreach. It's possible that a coffee has just one, or even no, pleasant aromas. Furthermore, it's quite possible that a coffee's aromas are indistinct. There's nothing wrong – and everything right – with noting a generic term such as 'earthy' or 'berry' if the aroma is generic.

Some people will find specific aromas agreeable and pleasant, while others might find the same aromas disagreeable. This is largely a matter of context, personal preference and familiarity.

If you like a particular aroma that others find objectionable, there is little need for you to conform to the consensus. In fact, you've just identified a characteristic that you are more willing to purchase than others, so you are likely to be able to buy with greater value.

TIM'S TASTING TIP

Try to work swiftly. Your olfactory receptors become desensitized to new aromas, and it gets increasingly difficult to identify a coffee's distinct aromas. If this happens, take a couple of steps back from the cup and sniff the back of your hand or the top of your arm. This gives your nose a break by removing the coffee's aromas and helps you to reset using a neutral, familiar odour. If your senses are completely overwhelmed, take a short break and get some fresh air outside before tasting your next coffee.

The Aroma Map

ESTERS

BERRY
Strawberry
Raspberry
Blueberry
Blackberry
Blackcurrant

ORCHARD
Nectarine
Peach
Apricot
Plum
Cherry
Pomegranate
Red Apple
Green Apple
Pear

TROPICAL
Passionfruit
Lychee
Banana
Overripe Fruit
Mango
Papaya
Cantaloupe
Pineapple

DRIED FRUITS
Raisin
Fig
Prune
Date

ALCOHOL
Aged Spirits
Winey

FURANS

SWEET
Vanilla
Caramel

PYRAZINES

ROASTED
Toasted Bread
Roasted Nuts

NUTS
Pistachio
Almond
Hazelnut
Peanut
Cashew
Walnut

GRAINS
Barley
Bran
Wheat
Corn
Rice

LACTONES

COCOA
Cocoa Powder
Dark Chocolate

LIGNIN

FIBROUS
Paper
Wood

TERPENES

CITRUS
Orange
Blood Orange
Grapefruit
Lemon
Lime

FLORAL
Orange Blossom
Honeysuckle
Jasmine
Rose
Lavender
Chamomile
Lilac
Violet
Elderflower
Hibiscus

HERBAL
Basil
Thyme
Rosemary
Sage
Lemongrass
Mint
Coriander Leaf
Dill
Green Tea

ALDEHYDES

VEGETATIVE
Fresh Cut Grass
Green Bell Pepper
Cucumber
Spinach
Peas
Tea Leaf
Celery
Hay
Tomato Leaf
Tomato

PHENOLS

SPICE
Coriander Seed
Peppercorns
Ginger
Licorice
Anise
Cardamom
Nutmeg
Cinnamon
Clove

EARTHY
Leather
Rubber
Tobacco
Peat
Smoke
Soil

TERPENOIDS

MEDICINAL
Menthol
Pine Resin
Eucalyptus

HALIDES

MINERAL
Wet Stone
Sea Air

101 COMMON, POSITIVE COFFEE AROMAS BY DOMINANT AROMATIC COMPOUND

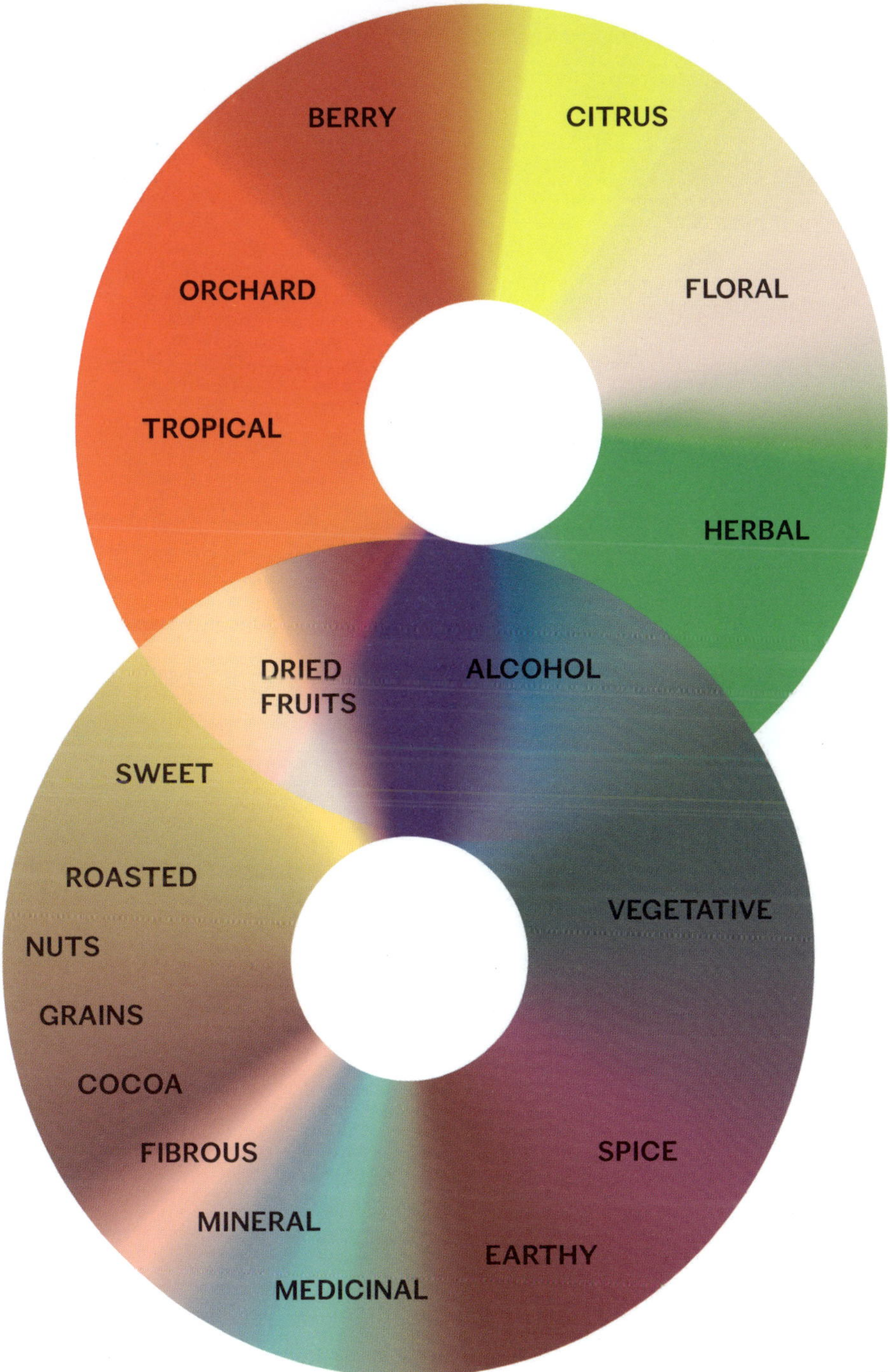

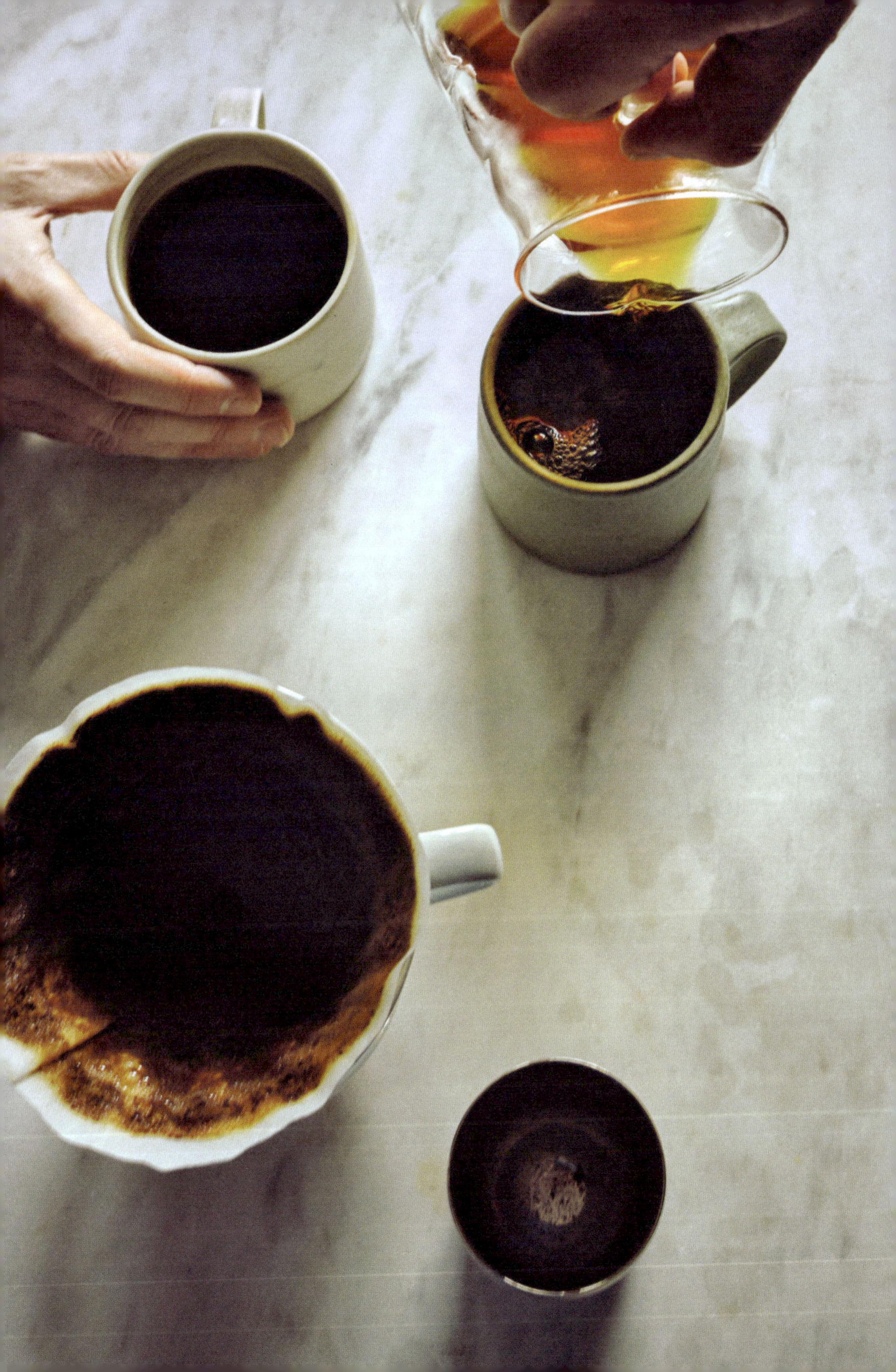

THE STRUCTURE OF A COFFEE'S AROMAS

Note each distinctive aroma. Depending on the coffee, it's typical to identify between zero and five aromas. Some coffees, mainly those that are of lower quality and darkly roasted, have no identifiable aromas other than smelling generically like coffee. Good coffees typically have at least two distinct aromas, and better coffees have many more.

Take a moment to consider the structure of the aromas. There are several common structures. Some coffees predominantly have aromas in the lower loop, and you might hear these coffees described using terms such as 'dark', 'low' and 'heavy', or as having 'bottom notes' or 'legs' and so on. Other coffees have aromas predominantly from the top loop, and these might have words ascribed to them such as 'bright', 'light' and 'fresh'.

In the centre of the Aroma Map are the heavy esters that typically smell of dried fruits and alcohols. Some coffees have next to no bottom or top notes but have a 'middle'. And, conversely, some coffees with high notes and low notes have no middle and offer the aromatic impression of being 'hollow'.

I'm not a fan of such indistinct terms, but the conceptualization of aromas potentially being present in the bottom, middle or top is very useful. Many pleasant coffees – though not all – have at least one aroma from the top loop and another aroma from the bottom loop.

Thinking about the structure of the aromas is both more revealing and more useful than an unordered list of aromas. Once you start considering each coffee's aromatic structure, you will quickly start to recognize structures you find pleasant. Plus, it might not be so much that you like nutty and cocoa-like coffees, as that you have fond memories of pyrazines and lactones. Empowered with these insights, you are liberated from solely buying coffees of the same origin – you can now look for coffees that have a similar aromatic structure or benefit from a similar dominant aromatic compound.

AROMA

GENERAL VERSUS SPECIFIC AROMAS

The Aroma Map incorporates only primary natural aromas. Your reference point might be more specific, for example 'Granny Smith apple' or 'strawberry patch'. Granny Smith is a secondary descriptor, as it is a more specific than 'green apple'. Strawberry patch is a compound descriptor because it is comprised of various primary aromas including those of strawberries, earth and hay.

In general, specific descriptors are better – as long as they are universally shared. The Granny Smith is an Australian cultivar and was a feature of my Antipodean childhood, but it's now widely available in Western countries. In this case, the more international the audience is, the more likely I would be to communicate this note as 'green apple'.

Compound descriptors require similar consideration. If the note is prominent and widely shared, it will be highly compelling. But deconstructing compound descriptors can both increase clarity and reveal structure. Taking 'strawberry patch' as an example, strawberry is a lightweight ester and is near the top of the Aroma Map. The aromas of earth and hay are in the lower loop towards the bottom. Breaking the note down into its constituent parts reveals that this coffee benefits from high highs and lower lows. It also poses the question: does this coffee have additional prominent aromas, especially from the centre of the Aroma Map?

Always deconstruct compound aroma notes so you can appreciate the structure and be open to identifying other aromas. If you are resisting breaking down a compound descriptor, it's probably because it's highly personal and compelling for you. Park that thought for a minute and start again with an open mind. It is all too easy to overlook other defining aromas once you've prematurely locked onto a compound aroma note. Then, once you have identified all the key defining aromas, you can use them to construct an accurate and compelling compound descriptor.

AROMA, TASTE AND FLAVOUR

Aromas provide only clues about each coffee's taste and flavour. Based on aroma alone, even experienced tasters struggle to predict how sweet, bitter and sour a coffee will be. We have very limited physiological capacity to smell a taste, if any.

Similarly, the coffee you are about to ingest could have very similar flavours to its aromas. Or it could be completely different. This creates a moment of palpable tension and a strong urge to start drinking this coffee as quickly as possible. But, before you do, hold out for a few seconds longer and make a prediction. Go on, take a punt – what do you think the prominent tastes will be? And what do you guess this coffee's defining flavours will be?

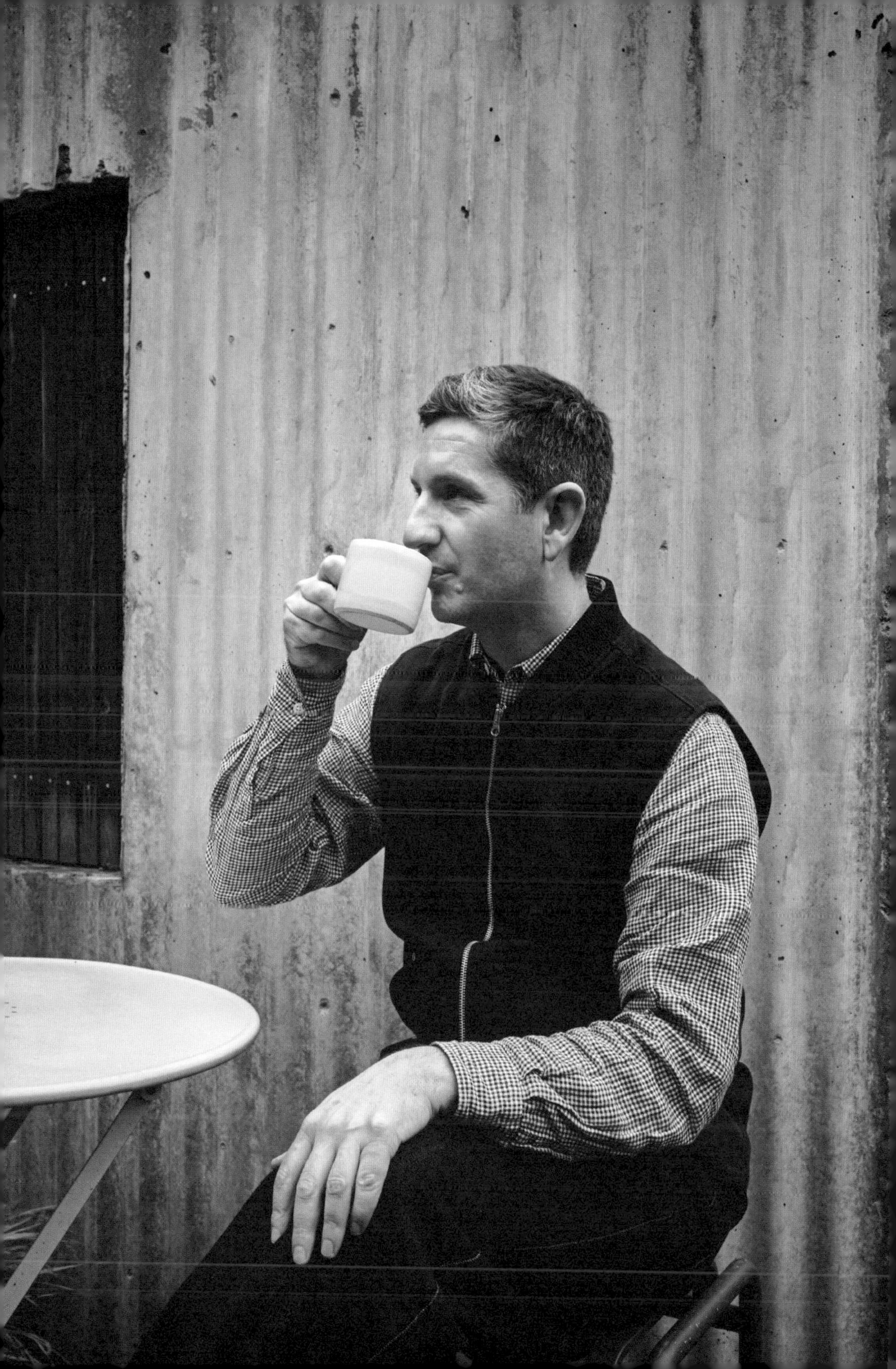

Assessing aroma

Raise the cup to your nose and smell the coffee.

1.

How intense are the aromas?

- Start by noting whether the aromas are more or less intense than is typical.
- If the aromas are less intense, it's possible the coffee wasn't freshly ground, was roasted too long ago or has been sitting in a warehouse for too long.
- If they are more intense, take a moment to consider the less bold notes.

2.

What does the coffee smell like? Use the Aroma Map to identify key primary aromas.

- Start by identifying the aroma's category. For example, it might be 'tropical' or 'earthy'.
- Is there is an accurate primary descriptor? For example, might a tropical note specifically be banana, mango or pineapple?
- Repeat for each prominent aroma, specifically identifying aromas from the top, middle and base.

3.

Are the aromas better described with secondary aromatic descriptors? Taking banana as an example:

- Might the aroma be more accurately described as overripe or underripe banana?

4.

Do multiple aromas combine to make compound aromatic descriptors? Taking pineapple as an example:

- Are there other aromas that in combination give a more compelling overall impression? For example, pineapple, coconut and alcohol might combine to create a compound descriptor of piña colada. Or strawberries and hay might combine to evoke a strawberry patch.

5.

Consider:

- How do the aromas compare with your expectations following the visual assessment?
- What is the structure of the aromas?
- How do the aromas shape your expectations of flavour?

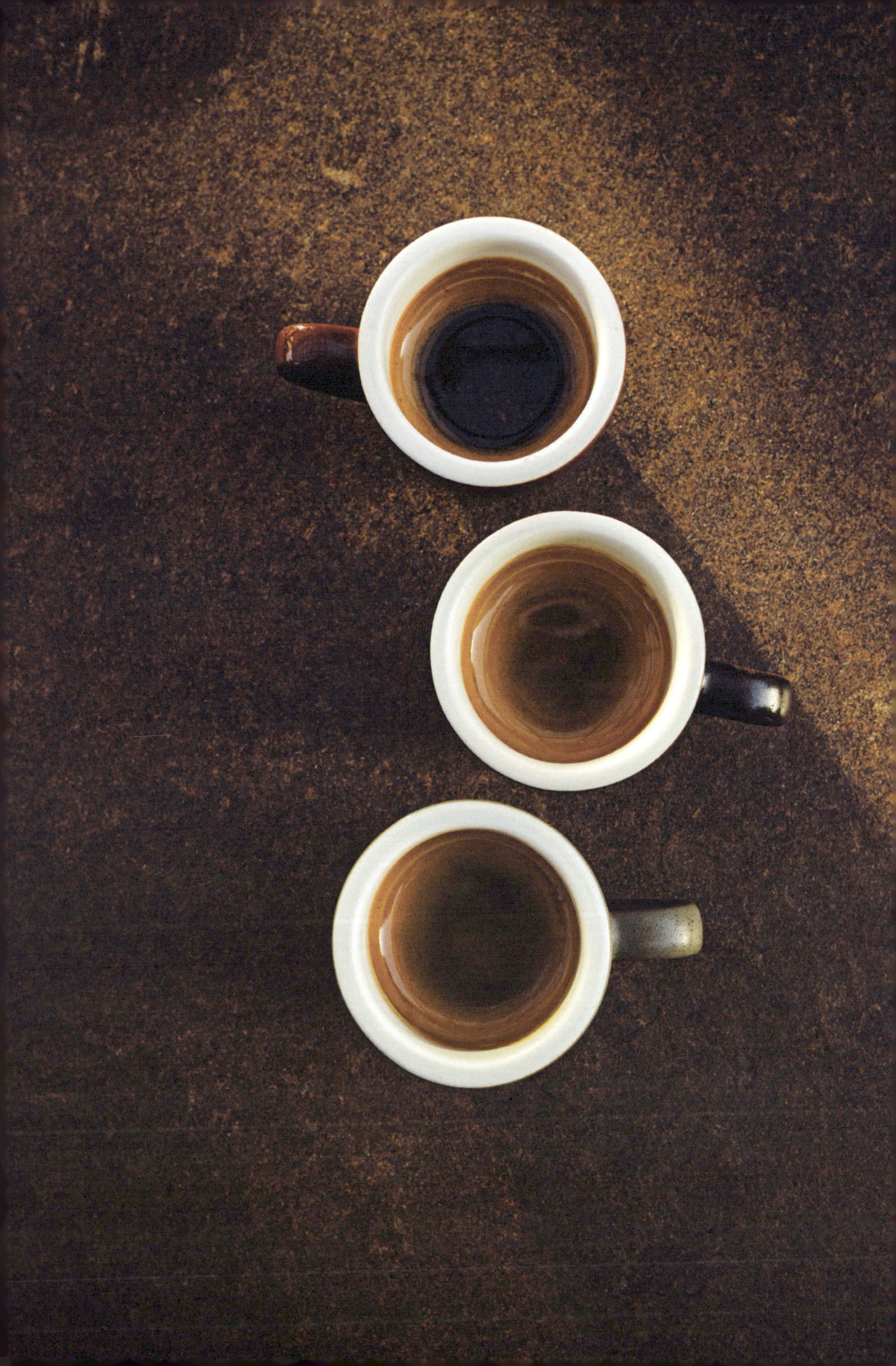

Defining Mouthfeel

MOUTHFEEL

THE TEXTURE OF COFFEE

Mouthfeel is sometimes referred to as 'body'. You may have seen tasting notes that include 'lightweight body' or 'silky body', for example. Mouthfeel is simply how, when you hold the liquid in your mouth, a beverage makes your mouth feel. We will assess each coffee on two attributes: weight and texture.

Our focus is on a subcategory of sensations detected by the trigeminal nerve (see illustration, page 63). The nerve has branches into your nasal cavity, mouth and throat. When you experience the cooling vapours of menthol, the crisp sensation of iced soda water or the burn in your throat from woodsmoke, these are trigeminal nerve endings responding to chemical irritants or temperature changes.

People are often well attuned to trigeminal sensations, even if they don't know what they are. Ask an everyday coffee drinker to describe a coffee's flavour and common descriptors will include terms such as 'smooth', 'round', 'full' or 'thin'. While none of these are flavours, it's possible to appreciate their meaning. Plus, it's notable that these drinkers have instinctively focused on mouthfeel. There's a good argument to be made that mouthfeel is the most important, overlooked aspect of tasty coffee. Delicious coffees always have a pleasant mouthfeel.

MOUTHFEEL

WEIGHT

Weight and texture often go together, but it's important to assess them separately. The perceived 'weight' varies with the quantity and type of compounds in the brew, which vary from coffee to coffee, as well as the fats and oils, which vary by brew method and roasting.

Darker roasts, finer grinds, hotter water and other techniques that boost extraction increase the quantity of total dissolved solids (TDS) in the cup, and your perception of the coffee's weight. Additionally, some brewing methods, such as pour-over drippers, use paper filters that remove more oils, fats and particles, resulting in a lighter-weight mouthfeel.

Espresso, which is brewed under pressure with more finely ground coffee, has 8–12 per cent TDS, ten times greater than filter coffee which typically has 1.2–1.5 per cent TDS. When preparing coffees for a tasting flight, it is best to uniformly brew each of the coffees. The objective is to assess the weight of each coffee, rather than the impact of the brewing method on the coffee.

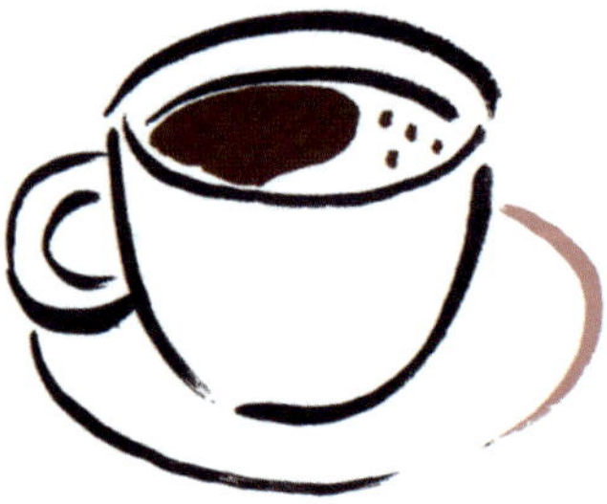

It's sufficient to assess each coffee on a three-point scale: light, medium or heavy. Learning to assess weight is largely a matter of calibration. Coffees are always weightier than water. So, you can identify a baseline by assessing the weight of the water you used for brewing. The closer the weight of the coffee is to the water, the more lightweight it is.

You have probably already drunk coffees with light, medium and heavy weights, but you possibly buy coffees of a similar weight and have forgotten about the span of weights possible. For filter coffee, a light mouthfeel approximates the weight of a lightly steeped green tea or a low-concentrate cordial while heavier weights are closer to fruit juices or milk.

TIM'S TASTING TIP

When first assessing coffee, it can be useful to prepare coffee with your normal brewing method, especially at home. You will have already calibrated your palate to appreciate lighter-weight and heavier-weight coffees. I like to taste coffees brewed on a Hario V60 or a Ratio brewer because they offer sufficient body to assess mouthfeel and sufficient clarity to assess flavours. See Brewing Coffee for Tasting (page 35) for more on brewing.

TEXTURE

If you are struggling to identify the weight, it's almost certainly because there is a distinctive texture. Mouthfeel textures that are perceived as pleasant include 'silky', 'smooth' or 'viscous', and textures generally perceived as unpleasant include 'astringent', 'watery', 'dusty' and 'rough'.

When assessing texture, you will instinctively respond to each texture as pleasant or unpleasant, and there is widespread agreement among coffee drinkers as to whether a coffee has a pleasant texture, or not. Roasters often use euphemistic terms to hint at unpleasant mouthfeels, so there are a multitude of terms in circulation. There is no need to cover all the textures here, but it is nonetheless useful to be able to identify the most common ones and appreciate what they mean.

Viscous

Emulsified oils and tiny suspended solids are dispersed throughout the liquid, increasing viscosity and contributing to a mouth-coating sensation. The more viscous a coffee is, the more it 'sticks' to the inside of your mouth. This often makes more viscous coffees feel 'thick'. Don't confuse viscosity with weight, even though they are frequently aligned. Most viscous coffees have a medium- or heavyweight mouthfeel. But it's worth separating these characteristics because it's possible for lightweight coffees to have notable viscosity, and not all heavyweight coffees are viscous.

Most people find viscosity pleasant. But that doesn't mean that greater viscosity is better. Occasionally, the viscosity is slimy, which is generally unpleasant. And when a coffee sticks to the inside of your mouth, the 'finish' is prolonged. A 'long finish' is positive, but you will perceive it as disagreeable if the viscosity prolongs unpleasant flavours.

Smooth and silky

When the water-binding molecules that create viscosity combine with proteins and lipids, the texture can be perceived as 'smooth' through to 'silky'. I am yet to meet a single person who doesn't find these textures pleasant. As well as being agreeable, these textures are more likely to be present with a desirable TDS ratio, which is an indicator that the cup has been well prepared.

The terms are similar but not interchangeable. Smooth textures feel 'rounded', and silky textures 'glide' across your palate.

The opposite of smooth and silky is 'rough', which is where the texture feels jagged and it is frequently not integrated with the coffee's taste or flavour. Some coffees have a rough texture, but it can also be a consequence of uneven extraction or channelling during brewing. If the brew is unexpectedly rough, consider brewing another cup more carefully.

MOUTHFEEL

Astringent

Astringency is the sensation of your mouth 'drying' out. Proteins in your saliva coat and lubricate the inside of your mouth. When higher concentrations of polyphenols are present in a coffee, they bind with the proteins, causing the inside of your to feel 'dry'.

It's best not to describe the coffee as 'dry'; instead use 'astringent'. 'Dry', or *sec* is often used in beverage tasting and means 'not sweet'. As we will discover, all coffees are 'dry', in the sense that they have a very low sugar content.

By contrast, astringency in coffee is pleasant only when is has limited intensity, has a fine-grained texture, and is short-lived because the polyphenols are smaller in size. This texture is relatively close to that of pleasant tannins in red wine or tea. Additionally, agreeable astringency is almost always aligned with an equally intense rumble of bitterness. By contrast, coarse, rough and enduring astringency is almost universally disliked.

Thin (and worse, 'thin with bits')

If the mouthfeel is lightweight with low viscosity, it might be described as 'thin'. This is typically unpleasant.

Additionally, if the coffee beans are old, poorly processed or roasted badly, the cell walls can be brittle. These beans are less soluble. With less to give, your brew often has a thin mouthfeel, plus you may feel small fragments of cell wall in the cup. A thin and bitty mouthfeel is very unpleasant.

'Thin with bits' is typically a sign of cheap coffee. I most frequently encounter this texture in circumstances where filter coffee is given away in a transient context: during breakfast service at a hotel, in-flight complimentary coffee, a coffee break at a conference and so on. When it occurs with a higher-quality coffee, it is almost always a sign that something has gone badly wrong during transport, storage or roasting.

Dirty, muddy, silty

The final key unpleasant mouthfeel you will encounter is 'muddy'. If 'thin with bits' is like dirt suspended in water, then 'dirty', 'muddy' and 'silty' are like a landslide damning your mouth. This sensation is universally disagreeable and most people habitually add milk to coffees that are dirty or muddy to dilute and soften the mouthfeel.

No texture

Not all coffees have a distinctive texture. In fact, many don't. Most coffees feel very ordinary. If the coffee doesn't have a notable mouthfeel, just assess the weight. Textures are important when they are a defining characteristic.

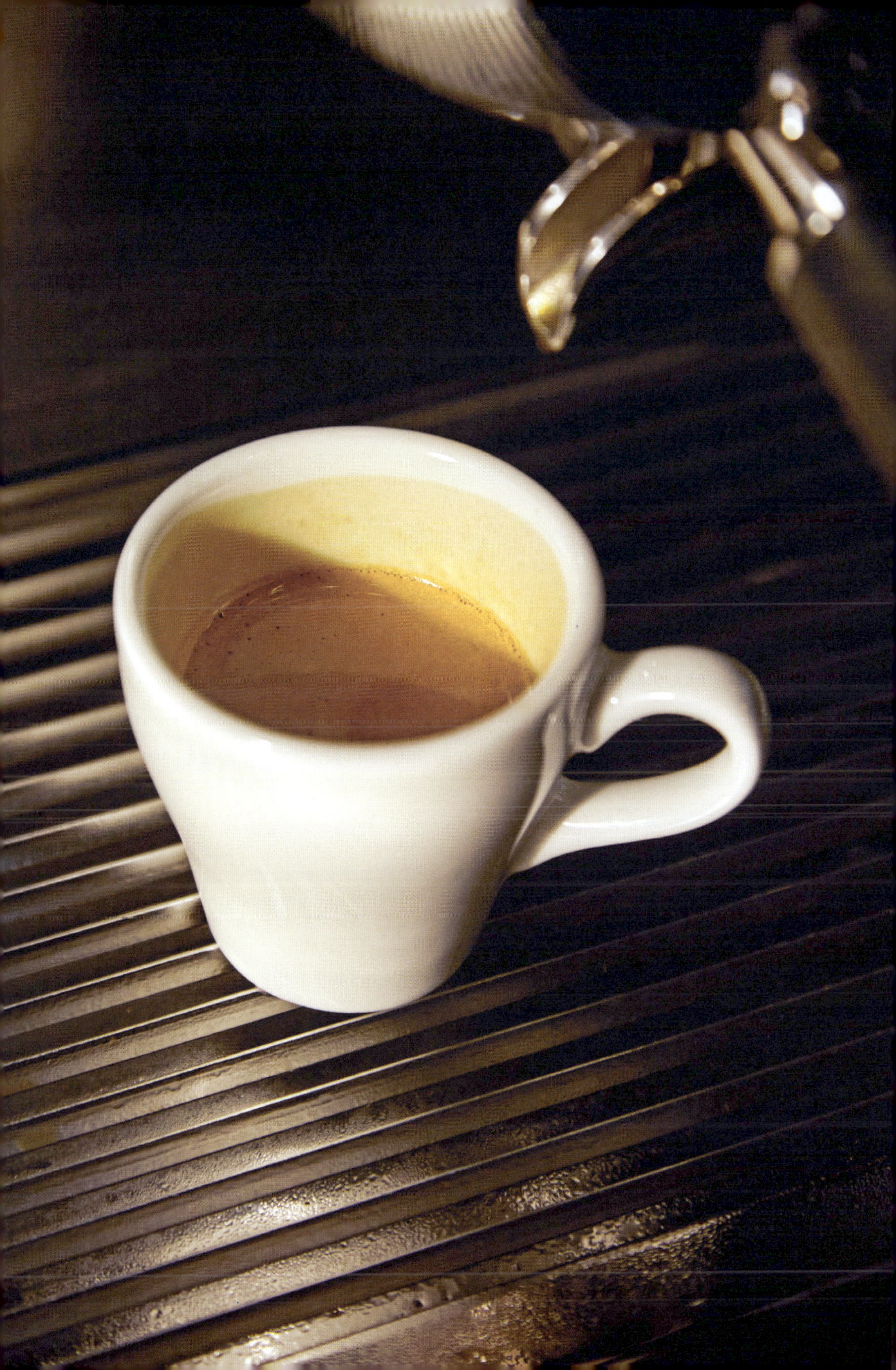

Assessing mouthfeel

1.

Take a sip.

- Take a small sip, say a dessert-spoonful of coffee into your mouth.
- Swirl the coffee around your palate by rotating your jaw and...
- Open your lips and let your jaw hang a little slack.

2.

How does the coffee feel in your mouth?

- Is it light, medium or heavy?
- The 'weight' is important when it is notable. For example, is the coffee particularly, or unexpectedly, light or heavy?

Swirl the coffee around your mouth.

3.

Does it have a distinctive texture?

- For example, is it effervescent, viscous or astringent?
- Some coffees have a lightly sparkling sensation, despite not being carbonated. Others are particularly syrupy on the inside of your mouth and can be labelled as viscous. Texture describes only the feel. For example, a coffee could be both light-bodied and viscous.

4.

Consider:

- Is the mouthfeel aligned with the colour or aroma?
- Is the overall mouthfeel pleasant?

ASSESSING A CUP OF COFFEE

Before we move on to taste, it's useful to point out that we are assessing *brewed coffee.* This places us, the coffee drinker, several steps removed from origin. Our assessment is of the cup of coffee, not the coffee farmer. There are multiple possible reasons why we may detect positive or negative traits.

For example, decisions made during roasting, such as about heat intensity and duration, shape the chemical reactions and impact the development of various compounds.

Equally, the temperature and mineral composition of the water, as well as the temperature of the water impact the extraction during brewing. Small differences can change which compounds become soluble and therefore affect your cup. Plus, all these chemical compounds interact with your saliva.

This means we are assessing a coffee, roasted by a certain roaster, brewed with a particular water and method and consumed in a specific context. Each of these variables influences the coffee's inherent aromas, textures, tastes and flavours by a matter of degree.

As tasters we seek to standardize these variables so we can more readily assess each coffee's unique and defining characteristics. As a barista, however, we would typically seek to optimize each coffee's characteristics for pleasantness by compensating for disagreeable traits. Baristas often seek to enhance coffees by tweaking the water, the brewing temperature, the coffee-to-water ratio and the duration of the extraction.

Coffee is an agricultural product, and, as we will discuss later, farmers need to able to sell their entire crop regardless of the challenges they faced during the growing season. It's important to be generous when assessing coffee, and especially so in our judgements of producers. If I am to pass judgement on a coffee, I typically judge the roaster. Out of all the coffees available in the world they have chosen *this* coffee. And, furthermore, they have total control over how they roast it. I appreciate that few things are perfect. Most of us are constrained by a range of factors including the weather, time, our budget and available information. I respect farmers, brokers, buyers and roasters seeking to navigate their constraints in the pursuit of value and quality.

You can often tell the difference between lower- and higher-quality coffee when assessing mouthfeel. It is simply not possible to roast old, defective or poor-quality beans in a way that enhances the mouthfeel.

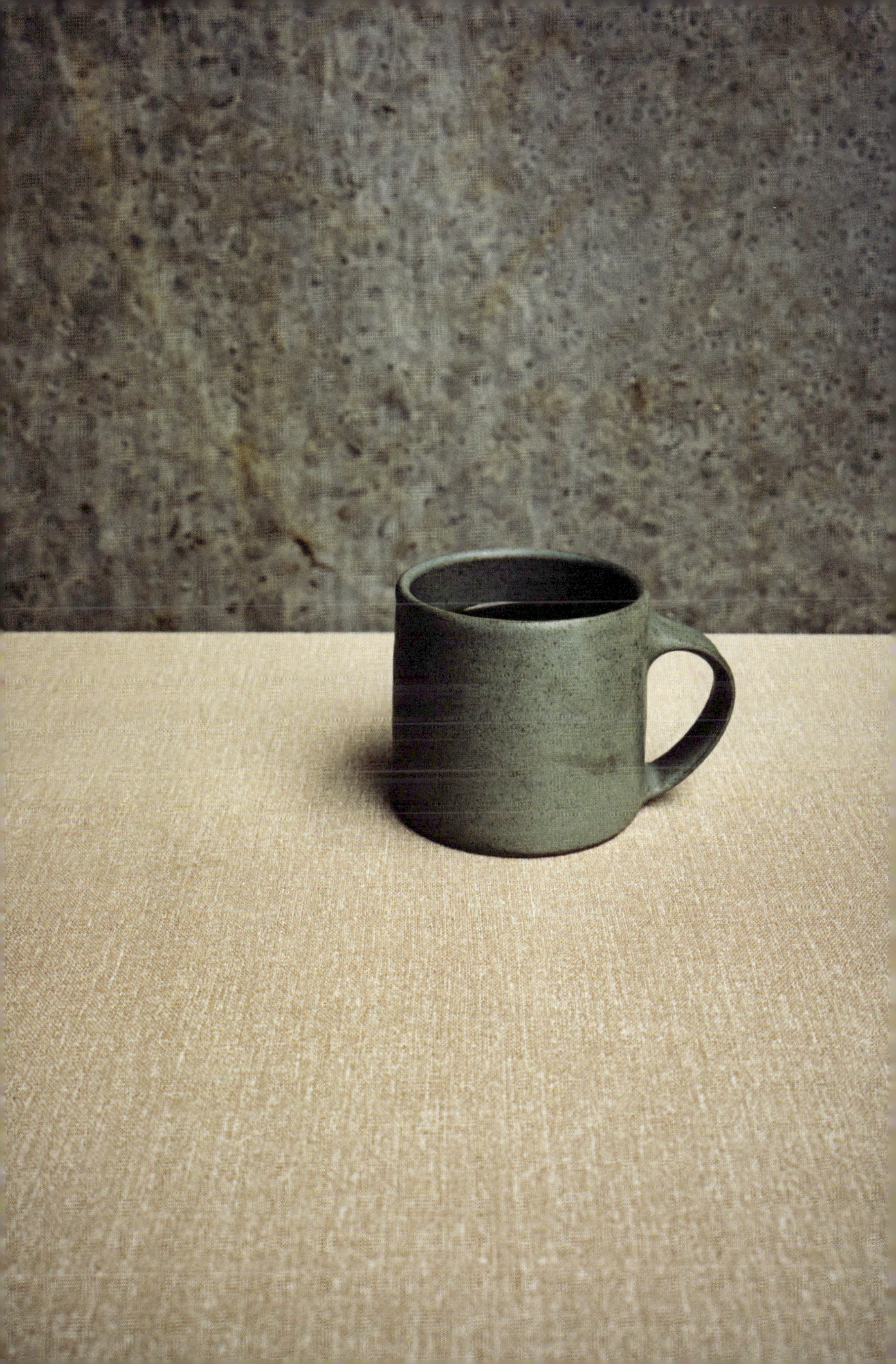

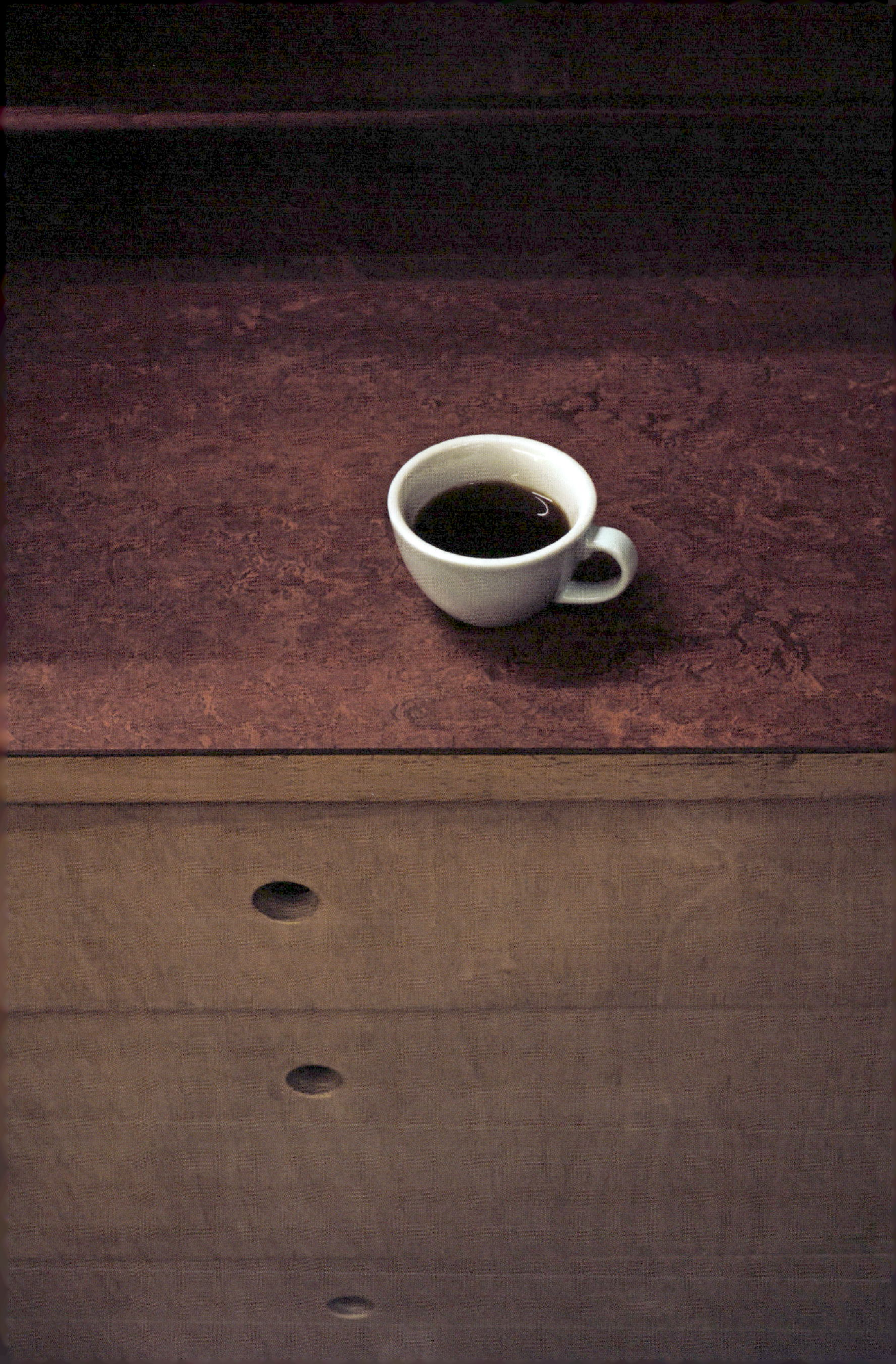

The Five Basic Tastes

TASTE

THE HARMONIOUS BALANCE OF TASTES

Taste is a delicate balance. Imagine you are standing on a star-shaped board placed on top of a ball. If the points are evenly weighted, it's possible to stand upright. If they are unevenly weighted, you will topple off.

A harmonious balance of tastes is not quite so simple, but it's close. This chapter focuses on identifying the key basic tastes, ascertaining whether they are sufficiently balanced to be tasty, and exploring why some taste combinations are more agreeable than others.

There are just five basic tastes: sweet, salty, sour, bitter and umami. All these attributes are detected on the tongue. Acids are present in all coffees and are perceived as sour, and all coffees have some bitterness. Well-roasted quality coffees usually benefit from some sweetness. Saltiness is rare. Umami is becoming more common with the increased prevalence of fermentation processing methods. A harmonious balance should be achieved between at least two of the basic tastes.

BITTER

The perception of bitterness evolved as a warning system for humans and a defence mechanism for plants. A range of toxins and secondary metabolites in plants have a bitter taste. The naturally occurring insecticide in coffee shrubs, 1, 3, 7-trimethylxanthine, is bitter. This compound is better known as caffeine.

There has been reluctance among quality coffee roasters to mention bitterness in tasting notes, largely because of its association with low-quality coffee. But not all bitterness is equal. Bitter vegetables such as radicchio, kale and roquette (arugula) are known for their sophisticated flavours and nutritional value. The gin and tonic celebrates the bitterness of quinine. And the foundational ingredient of chocolate is, of course, predominantly bitter.

Bitterness in coffee can be divided into two categories: bitterness present from coffee production and bitterness introduced from roasting.

Bitter chlorogenic acids are present in high levels in green coffee and are largely broken down during roasting. The residual compounds add a bitter sophistication and balance to a cup of coffee. And because these compounds are acids, they have a sour edge too. This type of bitterness is correlated with an astringent mouthfeel, as chlorogenic acids are phenols. When the resulting astringency is fine-grained and short-lived, the combination of the bitterness and gentle astringency is typically pleasant.

The second category of bitterness is introduced during roasting. Longer, dark roasts allow for the creation of more phenylindanes, leading to an intense, lingering, rough

It takes a wide range of tasting experience

taste. Some people perceive this bitterness as 'medicinal'; most people identify higher concentrations of phenylindanes in coffee as 'burnt'.

Because most people find a low level of bitter chlorogenic acids pleasant and higher concentrations of phenylindanes unpleasant, it follows that roasters should deploy roast profiles that maximize the pleasant bitterness and minimize unpleasant bitterness. However, this requires coffees that are of sufficient quality to withstand the flavour transparency that these roasting profiles offer. If a coffee is darkly roasted, it is probably because the roaster assessed that the bitterness that comes with roasting is more pleasant than the flavours that the bitterness masks.

It takes a wide range of tasting experience to discern between different types of bitterness. Some people are adverse to bitterness in any form. For them, the perceived threat of toxins triggers involuntary disgust. Children, for example, have a strong dislike of bitterness. It takes time and experience to distinguish between foods that are potentially poisonous and those that are delicious. Coffee, IPAs, broccoli, dark chocolate and black pepper are all described as acquired tastes.

Other coffee drinkers have grown accustomed to dark-roasted, bitter coffee. For them a strong bitter taste has become associated with the forthcoming caffeine kick. Of course, most people balance pronounced bitterness by adding a teaspoon, or two, of sugar to their coffee.

It's useful to understand your personal preferences and the quality implications of bitterness. If you have been denying coffee's bitter taste, an appreciation of chlorogenic acids can open up new possibilities for a harmonious balance of taste. If you are fearful of bitterness, you can rest assuring that roasted coffee is very safe for human consumption. And if you appreciate the intense bitterness of phenylindanes, there are alternate ways to balance coffee's sweetness or sourness.

to discern between different types of bitterness

SWEET

Sweetness is a cue for energy. Sweet-tasting foods contain sugars and carbohydrates, which are dense sources of fuel for our bodies. Today, we can readily buy sugary energy in countless forms but for our foraging forebears, sugars were available only from ripe fruit, tubers, nectar and honey. It was in a sugar-scarce environment that the human sense of taste evolved.

Brewed coffee has very few sugars, especially compared with other beverages such as fruit juice, soda, or even dry white wine. During roasting, most of the sugars are converted into aromas and flavours through a series of dynamic chemical reactions between the sugars and amino acids. Depending on the coffee and the roasting profile, 95 per cent of the sugars are decomposed, mainly into furans, aldehydes, ketones, melanoidins and pyrazines – all of which are on the Aroma Map.

Sugars are most likely to be present in lighter-roasted arabica coffees. Arabica beans have about twice the sucrose levels of beans grown on *Coffea robusta* shrubs (see page 132). Only higher-quality arabica beans can withstand the flavour transparency that comes with medium roasting. Other coffees are roasted darker to burn off rough flavours.

But when we talk about sweetness in coffee, we are referring to the perception of sweetness, rather than the presence of actual sugars. The perception of sweetness in coffee is a sensory illusion. The sugars in a cup of coffee are below the tongue's sweetness detection threshold.

A coffee may be perceived as sweet because of the presence of aromatics that the brain associates with sweetness, such as fruity, floral and caramel notes. Low levels of astringency further increase the perception of sweetness as does mouthfeel textures that are round, silky and smooth.

The perception of sweetness is simultaneously an indicator of skillful coffee production, precise roasting, a pleasant mouthfeel and specific aromatic compounds as well as our predisposition towards an energy-rich sugary taste.

It's little wonder that the perception of sweetness is highly prized by coffee tasters and typically liked by coffee drinkers. The fact that we perceive sweetness when there are no sugars is part of what makes us human. Understanding our physiological responses to aroma, taste and flavour is as much a part of tasting as the mastery of a well-calibrated palate.

It is therefore completely legitimate to assess a coffee's 'sweetness', consider how this balances with the other tastes and assess whether the overall perception is pleasant. In fact, one of the key reasons coffee is perceived as sweet is that it is not overwhelmingly bitter.

SOUR

Sourness is the telltale taste of acids, in the same way that sweetness is the taste of sugars. Sourness has a less straightforward nutritional and cautionary meaning. Acids can arise from many sources for a range of reasons. For example, sourness might signal the presence of vitamin C or gut-enhancing fermentations; equally, it might be a sign of unripe fruit or spoiled meat. Consequently, like bitterness, many people are deeply uncertain about sourness and may even recoil at the puckering sensation it causes in the mouth.

There are multiple acids potentially present in coffee, each of which feels different. But they all make you salivate. You may struggle to distinguish between sourness and bitterness, because both are 'strong' sensations in the mouth. A neat trick is to sip a small mouthful of coffee, swirl it around your mouth and then swallow; then open your lips, drop your chin to your chest, look at the floor and wait...

If you instinctively close your lips, it's because saliva is about to spill out of your mouth. You can associate this taste sensation as being caused by an acid and therefore being sour. Some coffees are very acidic, and you will have to purse your lips immediately. If the coffee has less pronounced acidity, it will take a moment or two for enough saliva to build up.

Different acids have different sensations. You may wish to calibrate your palate so you can readily identify them. Citric acid is present in citrus fruits like lemons. Malic acid is the acidity in green apples and causes less puckering. Acetic acid has a sharp, vinegar-like acidity. Lactic acid is present in sour milks and yoghurts, but you may also recognize it from beer. Phosphoric acid is the bright, light acid used to enhance the crispness of soda, and in coffee it is pleasant when aligned with some fruit flavours, such as berries.

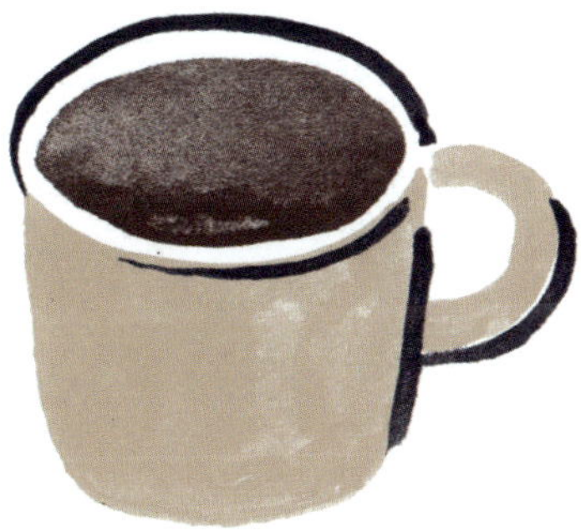

SALTY AND UMAMI

Saltiness and umami are uncommon in coffee, but they are worth mentioning both because they are noteworthy when present and have the capacity to amplify flavour.

In rare cases, coffees dried in coastal regions can absorb salt from sea air or saline soils. Trace salts can sometimes be found in Indonesian and Yemeni lots. In the case of Monsoon Malabar, coffees – traditionally from Karnataka or Kerala states in India – are dried on patios before being stored in open-sided warehouses along the Malabar coast during the monsoon. The beans are dried again and prepared for export. Monsoon Malabar is known for its heavy body, low acidity, deep flavours and occasional saltiness.

The detection of saltiness is often perceptual, triggered by associations of savoury flavours. If your coffees are consistently salty, check your water. Water with a high sodium content, or hard water that has passed through a softener that uses sodium ions, can impart a faintly salty taste.

Salt significantly reduces your perception of bitterness. If you add a little salt to a dominantly bitter espresso, the taste will be much improved. This is a reason why the salty Spanish sparkling mineral water Vichy Catalan is such a good complement to coffee.

The presence of umami is becoming more common with the advent of experimental fermentation techniques. Monosodium glutamate is to umami what salt is to saltiness. Umami adds a savoury, broth- or soy-like note reminiscent of mushroom or miso. Its presence, like that of salt, also punches up the perceived intensity of other flavours.

Coffees that have been processed using anaerobic, co-fermentation (see page 176) or yeast-inoculation techniques (see page 145) may experience amino-acid accumulation or glutamate formation, creating a perceptible umami or broth-like character.

Fruity-flavoured, acidic, sweet coffee lots with hints of umami are presently most likely to come from experimental processing in Colombia or Costa Rica while predominantly bitter coffees with traces of umami can be found in wet-hulled coffees from Indonesia.

TIM'S TASTING TIP
To calibrate your palate for bitterness, you can buy high-strength caffeine tablets. Dissolve one tablet in a cup of hot water. One tablespoon is sufficient to identify the unique taste and sensation of bitterness on your tongue.

We will learn more about both experimental fermentation and wet-hulled coffee processing in Single Origins (see page 151).

MULTIPLE TASTES

A coffee with a single dominant taste is almost always unpleasant, especially when it is bitterness or sourness. Multiple tastes are required to create balance. In coffee, this is typically sourness and/or bitterness combined with sufficient sweetness.

A balance of tastes doesn't demand that each taste be of equal intensity. Harmonious balances are created when there is sufficient intensity of a taste to counterweight another. Indeed, the dividing line between Comfort and Clarity coffees is the relative intensities of the tastes.

BALANCE OF TASTES

Comfort coffees typically have two dominant tastes – usually bitterness and sweetness – that are roughly equal in intensity. This is why Comfort coffees feel stationary and reassuring. By contrast, Clarity coffees have one taste that is more pronounced than the other. This is why Clarity coffees have a sense of momentum and – because the predominant taste is often sourness – vibrancy.

Harmonious balances are largely a function of the intensity of the bitterness and sourness. As there are imperceptibly low levels of sugar in coffee, pronounced bitterness quickly overwhelms any perception of sweetness. This is why coffees that are predominantly bitter are usually best classified as having a Classic, and not a Clarity, profile. Bitter–sweet balances are possible only when the bitterness is from the chlorogenic acids. Comfort coffee profiles often balance this gentle bitterness with the perception of sweetness. Bitter phenylindanes, which are introduced during roasting, quickly upset the delicate balance of Comfort coffees.

Coffees that benefit from a harmonious balance of sourness, bitterness and sweetness are almost always delicious. The balance of these three tastes demands the soft bitterness of chlorogenic acids, the perception of sweetness, and the right intensity of sourness.

The more the tastes are harmoniously balanced, the more consciously you will have to consider their intensity. A useful rule of thumb is that the introduction of another taste reduces the intensity of the first taste. For example, adding sugar to coffee doesn't just balance bitterness but also reduces your perception of bitterness. This is broadly true for all taste combinations, but it's worth noting that intensity of sourness is less masked by the other tastes. If you previously associated 'tasting' with identifying flavours, you might be wondering why we have spent all this time focusing on aromas, mouthfeel and tastes. But the payoff is about to come. As I have been hinting at, the most pleasant coffees benefit from strong alignment between their mouthfeel, tastes and flavours.

Assessing taste

1.

Which basic tastes are present?

2.

Is there a correlation between aroma and taste?

Hold your breath in your mouth and consider the prevalence of each taste.

3.

Are the tastes harmoniously balanced?

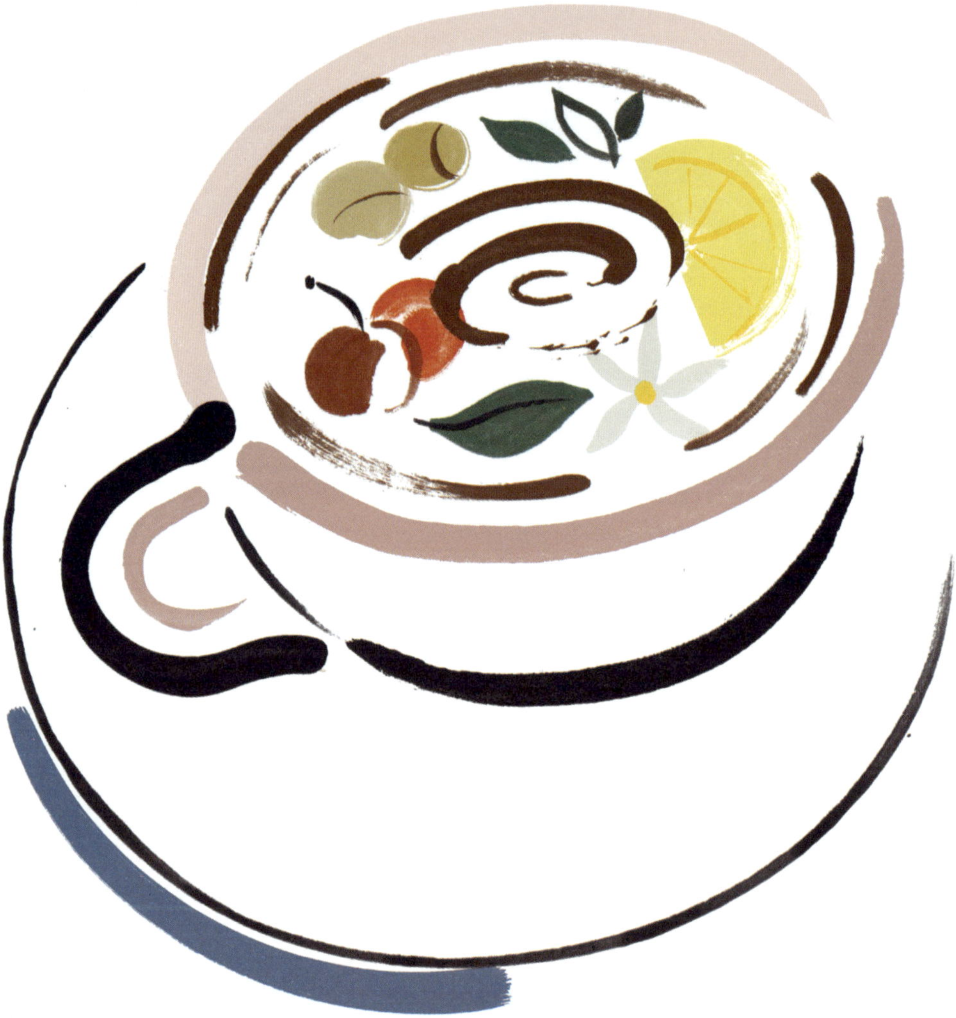

Exploring Flavour

COMMUNICATING FLAVOUR

This morning I drank a coffee that promised raspberry and mango flavours. There were, obviously, no chunks of fruit in the brew. These descriptors are a roaster's attempt to communicate that this coffee contains the compounds 4-(4-Hydroxyphenyl) butan-2-one and δ-3-Carene.

The problem with tasting notes is that every flavour is a reference to another. A coffee might be desired as 'winey', wines are often identified by their fruit flavours, some fermenting fruits are 'boozy', and some alcoholic spirits have a 'coffee' note. While there is a circular logic to flavour references, good notes are neither arbitrary nor subjective. A well-chosen flavour descriptor has the benefit of being both accurate and compelling.

THE COMPLEXITY OF COFFEE

Most beverages have similar aromas and flavours, but coffee is more complex. Roasted coffee contains an array of aromatic compounds extending from highly volatile gases to heavier soluble aromatic compounds. The soluble compounds are what gives brewed coffee its flavour. When assessing aroma, I frequently fail to guess the forthcoming flavours.

Both aromas and flavours are detected by the olfactory nerves in the nasal cavity. Aromas are detected when aromatic compounds arise from the brew, enter through the nose and reach the olfactory bulb in the nasal cavity.

Flavours, by contrast, can be detected only once the brew has been supped and is in your mouth. Some of the aromatic compounds are released from the liquid and rise into the nasal cavity where they are detected by the olfactory bulb. This is the process of retronasal olfaction and is the focus of this chapter.

While aromas and flavours are related, they are physiologically distinct. When assessing coffee it helps to appreciate that the more volatile an aromatic compound is, the less likely it is to be soluble in water – and vice versa. For example, coffee's most fragrant aromas, such as honeysuckle, rose and bergamot, seldom appear as flavours.

It is best practice to assess all beverages' aromas and flavours individually, but it is especially important for coffee as aromas and flavours are often different. Furthermore, when writing tasting notes you should always be specific about whether the descriptor is an aroma or a flavour. Mingling them together, or mixing them up, causes much confusion.

When you drink a coffee, some of the soluble aromatic compounds are released from the liquid due to the agitation of the liquid in your mouth and the aeration of your breath passing over it. Liberated, these compounds are free to rise from your mouth into your nasal cavity. This is why it helps to swirl the coffee around your mouth when you drink it. You probably do this intuitively. But there are tasters' techniques you can use to help you experience the full range of each coffee's distinctive flavours. This is the difference between gulping down a coffee and savouring it.

Understanding Aroma is covered on pages 61–73.

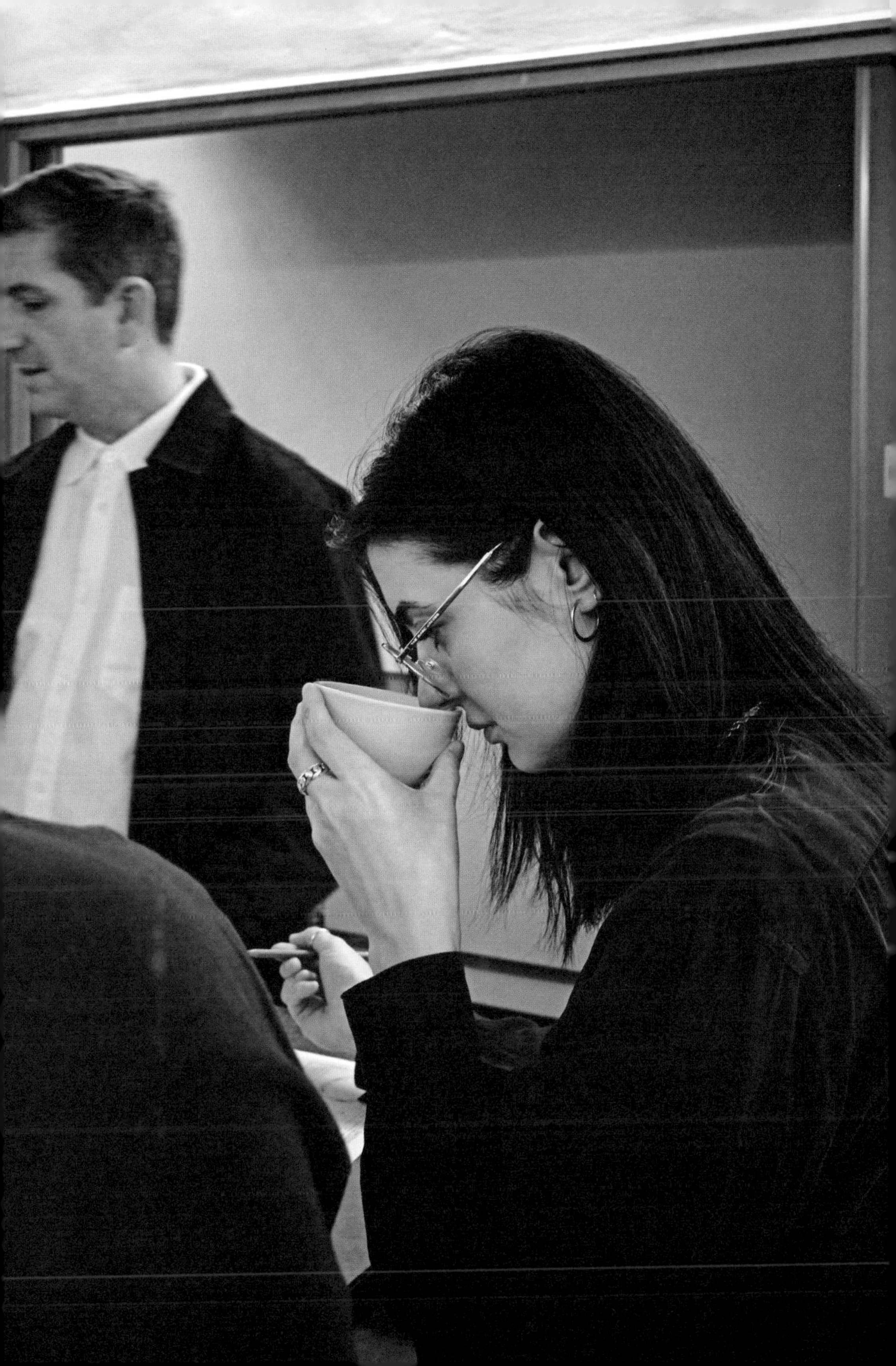

IDENTIFYING COFFEE'S FLAVOURS

Flavours can be both fleeting and delicate. The objective is to create two moments where trapped aromatic compounds have ample opportunity to rise into your nasal cavity. To give yourself maximum time for the compounds to build and for you to identify each flavour, you will need to coordinate your ingestion and breathing.

Each flavour reference is a proxy for a prominent aromatic compound. Very few people can categorize flavours by chemical compound. I once did a whisky tasting with a chemist. I felt like I was watching someone annotate music on a stave I didn't know. It was beautiful to watch, and I was completely out of my depth. Most of the time, most of us resort to likening one flavour to another. It's an approximation, but it works well. And, it's what we humans have been doing for millennia.

Start by breathing out, lift the cup to your lips, and sip enough liquid to fill the lower part of your mouth. It is natural to breathe in through your nose as you ingest the liquid, but, ideally, inhale through your mouth as well. This is easier if you have only a small volume of brewed coffee in your mouth.

After taking a sip, I close my lips and swirl the coffee around my mouth, without inhaling or exhaling. As the aromatic compounds rise, I experience a burst of flavour. This is the first opportunity to consider the flavours, and I pause for as long as possible to give myself ample opportunity to identify them.

The duration of this pause depends on how long I can hold my breath and the intensity of the flavours. If the flavours become overwhelmingly intense, you can dilute them by exhaling slightly through your nose.

I then swallow the liquid, breathe out and in again. Closing my mouth, I briefly hold my breath and then breathe out, forcing some of the air out through my nose. I pause again, trapping the remaining air in my mouth and nose. This gives an opportunity for the aromatic compounds to build up again, and I experience another burst of flavour. This second step is critical because it allows me to assess the 'finish'.

In the second phase, the flavours can be different from the first. The scientific tasting literature explains how aromatic compounds, after swallowing, are blown into your nasal cavity from the back of your mouth and throat as you exhale. This tallies with my experience. I find it much easier to consider all the flavours, as well as the finish, if I have swallowed at least a little of the coffee. After all, this is how you detect food's flavours. During chewing you get some of the flavour, but it's only once you swallow that the liberated aromatic compounds fill your nasal cavity.

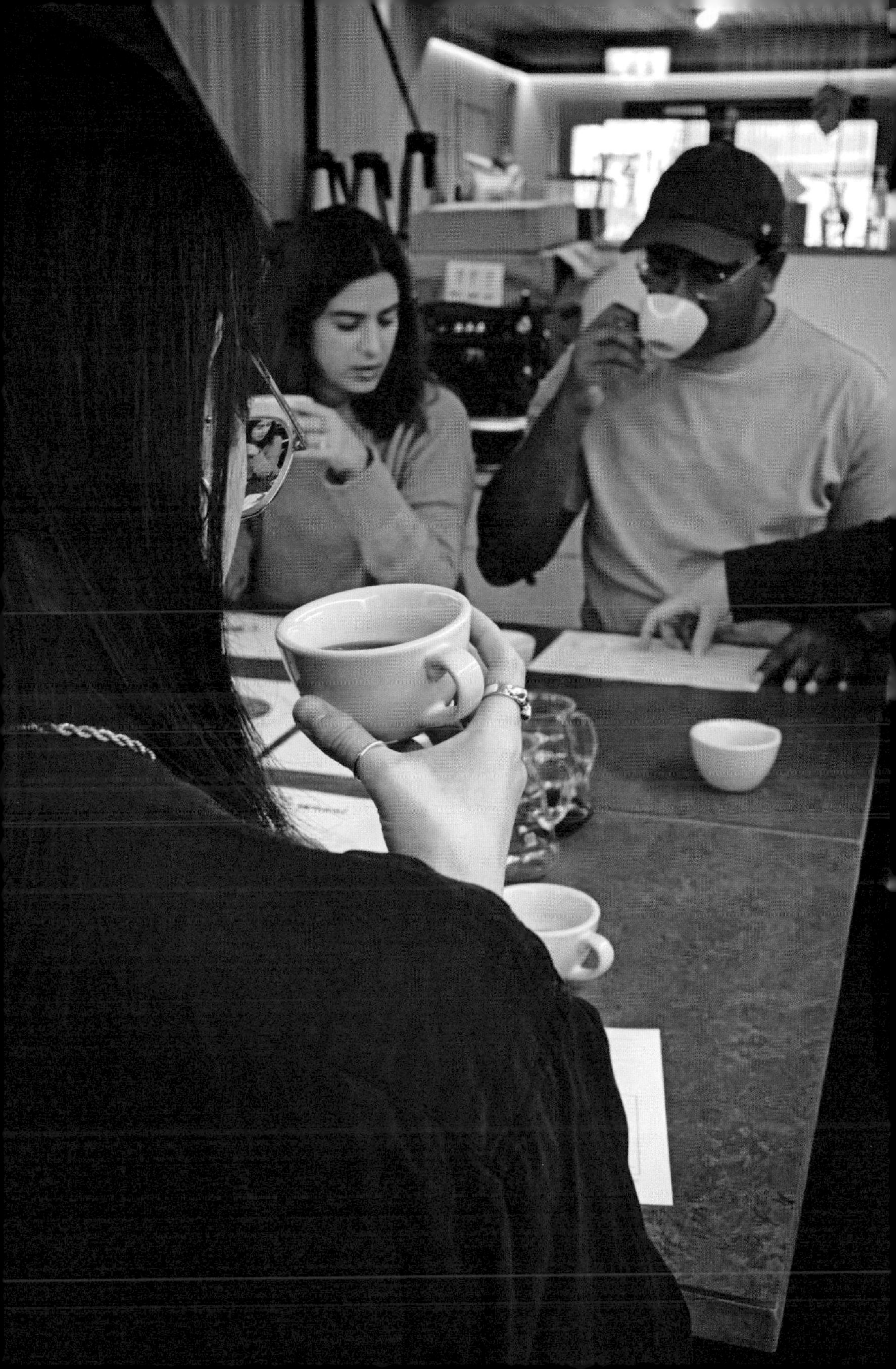

USING THE FLAVOUR WHEEL

Many coffees have only a generic flavour. For example, there are many coffees that have a spice note, but comparatively few have the specific flavours of nutmeg, clove or pepper. Similarly, many coffees have earthy, nutty or berry flavours, but fewer can be accurately written up as mushroom, tobacco, hazelnut or blackcurrant.

With the generic flavours agreed, consider if there are better flavour descriptors. The Flavour Wheel lists 73 common coffee flavours and is useful for considering both generic and specific flavours. For example, if a coffee has a nutty flavour, the Flavour Wheel lists the most common specific nut flavours of walnut, hazelnut, cashew, peanut and almond. All 73 flavours are arranged adjacently. If you detect a specific flavour, sense-check the proximate flavours to ascertain whether one of them might be even more accurate.

When considering coffee's flavours, start by identifying the flavour category. For example, a coffee might be nutty with a hint of spice and a vibrant berry flavour. As a rule of thumb, in a group tasting, everyone should be able to agree the presence of these generic flavours.

Of course, with so many possible aromatic compounds, not every coffee's flavours will be found on the Flavour Wheel. The Flavour Wheel comprises only the most common flavours from a cache of professional tasting sheets. For example, you might be familiar with yuzu, persimmon or rambutan and think that one of these descriptors more precisely communicates a coffee's flavour. Feel free to use the descriptor but only when it is also appreciated by your peers or audience. If your descriptor is unfamiliar to others, place it into the relevant flavour category on the Flavour Wheel and see whether a more commonplace descriptor resonates.

As an aside, I am amazed that so many people are familiar with the flavour of leather. But it does capture the essence of animal hide that is present in some coffees.

Specific tasting notes are enticing, and there is an urge to be as specific possible. Hazelnut, vanilla and raspberry sound better that nuts, sugars and berries. This creates an incentive for tasting notes to be hyper-specific. All too frequently, roasters' tasting notes overpromise and underdeliver. I think it is best to cite specific flavours only when they are clearly present and widely shared.

A useful rule of thumb is that smaller coffee lots have more distinct flavours. There are two factors in play. First, during production a decision has been made to keep the lot separate because it is sufficiently and distinctively tasty to command a price premium. Second, larger lots are comprised of multiple small coffee lots. Distinct flavours are amalgamated with other distinct flavours to create a coffee lot with generic flavours.

Some coffee lots, especially small ones, have very distinct flavours.

The Flavour Wheel

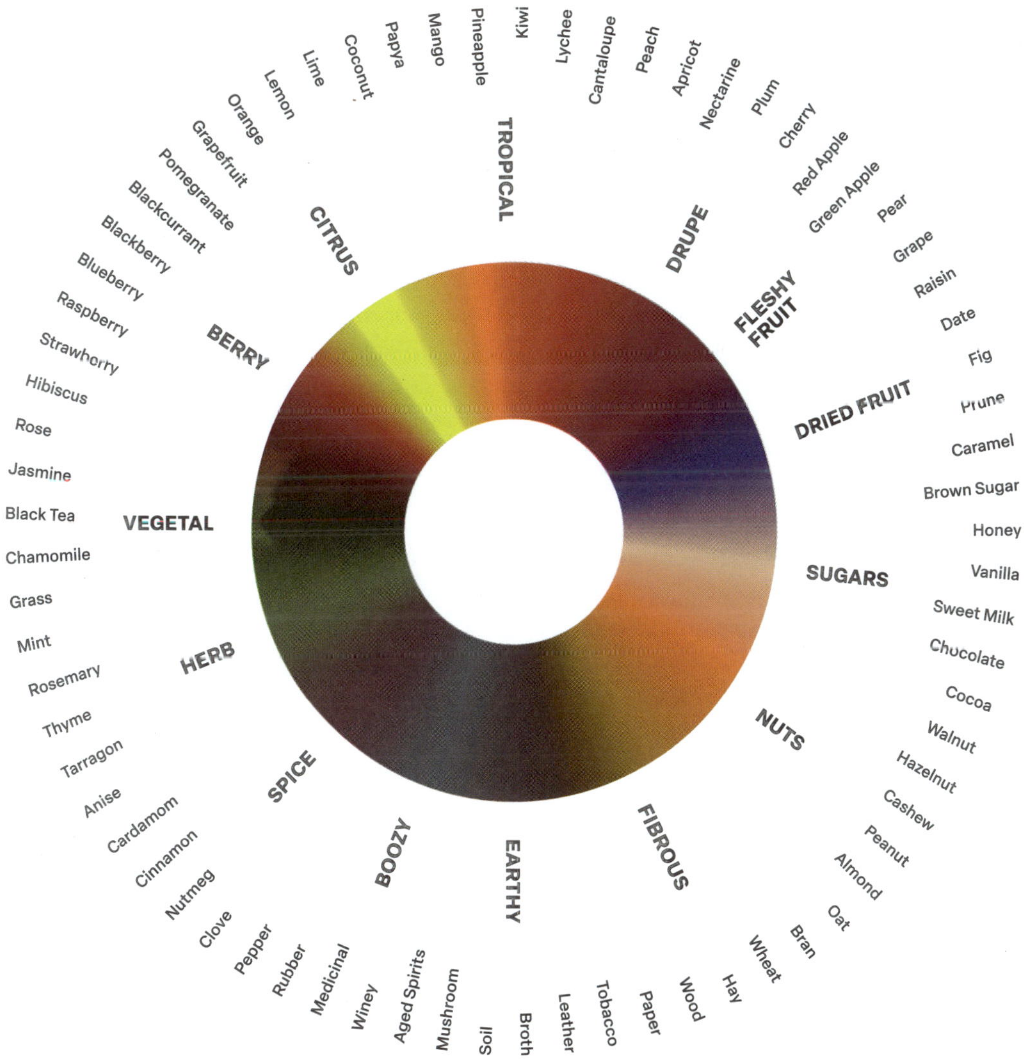

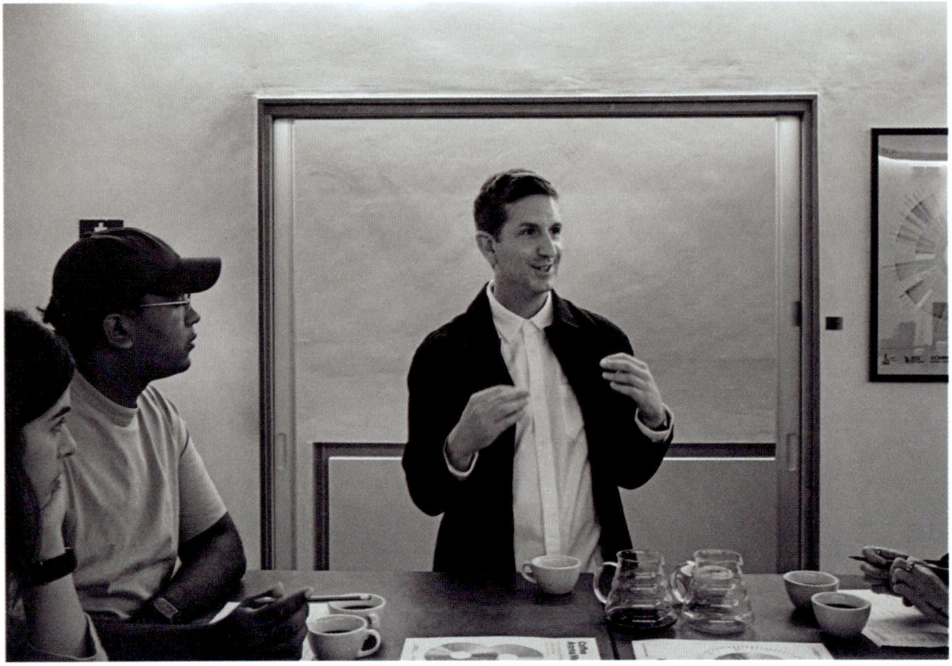

You might detect flavours of unripe raspberries, roasted cashews or even freshly picked mint. These are second-tier flavour descriptors, where the qualifications modify the 73 primary flavour descriptors. There are too many potential second-tier permutations for inclusion on the Flavour Wheel. As I explained with second-tier aromas, it's best to use second-tier flavours only when they are clearly present and widely agreed.

It is important to draw a distinction between second-tier flavour descriptors and compound flavour descriptors, which are an amalgam of multiple flavours, for example, iced fruit tea, rosemary oat shortbread and bittersweet fudge. Similarly to dealing with compound aroma descriptors, take the time to break compound flavour descriptions into their component parts so that you can sense-check whether there are other prominent flavours also present that you missed.

Each of the above examples are more revealing when the flavours are identified as peach, sugars and black tea; rosemary, sugars and oats; and caramelized sugars and vanilla with potentially an earthy base note. Breaking compound flavour descriptions down into their constituent parts helps you better consider the structure of the flavours.

STACKS OF FLAVOUR

Flavours can be conceptualized as being lighter or heavier. For example, raspberry is commonly perceived to be lighter than either leather or cloves. The spectrum of the stack extends from citrus and berries at the top to earth and fibrous things, such as wood and paper, at the bottom. In the middle might be dried fruits, nuts and vegetal flavours.

When assessing flavours in this way, it's easier to consider the *structure* of the coffee's flavours. If you have identified a roaster whom you like and trust, it's possibly because they buy coffees with a flavour structure that appeals to your preferences.

For example, among the high-profile coffee roasters in my city, one continually sources coffees that have pronounced flavours in the middle and little at either the top or the bottom. By contrast, another seeks out coffees that have maximum vertical range of flavours. No matter how dark or low the coffee's flavour profile might be, there will always be a burst of fruit at the top. Similarly, all their coffees have a ripple of earth or spice at the bottom, even when the most dominant flavours are at the top or centre.

And yet another roaster buys coffees that have several very prominent readily identifiable flavours, regardless of whether they are at the top, middle or bottom.

Our sense of some flavours being lighter than others isn't completely arbitrary. In many cases, there is a correlation between the molecular weight of the aromatic compounds and our perception of whether these flavours are lighter or heavier, even though our palates are not atomic weighing machines. For example, the molecular weight of raspberry ketone is lighter than the molecular weight of agaritine, an aromatic compound found in some mushrooms, or eugenol, the key aromatic compound in cloves. For flavours at the 'top' I like the term 'light' since it is grounded in the chemistry, but other tasters may refer to these flavours as 'high'. Base flavours are often referred to as 'dark', 'bottom' or 'heavy'.

The lack of standardized nomenclature can be tricky. To be explicit, I solely use 'light' to describe flavours at the top of the Flavour Wheel, whereas I would describe a flavour that is not pronounced as 'low intensity' or 'faint'.

TIM'S TASTING TIP

Tasting coffees with unpleasant flavours and rough mouthfeels can be challenging work. After an unpleasant coffee, a slice of apple or a cube of hard cheese can cleanse your palate. The acid and the proteins help to reduce the phenylindanes or other compounds stuck on your palate.

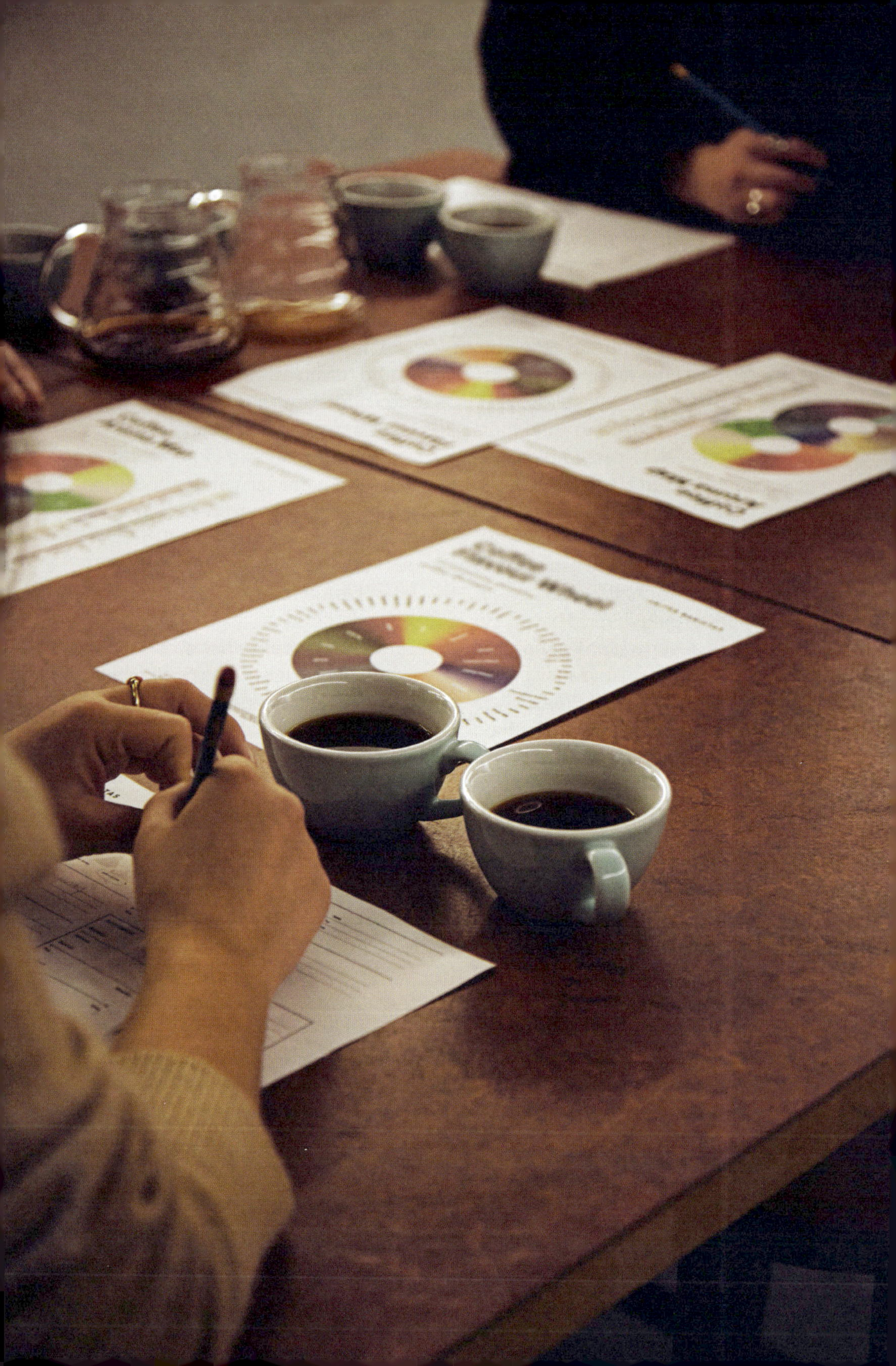

COMPLEXITY

Some coffees have more readily identifiable flavours than others. A coffee that has either no distinct flavours or just one can be labelled as 'simple'. Some coffees have four, five, six or even more clearly identifiable distinct flavours, and these can be classified as 'complex'. Complexity is a signifier of quality, and coffees with multiple distinct flavours typically score higher and cost more. Multiple, distinct flavours are often found in smaller lots. But, as we shall see, complexity is not the sole criterion of quality and neither is it the primary driver of pleasure.

Multiple flavours have the effect of suppressing the perceived intensity of each flavour. For example, the mango note in a coffee with flavours of raspberries, mangoes and tobacco is perceived as less intense than a coffee with flavours of just mangoes and tobacco – even when the same quantity of δ-3-Carene is present in both coffees. This is because your brain seeks a reference to the specific amalgam of flavours, rather than assessing them individually.

This is why tasting in a group can be useful and fun, especially for complex coffees. Often, people struggle to identify all prominent flavours, especially when the combinations are uncommon, For example, how often have you simultaneously tasted kiwi, raspberry, red apple, cocoa nibs, hazelnuts and tobacco? Your brain starts scanning for the previous time you experienced this unique combination. It takes conscious effort to individually identify each of the flavours. But you may have experienced the enlightening moment when someone calls out the flavour descriptor you have been struggling to identify.

Complexity is a signifier of quality, and coffees with multiple distinct flavours typically score higher and cost more

Assessing flavour

1.

Let air mix with the brew while it's in your mouth. What are this coffee's defining flavours?

2.

Use the Flavour Wheel to identify key *primary* flavours. Good coffees have at least one readily identifiable flavour; great coffees often have four or more.

Swirl the coffee around your mouth. More flavour compounds will be liberated from the liquid and rise into your nasal cavity.

3.

Are there more specific *second-tier* flavours? For example, might a peach flavour be unripe or ripe? Or even a particular variety?

4.

Do flavours and tastes combine into *compound flavours*? Might cocoa plus sweetness evoke chocolate?

5.

Don't overreach for flavours. If a note is faint or dull, it's not worth recording.

6.

Consider:

- Do colour, aroma and flavour align?
- Do flavours linger? A long, pleasant finish is more tasty.
- Are tastes and flavours aligned?

The most desirable finish is one that both lingers and continues to metamorphose through various flavours

FINISHING UP

Don't expect to experience all the flavours simultaneously. Some flavours may be more pronounced when you hold the brew in your mouth; others once you have swallowed and exhaled. And even then, the various flavours may come and go as the aromatic compounds persist in your nasal cavity.

Some coffees are very 'short' – that is, the flavours come and go quickly. Sometimes, the flavours pass in just seconds. Other coffees have a 'long' finish where the flavours linger. Long finishes are widely esteemed. More specifically, a long finish is a sign of quality when the flavours are pleasant. The most desirable finish is one that both lingers and continues to metamorphose through various flavours, especially in combination with a pleasant, lingering mouthfeel. Delicious coffees are almost always complex with a long finish and a pleasant mouthfeel, regardless of the specific flavours.

This is the point where our step-by-step assessment of a coffee finishes. With aroma, mouthfeel, taste and flavour now assessed, it's time to aggregate these attributes and consider what they mean for quality and – more importantly – your coffee-drinking pleasure.

A note on notes

A tasting note is a concise description that communicates a coffee's distinctive characteristics. Often tasting notes are several sentences long, but can be as short as three or four well-chosen words. The word 'note' has somehow morphed, and people sometimes say things such as

'I'm getting a note of _______'

or

'This coffee has notes of _______' like they have perfect pitch and are identifying musical notes. This collapses sensory information into metaphor, which quickly becomes problematic as flavour descriptors are already proxies for aromatic compounds.

It is more elegant to say something like

'I am detecting a _______ flavour'

or

'This coffee has flavours of _________'.

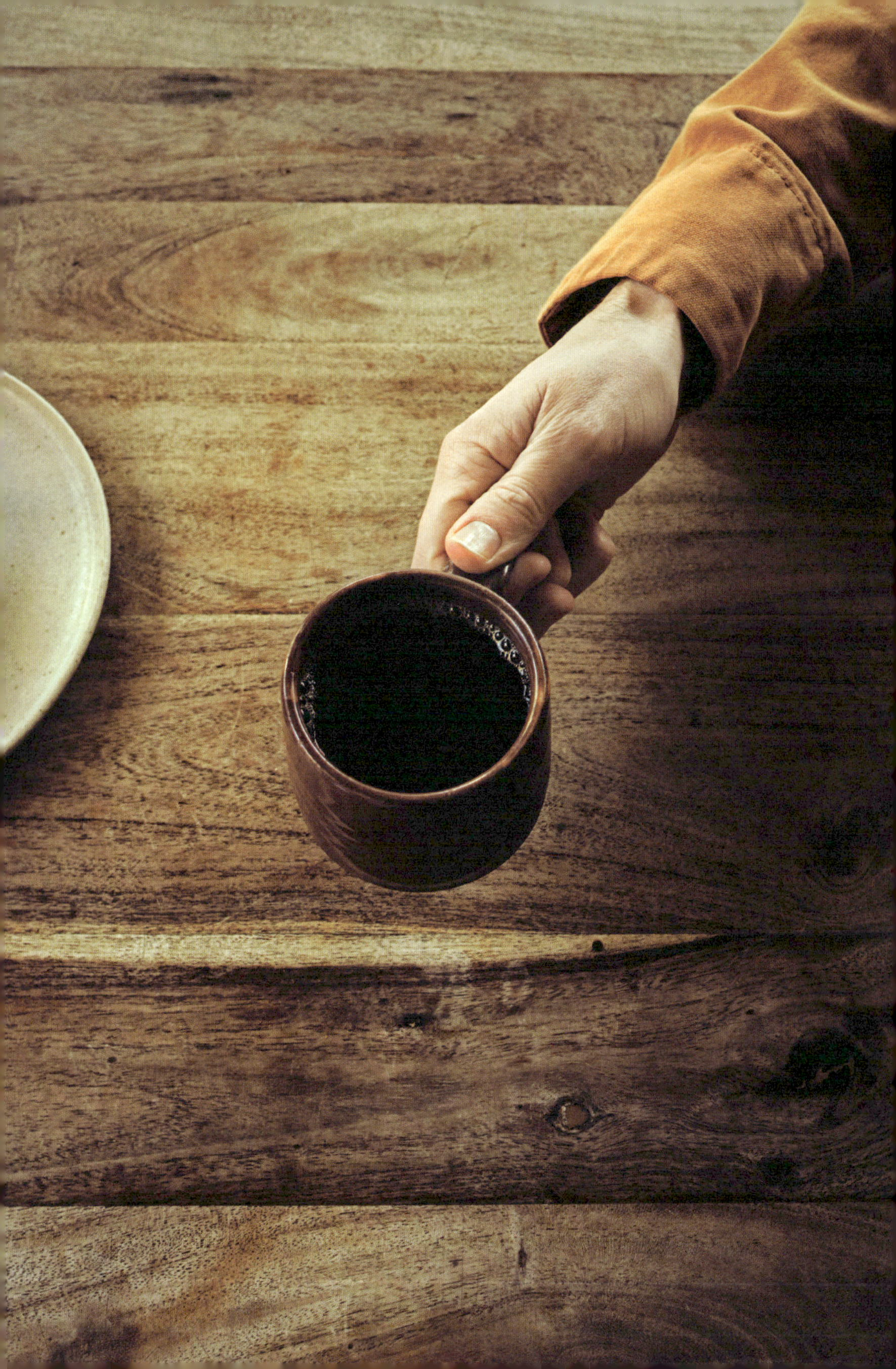

Introducing Alignment

WHEN MOUTHFEEL, TASTE AND FLAVOUR COMBINE

Most people prefer coffees that are 'well aligned'. Alignment is an assessment of how mouthfeel, taste and flavour integrate. Think of alignment as a scale that extends from no integration and runs through 'some alignment' and 'good alignment' to coffees that benefit from 'strong alignment'.

Alignment can occur between each of mouthfeel, taste and flavour – as well as across all three. A coffee that has a slightly viscous mouthfeel, tastes sweet and has a corresponding sweet flavour with the appropriate intensity, say, of plum is more pleasant to drink than a coffee that has a thin mouthfeel, tastes sour and has tobacco as its dominant flavour.

Alignment is a useful concept because it allows us to move past personal preferences. For example, a sweet, plummy coffee can be just as pleasant as a slightly astringent, slightly bitter, nutty-flavoured coffee, but the nutty coffee is likely to be significantly more pleasant than the tobacco-flavoured coffee example above, because of its stronger alignment.

Wine drinkers might consider this concept similar to balance, but 'balance' is a term we reserve solely for a harmonious combination of tastes. A coffee can be 'balanced' but suffer poor alignment, or have strong alignment but not be balanced. Understanding these distinctions is essential for categorizing a coffee's profile and identifying coffees that are to your liking.

TASTE AND FLAVOUR

The primary criterion of alignment is the relationship between taste and flavour. Tastes are detected on the tongue, and flavours are perceived as aromatic compounds rising from the back of the mouth into the nasal cavity. Coffees are more pleasant when they benefit from a corresponding flavour that matches the intensity of each taste, and vice versa. For example, a coffee with notes of milk chocolate or stone fruit should be sufficiently sweet to have good alignment. And, to be agreeable, a coffee that tastes bitter should have a flavour, such as walnut, cocoa nib or tobacco, that has corresponding bitterness.

Often it is easier to identify the tastes first and then assess the flavours. Your brain typically finds it easier to identify the intensity of each taste than it does to identify multiple flavours. For example, if a coffee has a balance between sour and sweet, be on the lookout for flavours from the fruit categories.

Most naturally occurring flavours have more than one taste. For example, raspberries are both sweet and sour. If a coffee distinctly tastes of raspberries, it should have both sufficient sweetness and sourness to benefit from good taste–flavour alignment.

Many people say that they find sour-tasting coffees disagreeable, but tangy coffees can be very pleasant when the acidity is aligned with flavours of, for example, kiwi, apple or blackcurrant. In fact, where these flavours are present, some sourness is required to achieve alignment. However, acidic coffees without distinct sour flavours are often unpleasant.

One of the benefits of using alignment to assess a coffee is that it is neutral on judgements of pleasant flavours. Strong alignment can occur between any of the primary tastes of sweet, sour, bitter, salty and umami, and the multitude of flavours possible in coffee. Some common taste–flavour combinations include sweetness with chocolate or stone fruit; sourness with berries or tropical fruit; and bitterness with spice or earthy notes. Whatever your personal flavour preferences, all can be understood to be agreeable with sufficient taste–flavour alignment.

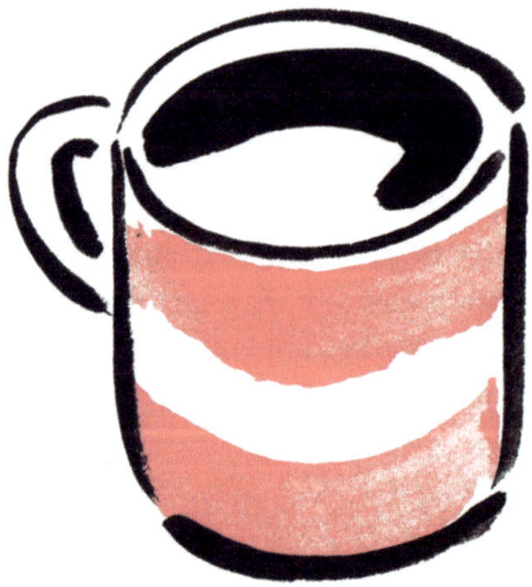

Most naturally occurring flavours have more than one taste

You are now quite possibly considering the many coffees you have drunk that don't have good taste–flavour alignment – and you'd be right. As a coffee's flavours are created during a combination of production, roasting and brewing, there's a good possibility that it will suffer from inadequate alignment.

Alignment also gives us an insight into why some flavour combinations in coffee are weird. I opened the previous chapter with the example of a coffee that had tasting notes of raspberry and mango. Intuitively, you might find these two flavours unattractive together. To be agreeable, there would need to be sufficient sourness and sweetness for the raspberry flavour to align with its tastes, but the requisite sourness seems like a poor fit for the overwhelming sweetness of mangoes.

When I read the tasting notes, I thought it likely that the coffee would have only one of these two flavours. However, it had both, but it lacked sufficient acidity to be pleasant. It would best be categorized as a Curious coffee because of the poor taste–flavour alignment. And it would be more pleasant with greater acidity, even though it would still lack taste–flavour alignment.

MOUTHFEEL AND TASTE

The next most important alignment is between mouthfeel and taste. Some coffees that have low taste–flavour alignment are nonetheless pleasant because they have sufficient alignment between their texture and taste. Mouthfeel–taste alignment is particularly important for simple coffees that have few, or no, clearly identifiable flavours.

The alignment between the level of astringency and bitterness is often the defining alignment for Classic coffees. Several alignments are possible including viscosity and sweetness; smoothness without tart sourness; and astringency with bitterness. For example, either pronounced astringency or bitterness is generally unpleasant, but some coffees – especially those with few, or no, distinct favours – can be agreeable when a gentle astringency is paired with a little bitterness.

We have already ascertained (see 'Astringent', page 78) that astringency can be pleasant when is has limited intensity, has a fine-grained texture and is short-lived. The parameters of pleasant astringency help to define the limits of the bitterness's intensity. If the bitterness is too intense, the mouthfeel–taste alignment is too low for the coffee to be pleasant.

While these examples would be tastier if the coffees were more complex or benefited from greater balance; these coffees can be perfectly pleasant and great companions to sweet baking.

AROMA AND FLAVOUR

It's also worth mentioning the potential alignment between aroma and flavour. Some coffee drinkers value strong alignment between aroma and flavour, and, indeed, these coffees are often readily approachable. However, firmly implementing this criterion culls the vast majority of coffees produced.

I have come to see a coffee's differing aromas and flavours as a feature rather than a bug. Coffees that have a wide range of aromatic compounds are more complex and often tastier. It's a quirk of chemistry and our bodies that some of these compounds are detected through the nose and others through the mouth.

In fact, the difference between aroma and flavour is one reason why coffee is beguiling to drink. Just when you start to successfully predict what the coffee might taste like, along comes a sample from an origin, variety and process method combination that conspires to confound your expectations.

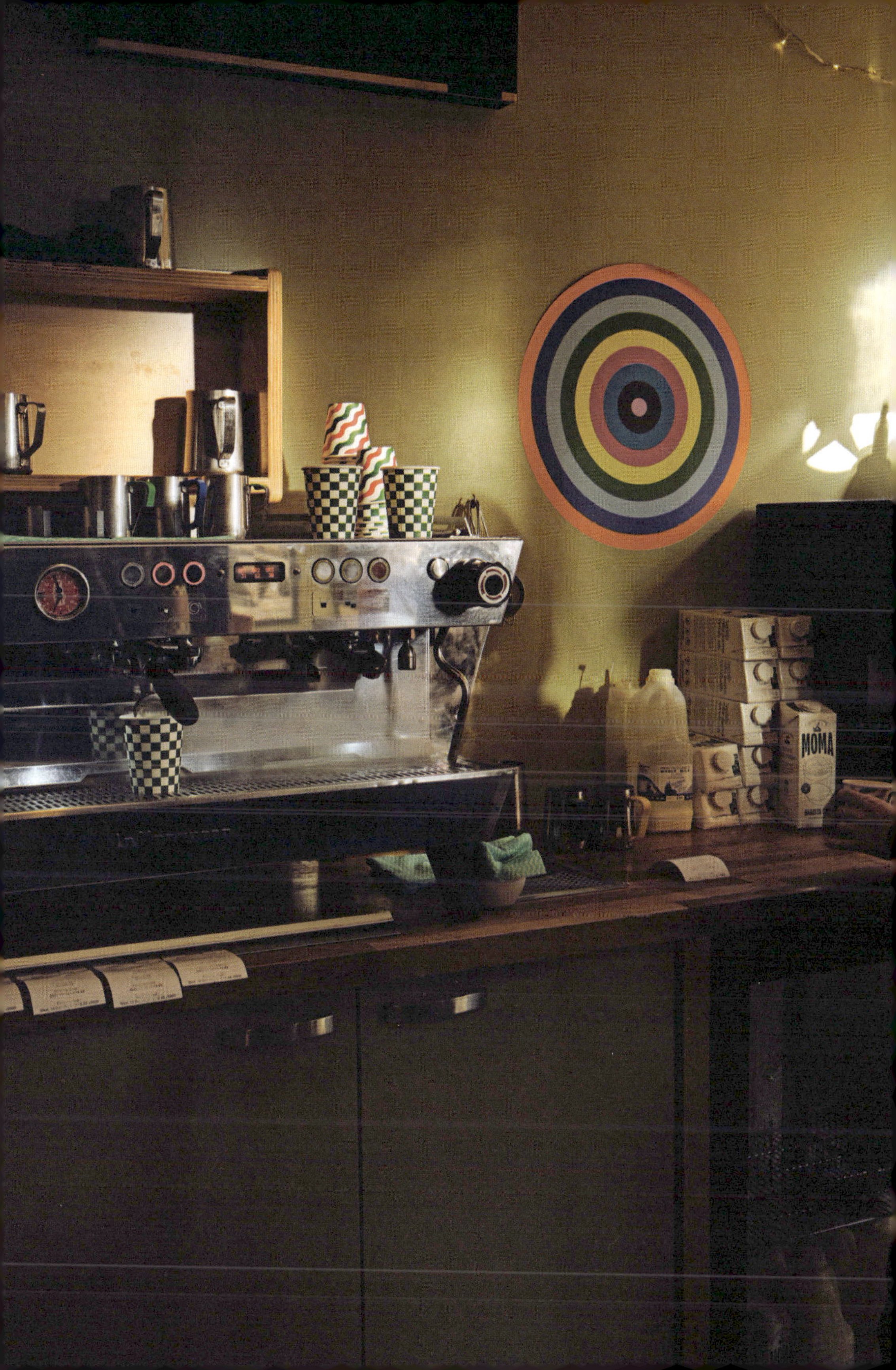
MOMA

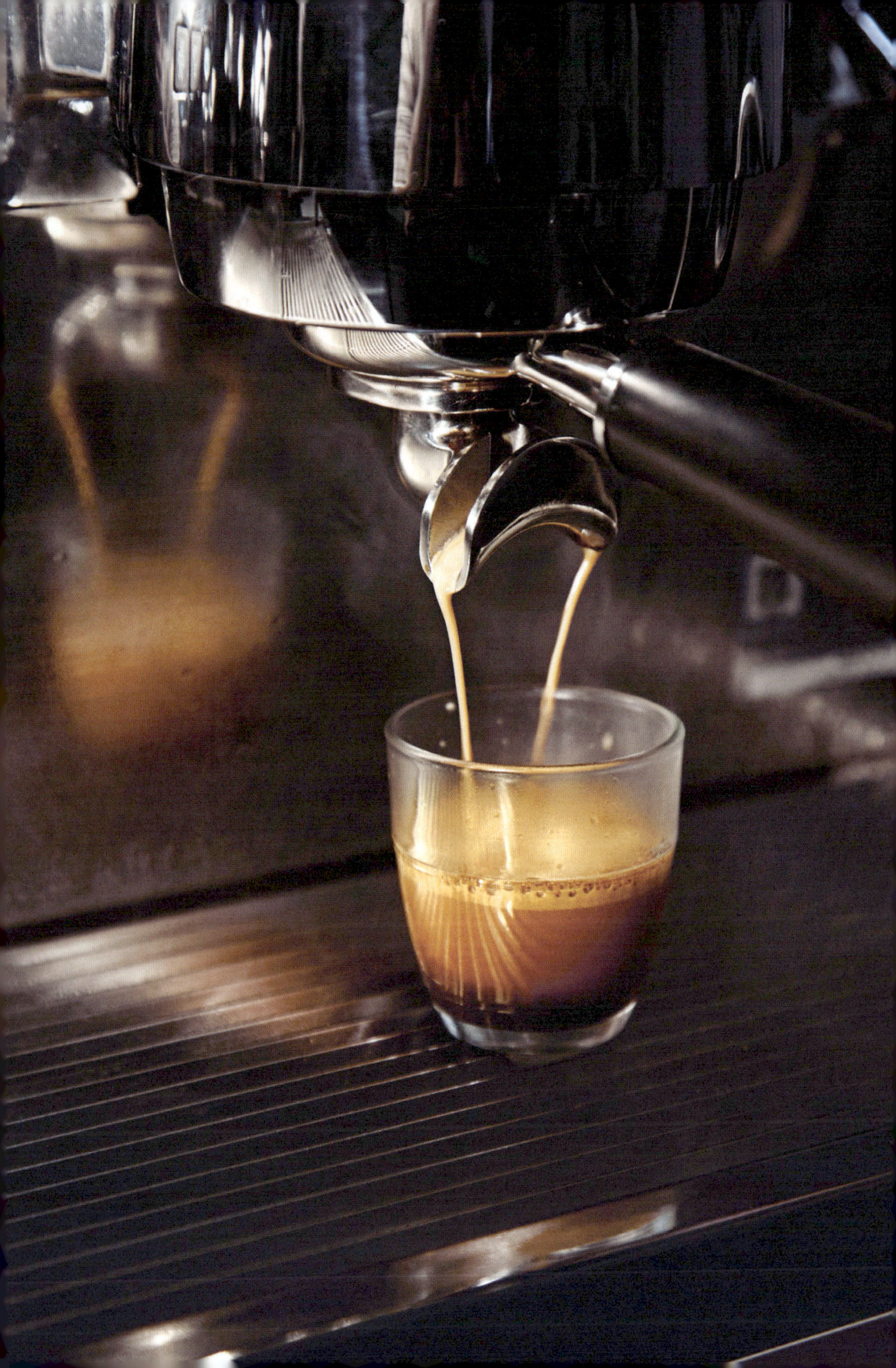

An understanding of alignment is also essential to consider a coffee's profile and appreciate your own preferences

ALIGNMENT AND PLEASANTNESS

Using alignment as a factor of pleasantness equips the coffee taster to appreciate coffees that others find pleasant, even if it does not conform to their own preferences. For example, if you prefer Classic coffees, you can still appreciate that a predominantly sour-tasting coffee with a distinct pineapple note will be agreeable to other people, if it is well aligned. Or if you prefer Clarity coffees, you can understand the attraction of a coffee that has a soft astringency, a little bitterness and sweetness, and a predominant flavour of nuts.

Alignment also provides an insightful critique of a poorly structured coffee regardless of your preferences. For example, for people who are adverse to sour coffees, it's more insightful to realize that few people like acidic coffees without corresponding flavours and that predominantly sour coffees with aligned flavours of equal intensify are well structured.

An understanding of alignment is also essential to consider a coffee's profile and to appreciate your own preferences.

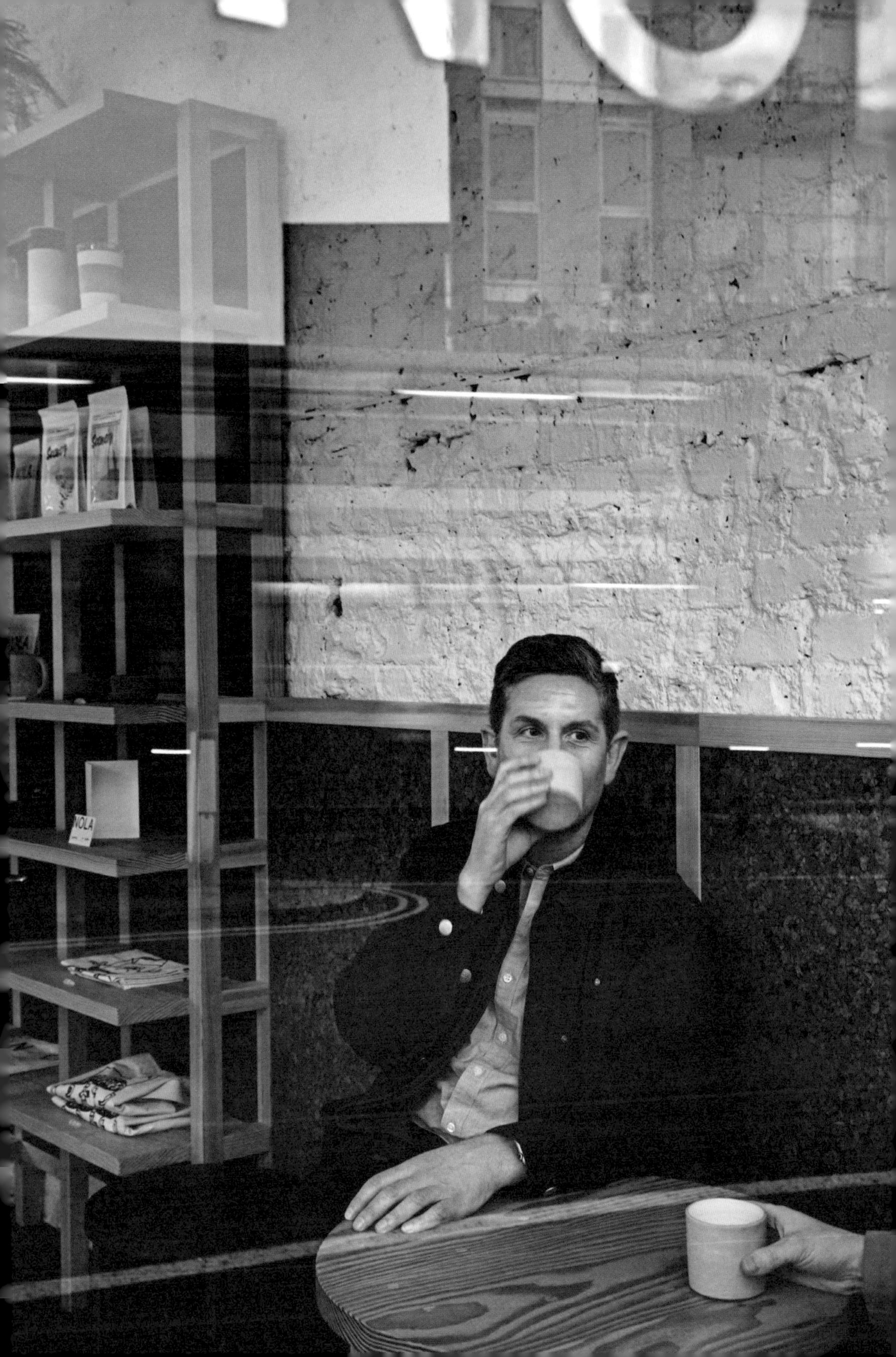
NOLA

Appraising Coffee

WHY SOME COFFEES ARE TASTIER THAN OTHERS

Identifying each coffee's profile is useful. In fact, it's mission critical. Appreciating each coffee's profile enables us to achieve our two interconnected objectives: to equip you to identify coffees that bring the most pleasure and to understand why some coffees are tastier than others.

Whether a coffee might be best categorized as Classic, Comfort, Clarity or Curious is a function of its balance of tastes and alignment. To assess how tasty the coffee is, we also need to consider its mouthfeel, balance, alignment and complexity. There are lower-quality and higher-quality coffees in each of the four coffee profiles. So whether you enjoy a coffee is a combination of whether the profile matches your preferences and whether the quality is sufficiently high enough for your enjoyment.

THE FOUR-POINT SCALE

There are deliberately no intervals on the tasting sheet's grading scales. This is because not all scales have equal intervals and not all tasters have an equal ability to assess each attribute. For each of the following five assessments, at least when starting out, I suggest you use a four-point scale.

Having only four options forces you to commit to whether something is above, or below, average. If you give people a five-point scale, they default to the middle option all too frequently.

Start by considering whether the coffee is among the best 50 per cent of coffees you have drunk for this attribute, or the worst 50 per cent. Let's say I'm assessing mouthfeel, and the coffee benefits from little to no astringency, is medium weight and has a silky mouthfeel. This coffee deserves to be in the upper half of the scale. Next, I can consider whether the mouthfeel is in the best 25 per cent of coffees I have ever drunk. For this example, let's say it isn't. Using a four-point scale empowers tasters to assess each attribute confidently.

You will quickly discover, or already appreciate, that few coffees are average or consistent across all attributes. Chances are, by the time you have encountered an outlier, you will be sufficiently proficient to make a judgement for yourself. For the sake of clarity, I am going to refer to the scale as extending from one to four, where one is the lowest and four is the highest.

1.

Mouthfeel

Some mouthfeels are more pleasant than others. If the mouthfeel is either noteworthy or pleasant, it deserves to be graded in the upper half. If the coffee has a notably pleasant mouthfeel, and especially if it is a defining attribute of the coffee, grade it a four. If mouthfeel is not particularly pleasant but unobjectionable, grade it a two. If it is overwhelmingly or distinctively astringent, grade it a one.

There is no direct correlation between the weight and the grade. All weights can be pleasant with the appropriate alignment. However, bitty, thin and especially thin with bits are always unpleasant and should be marked as a one.

2.

Balance

There must be at least two of the basic tastes present to achieve balance. If there is only bitterness, grade the coffee a one, especially if it is associated with a burnt taste and a rough mouthfeel. This is an indication that bitterness is from phenylindanes, which develop during roasting.

If there are multiple tastes, but one dominates, the grade will be a one or a two. As a rule of thumb, if there are two tastes and they have a degree of balance, grade the coffee a three. Reserve grade four for coffees that either have an excellent balance between two tastes or at least a good balance between three tastes.

A harmonious balance of taste doesn't require them to be of equal intensity, only that there is sufficient intensity of each taste to create balance. Many coffees will have one taste that is more pronounced than others; you should judge whether it is so dominant that it upsets the balance.

As sweetness is typically perceived in coffees that are not bitter, it's very unusual – nay, almost impossible – for there to be a harmonious balance between intense bitterness and intense sweetness. As a consequence, high-scoring, harmonious balances are typically built with combinations of sourness, sweetness and bitterness.

3.

Alignment

Summarize the alignment assessments into a single measure. As the taste–flavour alignment is of primary importance, reserve grade four for coffees that benefit from a strong alignment between taste and flavour. If a coffee has adequate alignment, grade it a three.

For coffees that have little, or no, taste–flavour alignment, but have mouthfeel–taste alignment, the maximum they typically score is a two. Many of these coffees are slightly astringent, have mild bitterness and no distinctive flavours. Coffees that suffer poor alignment can be graded a one.

4.

Complexity

Review the number of distinct aromas and flavours that you identified. Simple coffees have one, or even no, distinct aromas or flavours. Complex coffee have four, five, six or even more distinct aromas and flavours.

Score simple coffees as a one and coffees with one or two distinct aromas or flavours a two. For a coffee to be graded a three or higher it should have at least one or two distinct aromas and flavours. Reserve grade four for coffees that have multiple aromas and flavours.

If the coffee has a long and pleasant finish, consider bumping the coffee up a grade. And if the coffee has aromas and flavours at the top, middle and bottom, also consider increasing the grade, but this – obviously – requires at least three distinctive aromas and flavours.

IDENTIFYING THE COFFEE'S PROFILE

Balance and alignment are the key criteria for identifying each coffee's profile. Start by considering the balance of tastes and the structure of the alignment.

CLASSIC

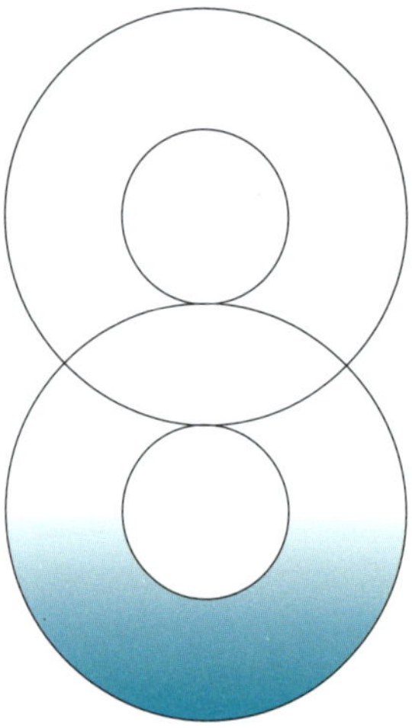

COMFORT

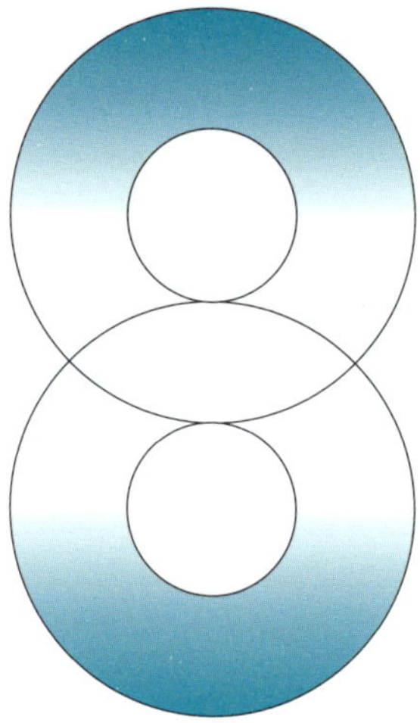

CLARITY

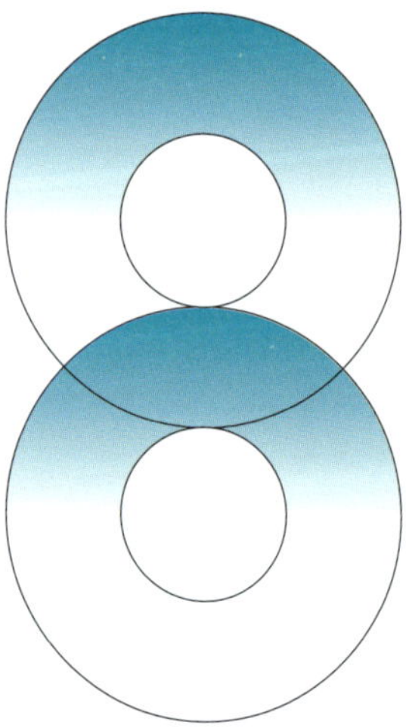

CURIOUS

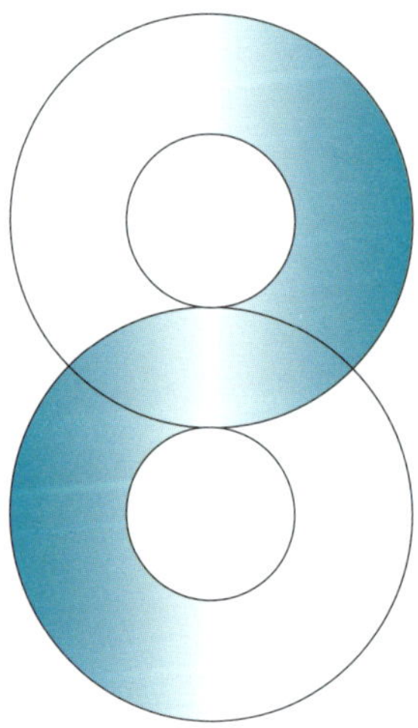

	CLASSIC	COMFORT	CLARITY	CURIOUS
Balance	Often predominantly bitter.	Balance of sweetness, sourness and bitterness.	Balance of sweetness, sourness and bitterness.	Can be unbalanced, usually with dominant sourness.
Note on taste	Classic coffees are often defined by being dominantly bitter, but may have adequate sweetness or sourness to achieve balance.	Comfort coffees have two tastes that are equally intense. There is usually sufficient sweetness to achieve balance. Balances are most commonly between bitterness and sweetness.	Clarity coffees often have a harmonious balance, but with tastes that are not of equal intensity. Clarity coffees are usually predominantly sweet or sour.	If balanced, Curious coffees usually balance sourness and sweetness. If unbalanced, Curious coffees are often dominantly sour.
Note on flavours	Classic coffees are often simple.	Comfort coffees range from simple to complex.	Clarity coffees range from simple to complex.	Curious coffees are often complex.
Alignment	Not always aligned.	Good versions benefit from taste–flavour alignment.	Good versions benefit from taste–flavour alignment.	Do not always benefit from taste–flavour alignment.
Note on alignment	Often the alignment is between mouthfeel and taste. An astringent–bitter combination is common.	Look for an aligned flavour with each taste, and vice versa.	Look for an aligned flavour with each taste, and vice versa.	Tasty Curious coffees are either balanced or aligned. If a coffee is both balanced and aligned, it might be better categorized as a Comfort or Clarify coffee.

TASTINESS

Coffees that are pleasant to drink typically benefit from a pleasant mouthfeel, have a harmonious balance of taste and have adequate alignment. Tastier coffees score higher in these scales plus benefit from greater complexity.

For example, if a coffee has a smooth, viscous mouthfeel, is balanced between sweet and sour, benefits from strong alignment, and has aromas and flavours at the top, middle and bottom of the stacks, it's likely to be among the most pleasant coffees you ever drink. Savour it. And if it is good value, buy a good amount of it while it's available.

Conversely, if a coffee scores poorly on mouthfeel, balance, alignment and complexity, it's probably not pleasant to drink and not worth buying again – especially if it is comparatively expensive.

Most coffees, however, score higher on some of these metrics that others. There are two ways to approach grading pleasantness, each suitable for a different purpose.

Grading quality

Often, I grade coffees on a four-point scale that runs from good to outstanding. If a coffee doesn't pass this baseline standard, then something has gone wrong across the production, grading, transportation or roasting of the coffee. If a coffee is unpleasant, you can opt not to give it a grade.

One of the joys of being a coffee drinker is embracing the fact it is someone else's job to do quality control. If a roaster sources, roasts and sells a coffee, they are putting their stamp of approval on that coffee. It is their reputation – not the farmer's – that is on the line. If the coffee is less than good, or significantly overpriced for its pleasantness, I judge the roaster. There are many good-tasting coffees available at reasonable prices, and I think it's important we support farmers, importers and roasters who deliver value both for themselves and others across the supply chain from crop to cup.

Quality and profile

Using an all-time approach to grading limits the potential score for Classic and Curious coffees. Classic coffees, by definition, don't have sufficient balance or complexity to be graded outstanding. Equally, Curious coffees lack taste–flavour alignment or balance to also be outstanding. For example, a coffee with a balance of sourness, sweetness and bitterness and a complex array of aligned flavours would almost certainly be better categorized as a Comfort or Clarity coffee.

In most instances, this is entirely acceptable and even desirable. It permits us to taste, say, a poorly aligned Curious coffee and appreciate that it would be more pleasant to drink if it benefited from stronger alignment.

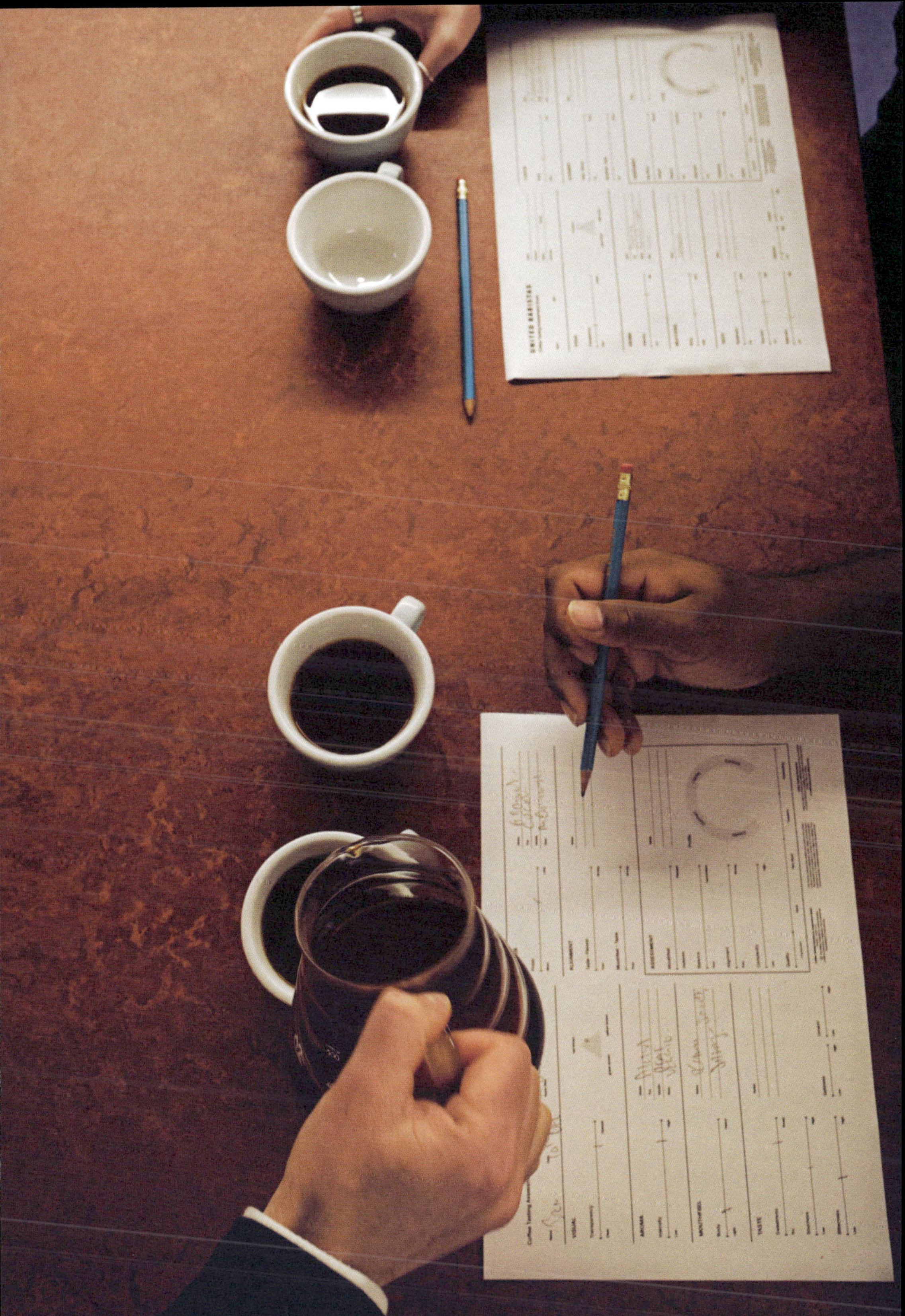

You can develop your coffee-tasting skills at home, while frequenting a coffee shop or even when drinking coffee in the office

EXPERIENCE AND REFERENCE POINTS

In basic coffee-tasting training, I offer a dozen diverse coffees over several tasting sessions. This is typically more than enough for people to calibrate their palates and confidently grade each attribute and assessment.

When working with people who have tasted a lot of coffee, it typically only takes two or three coffees of different profiles for them to familiarize themselves with the approach.

You can develop your coffee-tasting skills at home, while frequenting a coffee shop or even when drinking coffee in the office. If you can categorize six or twelve coffees that represent the breadth of the coffees available, then these tasting techniques and concepts will quickly become second nature. At that point there is little need to print out a Coffee Assessment Sheet and dedicate time to assessing each coffee. I frequently assess coffee while working, socializing or in a meeting.

When calibrating your palate, can I encourage you to buy some nice coffees from a reputable roaster. In the next chapters we explore the range of the extraordinary range of origins, processes and varieties that are available. You can start by getting three or four coffees that are archetypical examples of their origins.

APPRECIATING COFFEE

Assessing coffees using the attributes of mouthfeel, balance, alignment and complexity enables us to recognize why some coffees are tastier than others. Equally, it allows us to better appreciate quality coffees that don't fit with our own personal preferences and to respect the preferences of others.

Most people will broadly agree on a coffee's attributes. A tasting methodology has the benefit of both creating a common language and removing subjectivity from the assessment. That doesn't mean having a structured approach hampers or constrains your personal preferences. Rather, it shines a light that enables you to appreciate them in a broader context.

It then becomes more interesting when someone likes something that you don't, or vice versa. Equipped with the language to understand what you are tasting, it's possible to identify the specific characteristics that are divisive.

Assessing coffee has also helped me appreciate how my preferences shift, throughout the day and from day to day. As well as understanding coffee, I now also better understand myself. For example, when I am busy with work, it's not uncommon for me to pick up a bag of delicious complex coffee that neatly fits a Clarity profile, only to put it down and opt for a simpler coffee that has a Comfort profile. In this minute I am clearly seeking straightforward reassurance.

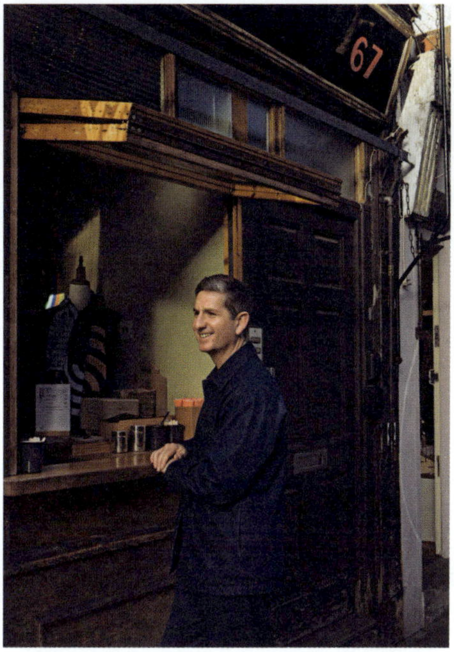

Picking the right coffee for the right moment is a theme we will return to. But now that we can identify and appreciate the wonderful range of aromas and flavours in each cup, it's valuable to consider the people who create these flavours – coffee farmers and producers.

ASSESSMENT

Choosing & enjoying coffee

There are dozens of stages across the coffee supply chain. At each step, people make decisions that shape a coffee's flavours. In this final section we journey from crop to cup, to empower you to choose coffees that you'll like.

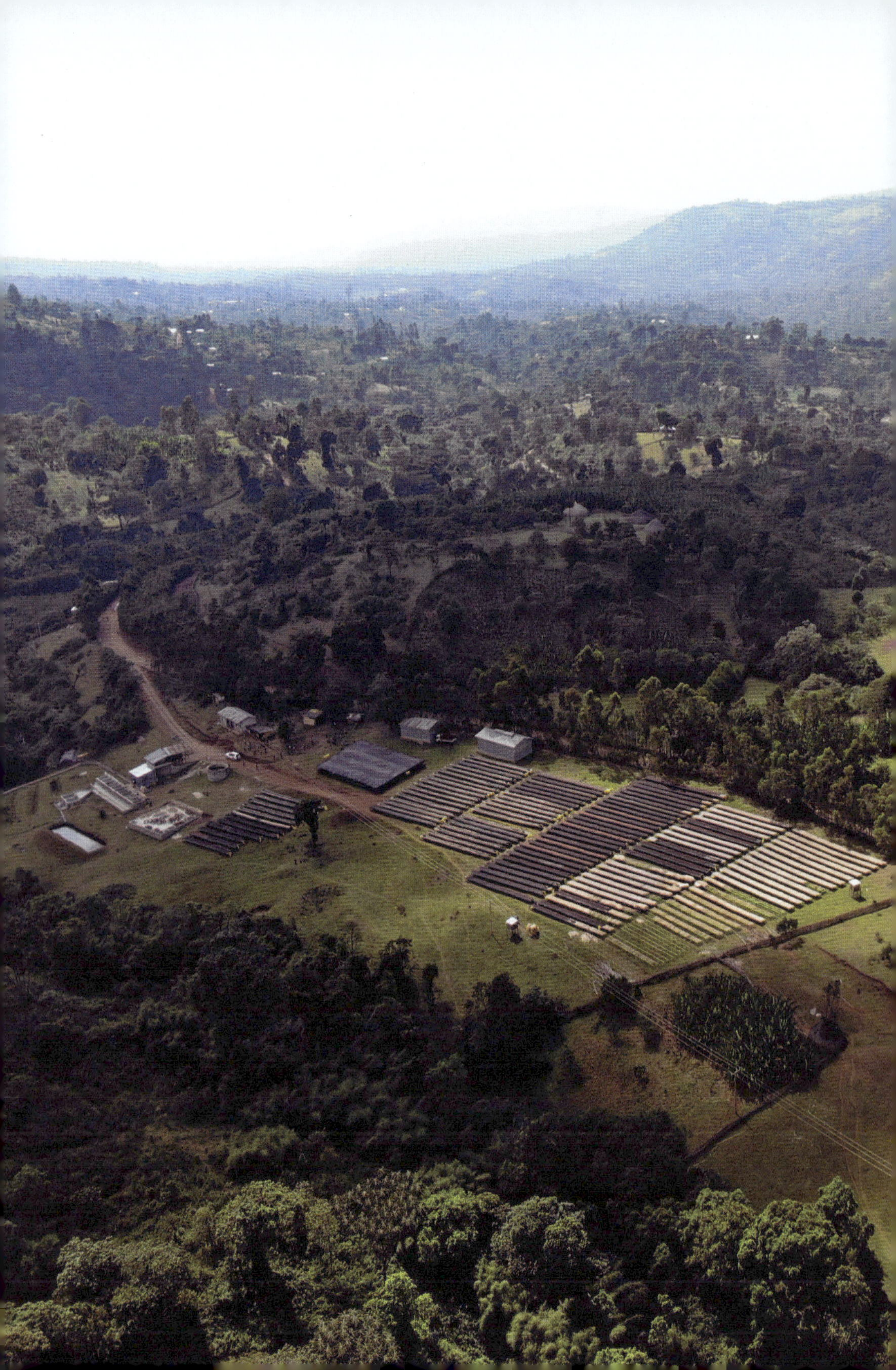

Terroir and Taste

COFFEE VARIETIES

People drink coffee throughout the world, but coffee shrubs grow almost exclusively in the tropics. Where each coffee is grown and how it is processed clearly shape each cup's flavour. It is tempting to liken coffee to wine, where each variety and appellation have distinct, defined flavour profiles. But, for a range of factors, coffee is more fragmented, more diverse, not as well defined and significantly less regulated.

The resultant patchwork is complex, not easily categorized and riddled with exceptions. While some coffees can be traced to a single point of origin, it's not always clear how the coffee's terroir shapes its flavour. It is often, in fact, agricultural, social, environmental and economic forces that influence the array of coffees globally available. Without this understanding, it's difficult to appreciate the range of flavours available from each coffee-growing region.

THE DELICACY OF COFFEE SHRUBS

Coffea arabica is widely regarded as the tastiest of the commercially grown coffee species. It demands similar conditions to its ancestral environment in the Ethiopian Highlands and neighbouring regions such as the Boma Plateau.

Arabica is best grown in locations with an average temperature of 18–22°C (64–72°F). An annual rainfall of 1,200–2,200mm (46–87in) is desirable, but there needs to be a short dry spell to trigger flowering followed by a wet season to maximize fruit growth. The soil needs to be mildly acidic, well-draining and rich in nitrogen, potassium and calcium.

Having evolved under the canopy of larger trees, *Coffea arabica* shrubs will wilt when temperatures rise over 30°C (86°F), but demand sufficient direct sunlight to produce cherries. The shrubs are also fragile and don't cope well with wind, will die with prolonged exposure to low temperatures, and are easily frost-damaged. Further compounding the challenge is the narrow gene pool of commercially grown arabica varieties, which makes shrubs susceptible to disease and pests.

Suitable growing conditions are found at higher altitudes closer to the equator and at lower altitudes farther away from the equator. *Coffea arabica* is typically grown at elevations between 1,000 and 2,200m (roughly 3,300–7,200ft) on aspects that have sufficient sun. But there are viable coffee farms situated in elevations as low as 600m (roughly 2,000ft) and as high as 2,800m (roughly 9,200ft), which have complementary factors to provide adequate warmth, protection and sun.

Coffea robusta is the hardier of the two most common commercially grown coffee species. It evolved in the lowland rainforests of Central and West Africa and has an optimal growing temperature range of 22–26°C (71–79°F), but it can survive at temperatures of up to 34°C (93°F) with sufficient watering. Suitable conditions can be found at elevations ranging from sea level up to about 1,000m (3,300ft). In these hotter conditions, the plants require greater rainfall and high humidity, but still demand free-draining soil and adequate nitrogen and potassium for cherry growth.

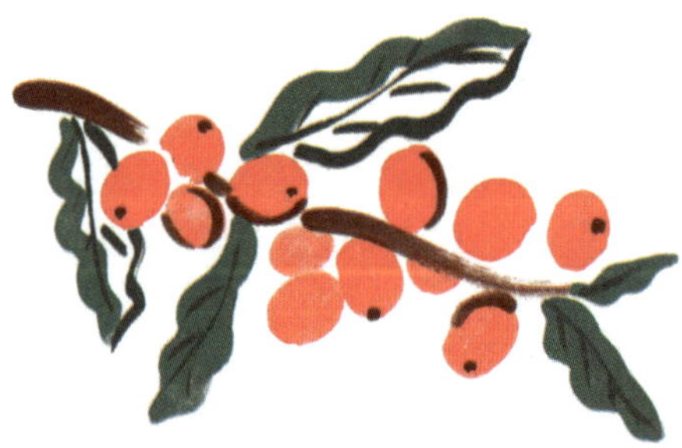

THE SELECTION OF VARIETIES FOR YIELD AND DISEASE RESISTANCE

Growers with suitable land must select from several dozen mainstream varieties, plus many more besides. Each variety prefers slightly different climatic and soil conditions and has a different yield and varying types of disease resistance. The grandfather of arabica varieties is Typica. Some varieties, such as Bourbon, Mundo Novo and Caturra are mutations or naturally occurring hybrids. Others, such as SL-28, Pacamara and Kent are cultivated varieties as the result of breeding programmes.

It makes financial sense for a farmer to plant coffee shrubs only when this provides better monetary returns than other crops. One of the many challenges facing the coffee industry is that alternative crops can be more lucrative. Many farmers choose to grow coffee for family, historic or personal reasons as much as for the financial incentives. With tight margins, for the farmers that choose to invest in coffee, the primary criteria for choosing varieties are often yield and resilience.

Yield is the quantity of cherries produced and is typically measured in kilograms per tree when considering the farm agronomy and in tonnes per hectare when evaluating financial performance. As a rule of thumb, once processed, dried and roasted, it requires 6–7kg (13–15lb) of cherries to create just 1kg (2lb 5oz) of roasted coffee. In other words, for every kilogram of coffee you drink in a year, a farmer has had to maintain and harvest a coffee shrub. At two or three coffees per day, I am paying for several dozen coffee shrubs to be fertilized, watered and harvested.

The upfront investment is made by the farmer, who must buy in juvenile shrubs, plant them and tend them at a financial loss until they start to produce cherries. Received wisdom is that shrubs bear fruit three to four years after planting. However, there are stories of shrubs producing cherries at 18 months with intensive fertilizer application and care. Planting new shrubs, and especially a new variety, is both a significant risk and a long-term investment

Farmers hedge their bets by growing multiple coffee varieties. This enables them to see what grows best on the land and helps to derisk against outbreaks of disease and pestilence that may affect a single variety. The productive life of a coffee shrub is typically 20–25 years, but there are shrubs producing cherries that are much older, admittedly with significantly reduced yields. The upfront investment and long tail of income disincentivizes prematurely switching out shrubs with alternative varieties as market trends change. Many coffee farms have plots of legacy varieties that may have either suboptimal flavours or yield, but which on balance continue to support the viability of the farm.

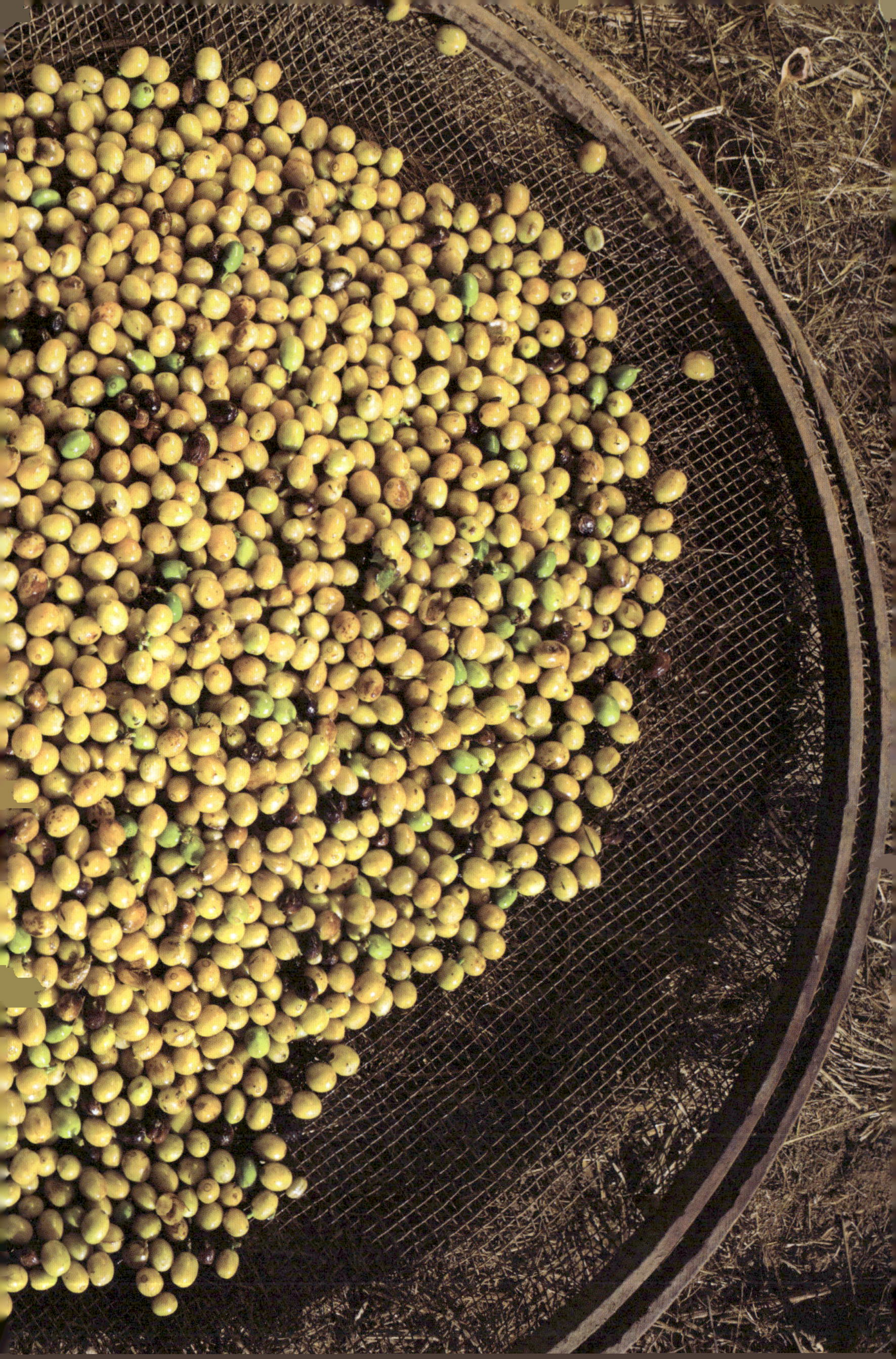

COFFEE AS A GLOBAL COMMODITY

The lag between planting and first harvest also highlights the boom-and-bust nature of the global coffee commodity market. When demand outstrips supply, prices rise and it is worth farmers investing in new shrubs. However, three or four years later there is often an oversupply of coffee as the recently planted shrubs start producing cherries. With coffee supply now outstripping demand, prices fall.

There is a long history of market-distorting practices, such as governments buying up excess supply, and centralized attempts to coordinate production in an effort to balance supply and demand. All have ultimately resulted in failure or proven to be unsustainable. Coffee roasters oscillate between hand-wringing about the plight of coffee growers when the price is low and then complain about the high cost of green coffee as prices rise. Don't feel sorry for them: they take comparatively little risk, are free to contract forward when prices are low, and can buy on spot when prices are high. What's more, many roasters end up trading down and buying lower-quality coffee as prices rise to keep consumer prices stable.

By contrast, coffee farmers operate in the face of the vicissitudes of the weather, climate, trends and the commodities market, and, moreover, must manage an investment that spans decades. The International Coffee Organization (ICO) collates and disseminates coffee statistics, especially on production and export volumes. More recently, the *Specialty Coffee Transaction Guide*, published by the Goizueta Business School at Emory University, Atlanta, Georgia, in the USA, is an annual report documenting the free-on-board (FOB) price paid, broken down by grade, origin and lot size.

Neither are perfect measures. The ICO has recently updated its methodology to better estimate global volumes and the FOB price is a record of what was paid for the coffee when it is delivered to the port in the country of embarkation. The price typically covers growing, processing and transportation costs from mills or warehouses to the port of origin, but not any subsequent cost. So the FOB price is neither a reflection of farmers' incomes nor the landed cost of green coffee.

It is, however, both convenient and nearly universal, as there is export paperwork created by the international coffee trading houses that are responsible for much of the world's coffee logistics, regardless of the quality, origin or who the farmer and roaster might be. Despite all the fragmentation of coffee growing and roasting, there are only several key companies that finance and manage international coffee exports. These corporations are the present-day iteration of the 16th-century Yemeni coffee merchants.

THE GLOBAL SPREAD OF VARIETIES

Most varieties are grown in multiple countries, and a range of varieties are found in most coffee-growing regions. Few regions are dominated by a single variety. At the global level, the trend is for farmers to grow more varieties, rather than to specialize. This trend is driven by consumption trends on the one hand and the emergence of new varieties on the other. The result is that coffee production is becoming more fragmented and further away from the appellation-style systems that define wine, cheese and spirits.

One of coffee's great untold stories is the occasional informal spread of coffee varieties through personal networks that connect the global coffee supply chain. In the spirit of Baba Budan, seeds have been transported around the world both by coffee brokers visiting farms and between networks of farmers who share agronomy tips and market information. Many countries have agricultural import or export controls, so seeds have been concealed within shoes, garments and other items. It takes only a single viable seed to grow a viable shrub, which in turn can produce dozens of seeds. For example, seeds from wild-growing shrubs in the Ethiopian Highlands might end up in a shrub nursery in the Americas, whence plants can then be sold throughout the continent. Once a nursery develops a reputation for hardier shrubs with strong yields, word quickly spreads among farmers.

The consequences are profound – largely positive but a challenge to the industry's narrative of transparency. The coffee industry has long prized 'traceability' – that is, line-of-sight back to the producer and the documentation of the varieties and process methods used. But it is possible for a farmer to not know the variety of some of their shrubs, and, even if they do, they may not wish for it to be public knowledge. Coffee produced from these shrubs is often labelled by the farmer as a commonly grown variety.

Additionally, sometimes there is confusion, as unknown shrubs are labelled as a specific variety for no other reason than they have similar proportions, leaf shapes or cherries. And these misclassifications are before human error, blended lots or fraud come into play. Without genetic testing, often no one is certain. In most cases, the variety listed on the bag is simply what the farmer told the mill or exporter.

In general, we can take the variety listed on a retail bag of coffee at face value, but it is useful to appreciate the multi-step supply chain creates room for confusion, mistakes and deception. For example, a coffee buyer recently relayed a situation in which a farmer had coined a name for a variety of which they were uncertain. The coined name was a portmanteau of two existing varieties because these shrubs had characteristics of both. The specific challenge was that the naming convention implied a new naturally occurring variety, but in reality this was likely to be an unidentified pre-existing variety. Consequently, there was a choice between (1) labelling the coffee with the farmer's term, (2) not labelling the coffee variety or (3) guessing what the variety was likely to be.

If seed smuggling is a grassroots endeavour to identify varieties with good yields and resilience, a top-down science-led project is under way conducted by World Coffee Research (WCR). It both catalogues existing varieties and breeds new cultivars. The project is financed by some of the largest coffee companies in the world as well as several smaller ones. The impetus for collective action is the recognition that climate change fundamentally threatens coffee production.

Hotter temperatures and changing weather patterns place added stress on coffee shrubs and make them more susceptible to disease. Part of the solution to growing coffee in a warmer world is for new varieties to be bred that are sufficiently tasty, have good yields and show resistance to disease and pests that are more common with warmer, wetter growing seasons. To date, there are well over 60 varieties in the WCR arabica catalogue and more than 40 in the robusta catalogue.

Global efforts to prepare the coffee supply chain for climate change have also led to the reappraisal of the coffee species *Coffea eugenioides* and *Coffea congensis* as well as the rediscovery of *Coffea stenophylla* and *Coffea liberica*. In the UK, London's Royal Botanic Gardens, Kew, is playing a key role in both identifying sidelined coffee species and facilitating breeding programmes to create new varieties that are better suited to the growing conditions in a world impacted by climate change. Excitingly, these species are already available to coffee drinkers and new varieties are coming to market.

WHAT IS A COFFEE'S TERROIR?

Ethiopian garden coffee

The vast majority of coffee produced in Ethiopia is grown by smallholders. Shrubs typically grow on domestic plots alongside fruit trees, such as mango, avocado and banana, as well as staples such as maize. Once the cherries have formed, they are picked and sold to a local mill for processing.

Mills sort, process and grade the coffee in preparation for export. Across the world it is common for smaller-scale growers to sell their cherries to mills. This means we need to draw a distinction between the coffee grower and the producer. Some farmers, especially of large estates, both grow and process their coffee to maintain control and increase margins, but this requires capital investment in processing infrastructure, additional skills and labour and an appetite for the increased risk. Many smallholders opt to sell their cherries as a cash crop.

Decentralized, smallholder coffee production occurs in many coffee-growing countries. This is why there are more than 10 million coffee farmers globally. Many smallholders are found in Ethiopia, Uganda and Indonesia, but domestic coffee growing is also common in Colombia, Kenya, Rwanda, India, Papua New Guinea and even Brazil.

The best coffee in Ethiopia is grown on the higher elevations of the mountainous plateaus. The regions of Yirgacheffe, Sidama and Guji are some of the most sought-after coffees in the world thanks to their floral aromas, crisp acidity and sweet fruity flavours. There is also frequently a hint of bitterness, which adds balance and sophistication.

The higgledy-piggledy nature of growing in Ethiopia reduces the consumers line of sight to the grower. Coffees are often named after the mill and because lots may contain any number of varieties, the variety is frequently categorized as 'heirloom'. Ethiopia is a good example of the complexity of the coffee supply chain and how it can be difficult to trace coffee further upstream than the mill. Many of these features are mirrored in coffee production globally.

It is also worth noting that coffee still grows in the wild in Ethiopia's mountain forests. As well as a source of income, these wild shrubs are also a resource of genetic diversity for breeders and a source of seeds for smallholders, mainly in Ethiopia but also throughout the world.

Only 5 per cent of Ethiopian coffee production occurs on commercial plantations, which are mostly in Oromia and southern Ethiopia. Elsewhere in the world, the climatic conditions are less ideal for growing coffee, demanding more intense fertilizer application and watering.

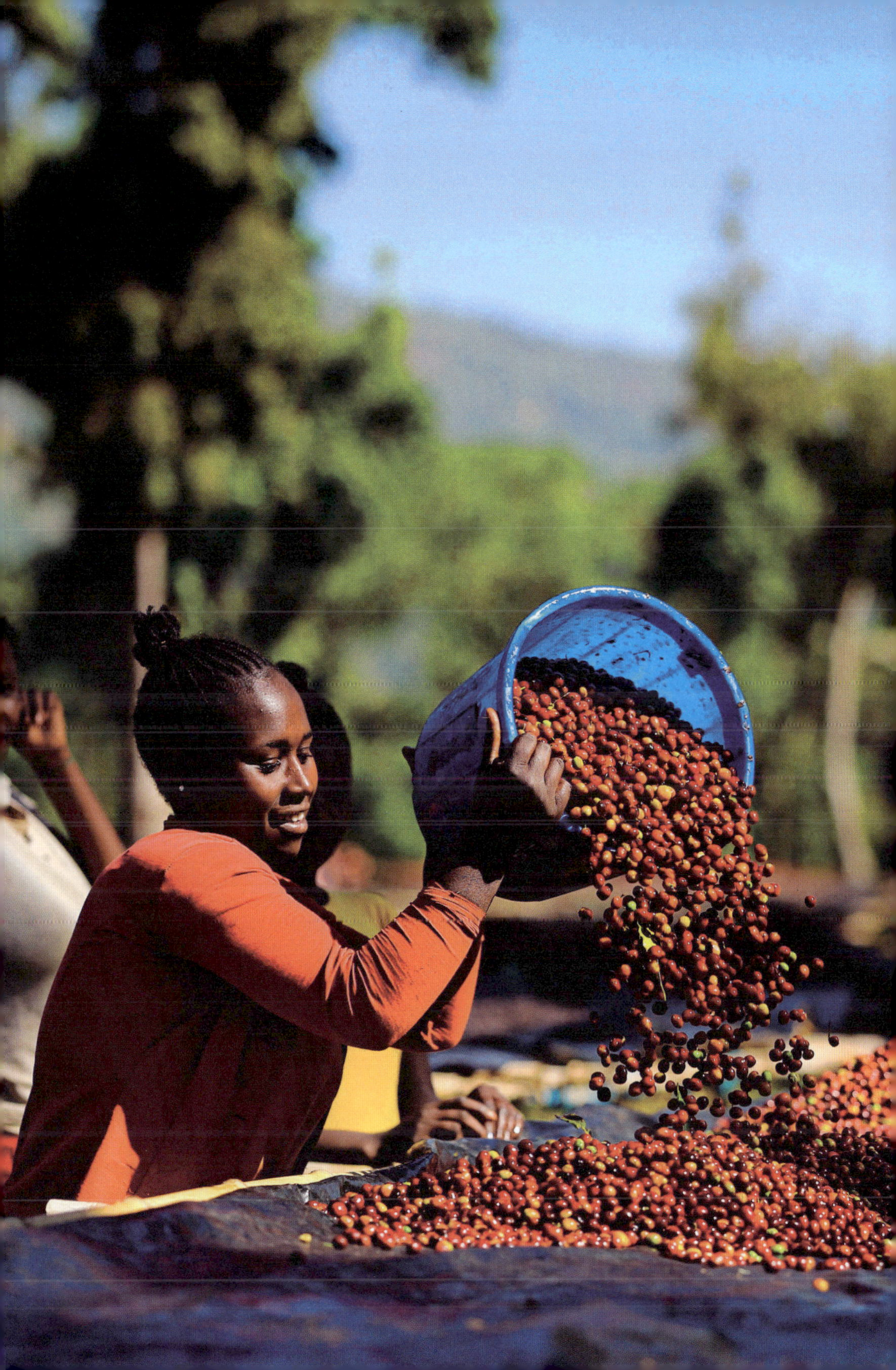

Commercial coffee in Brazil – advanced agronomy and mechanized harvesting

Brazil is the world's largest coffee producer and dominates the international market. Almost one in three beans is grown in Brazil. The country has suitable climatic and geographic conditions, and has accumulated the necessary agricultural and technological know-how, as well as the financial resources, to be a coffee superpower.

The country's flat plateaus are well suited to growing coffee and make mechanized harvesting possible. Coffee is planted in orderly rows, and shrubs are pruned so that harvesting machines can pick cherries.

Brazil will continue to shape the future of coffee growing and production. There are millions of hectares of degraded pastureland suitable for potentially deforestation-free expansion of coffee farms. As global coffee consumption increases, Brazilian farmers will further extend the land under coffee cultivation. The economic consequences are that Brazil sets the benchmark for the global arabica price and the country will continue to be the world's key coffee producer for the foreseeable future.

With limited water resources, coffee in Brazil is typically dried on flat terraces. Harvested cherries are thinly spread across concrete or brick patios to dry in the sun. The cherries must be turned regularly to prevent mould developing or rot setting in.

Drying coffee on terraces is usually called the 'natural process'. Because the cherries' flesh is in contact with the seed as the coffee dries, there is often some fermentation. The best-tasting natural-processed coffees are often fruitier. Tasty natural-processed Brazilian coffees often have flavours of stone fruits, such as plums or cherries. Fermentation can greatly add flavour, so it's also possible for the fruit flavours to be lighter, even berry-like. Pleasant Brazilian natural-processed coffees often have flavours that I associate with what I grew up calling scroggin, but which is more widely known as trail mix. Trail mix is a blend of dried fruits, such as raisins, sultanas and currants; dried pineapple, apple or banana; and nuts such as almonds, cashews and peanuts. The precise combinations and ratios are determined by the blender, and many people who create their own trail mix have their own recipe. The best versions in my childhood also contained chocolate.

It is difficult to control all the variables when drying coffees using the natural process. Cherries may be unevenly distributed, plus a cherry may be turned only to return to lying on the same side. Consequently, natural processing can be unpredictable. Like my childhood scroggin, you never really know what flavours you are going to get with each handful. While this processing method is used throughout the world, it is mainly used for processing larger volumes of cherries in drier locales.

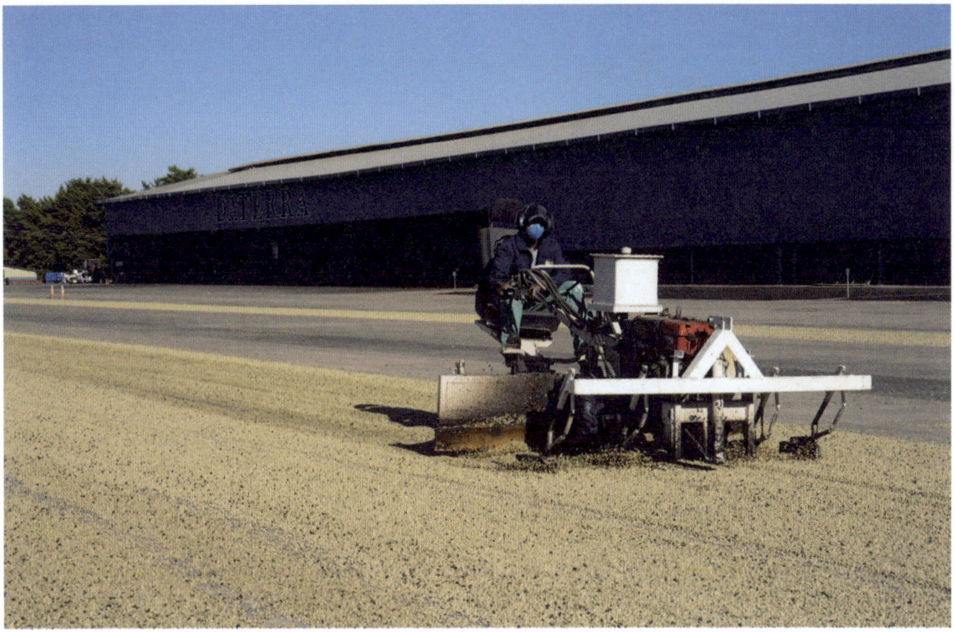

In some parts of the world it is more common for cherries to be dried on table-height frames with a wire-mesh surface. Often called 'raised beds', these structures enable better airflow and thereby reduce the risk of mould or rot; people can also turn the cherries more easily at table height.

Coffees grown at lower altitudes ripen more quickly in the heat and are generally less complex. Typical flavours include dried fruits, nuts and cocoa nibs, but they can equally be fibrous and earthy. The natural-process method can complement these flavours by enhancing the fruit flavours.

Unpleasant flavours as a result of growing and production are labelled as 'defects'. While some, such as insect damage, are clearly faults and taste bad, some fermentation processes have a finer line between taints and positive flavours. It is the job of exporters and buyers to grade the coffee lots; those with fewer defects are awarded higher grades and command higher prices.

A variation is the pulped-natural process, in which the cherries' flesh is mechanically removed before being dried on terraces. With no flesh remaining, there is a reduced chance of rotting and the coffee's flavours should be free from fermentation flavours.

With no opportunity for the flesh to rot after picking, washed coffees often have the benefit of more direct, linear flavours and fewer taints

Hillside coffees – commercial coffee farming with cherries that are hand-picked

As coffee production nears the equator, the necessary climatic conditions are found at higher altitudes. In Central America much coffee is grown at elevations of over 1,000m (3,280ft), with some coffees, for example in Colombia (which straddles the equator), grown at elevations of over 2,000m (6,560ft).

The cherries take longer to ripen at altitude, increasing the opportunity for complex flavours to develop. Colombia is the world's third-largest coffee-producing country. The key coffee-growing regions follow the Andean mountain ranges. Many farms are at elevations of 1,300–2,000m (4,265–6,560ft), and the terrain is often steep, with ridges and gullies.

Coffee grown on slopes must be manually picked. It's typically hard, hot work often carried out by itinerant labour as well as by the farmer and family members. Colombian coffee farms are close to the equator, and many farms pick twice a year: a main crop and a secondary 'fly' crop. In reality, selective picking often occurs across a long, continuous season with the cherries divided into two export shipments. Other counties that also straddle the equator, such as Indonesia, also have a main and a fly crop.

Many of the coffee-growing regions near the equator have abundant rainfall, and farms can either store or access sufficient water to make wet-processing methods commonplace. Plus, some coffee farms have their own processing equipment, or growers may pool resources and form a collective.

In wet-processed coffee, much of the flesh is removed using mechanical pulping before the seeds are tipped into a water tank. The remaining flesh breaks down and can be removed from the seeds, which are strained from the tanks before being placed to dry on either patios or raised beds. With less opportunity for the flesh to rot after picking, washed coffees often have the benefit of more direct, linear flavours and fewer taints. They are often described as 'clean' or as having greater 'clarity'. This term is derived from a conceptualization that coffee buyers often wish to taste the flavours originating from the cherry, not its processing.

High-altitude washed coffees often benefit from complex stone-fruit flavours such as cherry, peach or even nectarine. Other red fruits are also common, including red apple. These coffees are often predominantly sour, but benefit from some perceptible sweetness thanks to the combination of their fruit flavours and low levels of bitterness.

A wide range of flavours are possible. Across Central American washed coffees, it is easy to source crisp citrus examples, such as high-quality Gesha from Panama; sweet-tasting cherry, redcurrant and red apple examples from Huila, Colombia; and coffees with low acidity and chocolate flavours from, say, Guatemala.

DIVERSITY

Global coffee production is diverse and evolving, so there are many examples of coffee farming and production that do not fit neatly within the above artificially bounded examples. However, many farming arrangements or production techniques are either iterations or mixtures of these models. There are several interesting and notable examples that also highlight widespread practices within coffee production.

Not all commercial coffee is grown by large estates. For example, Vietnam is the world's largest robusta producer and second only to Brazil in total coffee exports. Its 650,000 smallholder farmers grow coffee intensively on small, flat plots of land that can be easily strip-harvested, where pickers work each row harvesting all the cherries regardless of each cherry's ripeness. While a typical plot is just a couple of hectares, Vietnam's centralized coordinated market economy and the combined scale of production make it distinct from both the Ethiopian garden coffee and Brazilian mechanized production.

While coffees are often identified by their country of origin, this method is almost always too generic and simplistic. For example, Kenya has both large coffee estates and smallholder growers. As the coffee estates often have their own processing facilities, it's possible to trace these coffees to a specific location. However, some of the tastiest coffees, with the archetypical crisp blackcurrant-profile, are often grown by smallholders who sell their cherries to mills. It is ineffectual to reduce this country's coffee production to this archetypical style because if you buy a coffee from this origin it might defy your expectations, regardless of its pleasantness or quality.

Furthermore, it's not always possible to be assured even of the country of origin. For example, it's estimated that a significant portion of the coffee grown in the Democratic Republic of the Congo (DRC) is smuggled into neighbouring countries, primarily Uganda and Rwanda. It's then mixed with domestic lots by local agents and exported under the assumed origin. The subversion is necessary and worthwhile because of the conflict in the eastern provinces of the DRC, which is one of the country's coffee-growing regions, as well as the Congolese state's higher taxes and complex bureaucracy.

There are also multiple iterations of processing methods. For example, a common technique in Costa Rica and El Salvador is the 'honey process'. After harvesting, cherries are coarsely mechanically pulped, sometimes with a little water, to leave more flesh around the seed before it is dried. The cherry's flesh is called *miel* in Spanish, which also means honey. Pulpers can be adjusted to retain various amounts of *miel*. A honey-processed coffee might be described as 20 or 60 per cent, referring to the quantity of retained *miel*. Or there are various labels including yellow, red and black honey, which refer to the quantity of retained flesh, in increasing order. The term 'honey processing' is evocative of sugars, despite the process not adding sweetness to the cup.

Finally, coffee producers are embracing experimental production techniques to enhance and punch up coffee's natural flavours. Most of these methods involve controlled fermentation. One of the most common methods is to allow coffee cherries to ferment in an airtight tank. Often labelled 'anaerobic fermentation' or 'carbonic maceration', removing oxygen from the tank fundamentally changes the biochemical pathways available to microorganisms like yeast and bacteria. The result is often pronounced red berries, red fleshy fruits or tropical fruit flavours.

There is a wide range of fermentation methods. The crudest form is no more complicated that putting cherries into a plastic bag. The most sophisticated methods involve multiple stages of controlled fermentation in large stainless-steel tanks, sudden changes in temperature to stop fermentation, and use of commercially produced yeast strains. Sometimes, these processes are shrouded in mystery. It is increasingly common for producers to restrict access for visitors for fear of their intellectual property know-how being stolen and their signature flavour profiles becoming widespread.

An alternative way for coffee producers to enhance flavour is to add fresh fruit to a tank in which coffee cherries are soaking. Commonly called co-fermentation, the flavours of the fruit are imparted into the coffee seeds and are present when drunk. Often, whatever fruit is readily available is used, so it is common for co-fermented coffees to have tropical fruit flavours, such as pineapple, mango and passionfruit; berry flavours, such as strawberries and raspberry; or even boozy or floral-associated flavours such as whisky or jasmine.

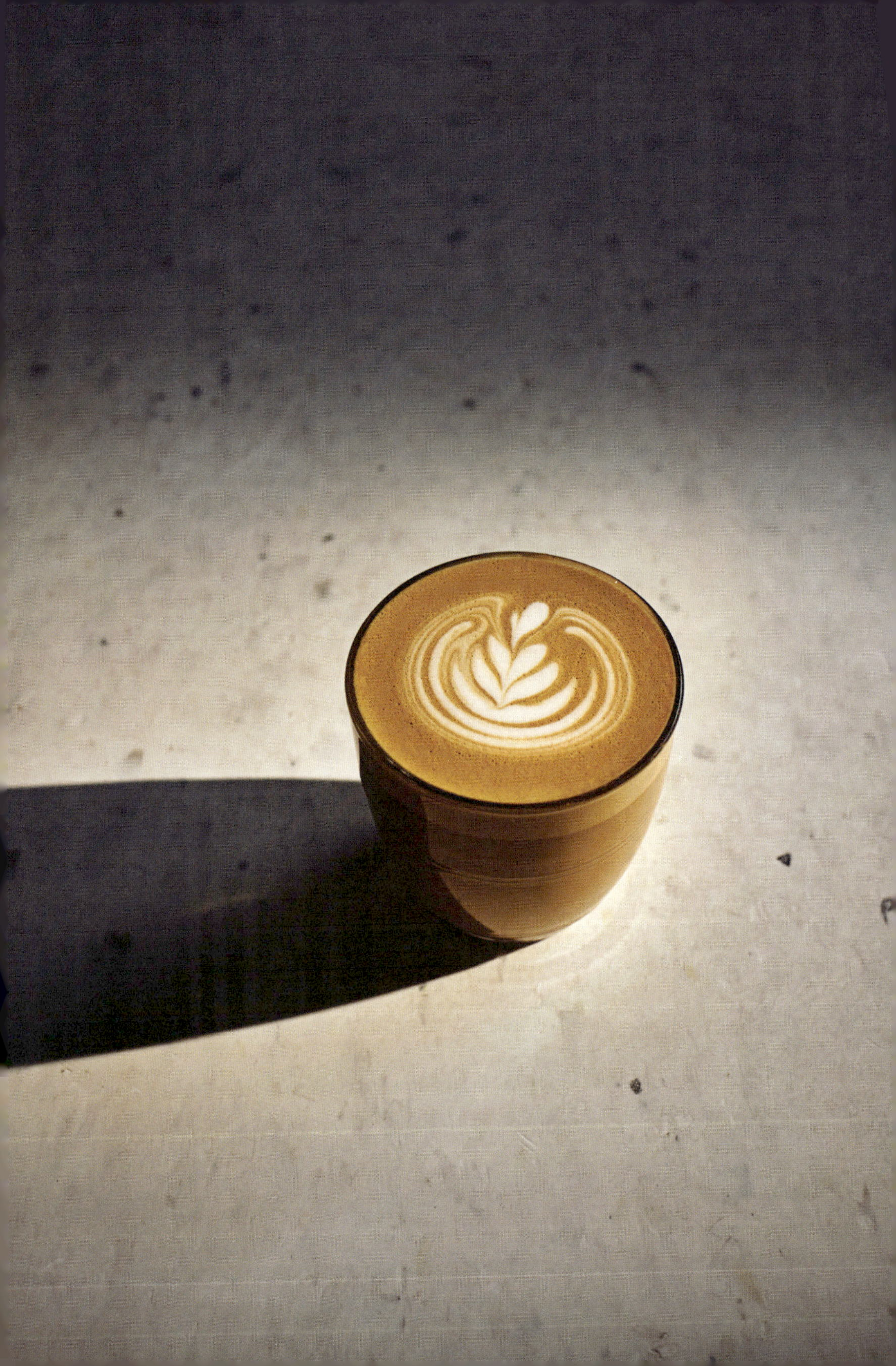

CULTURAL TERROIR

The complex tapestry of varieties, farming, production, experimentation and climate change means that there are challenges to drawing direct correlations between a coffee's origin and its flavour. It is always too reductive to artificially label a country as having a typical flavour profile. While there are specific regions that consistently produce specific flavour profiles with specific varieties, it often doesn't help to think about the entire coffee industry in this way. There are either an increasing number of exceptions to the received rules, or many archetypical characterizations of coffee flavours that were too arbitrary in the first place.

Where origins do have archetypical expressions, these are often a function of producers grading lots with those flavour profiles in mind and coffee buyers looking for lots that exhibit archetypical flavours. If 'terroir' refers to flavour imparted by the geography and climate, then flavours refined through a process of screening, grading and lot selection might be best described as 'cultural terroir'.

Cultural terroir plays a significant role within coffee production. For example, a significant portion of Gesha cherries grown in Panama are sold generically, or under an assumed varietal name, as they lack the desired flavour profile. Panamanian Gesha is arguably the closest analogue coffee has to an appellation-style flavour profile with appellation-like screening of production to protect the origin's reputation.

While Gesha is an extreme example, similar screening and grading occur throughout the coffee supply chain for most origins. A coffee's flavours are as equally shaped by each country's history, traditions and coffee-processing norms as they are by its land. In fact, cultural terroir often better explains coffee's flavours as well as why flavours and our perception of various origins' archetypical flavours are changing over time.

TASTE IS THE ULTIMATE CRITERION

With an extraordinary number of permutations possible from an array of varieties, agronomy, processes and norms, it has never been more important to be able to appreciate coffee's aromas, mouthfeel, tastes and flavours. It's this appreciation that enables you to understand how a specific origin, variety and process has culminated in a distinct set of flavours. Furthermore, tasting skills will help you navigate the complex range of coffees available, now and into the future.

Coffee production has always been fluid and dynamic. Farmers work endlessly to improve yields, reduce defects, derisk production, reach new export markets and maximize the value of their crop. Traceability is no substitute for tasting. In fact, as many of the best coffee buyers I know continually tell me, 'Taste is the ultimate criterion'.

HOW COFFEE FARMING AND PRODUCTION IMPACTS FLAVOUR

Altitude

Coffee grown at a high altitude ripens more slowly and benefits from greater complexity. They are also typically sweeter, which means they are also less bitter and generally more acidic. While there is no guarantee they will be more balanced or aligned, often they are. Lots are typically compiled from micro-lots and are blended to be tastier.

Coffees that are grown at altitude are frequently have a Comfort, Clarity or Curious profile. Notable countries that have significant coffee production at higher elevations include Colombia, Ethiopia, Honduras, Peru, Guatemala, Costa Rica, Kenya, Tanzania, Rwanda and Burundi. Many of the archetypical coffees from these origins are esteemed for their floral or fruit aromas and flavours.

It's easier to find nutty, cocoa and earthy flavours in coffees grown below elevations of some 1,400m (4,600ft). In these conditions, the coffee cherries ripen more quickly in the heat, and the coffees typically are less complex.

Processing

Coffees that are naturally processed – that is, where cherries are dried on terraces – may have flavours associated with fermentation. Natural processing can be a good complement to coffee grown at lower elevations.

Washed coffees are typically described as 'clean'. The cherries' flesh is immediately removed after harvesting through a combination of a mechanical pulper and flotation tanks.

Honey-processed coffees are mechanically pulped, sometimes in water, but not all the cherries' flesh is removed. They are deemed to be sweeter than washed coffees.

Traditionally, coffee was processed using whatever resources were available. Wet processing lends itself to locations with limited access to flat land but abundant rainfall. Natural processing is the preferred option in regions that have large tracts of flat land and where water is scarce. However, it has become increasingly common for coffee farmers and mills to produce coffees with a variety of processing techniques. More recently, farmers and producers are experimenting with fermentation techniques. These typically add fruit flavours that range from berries to stone fruit to tropical fruits.

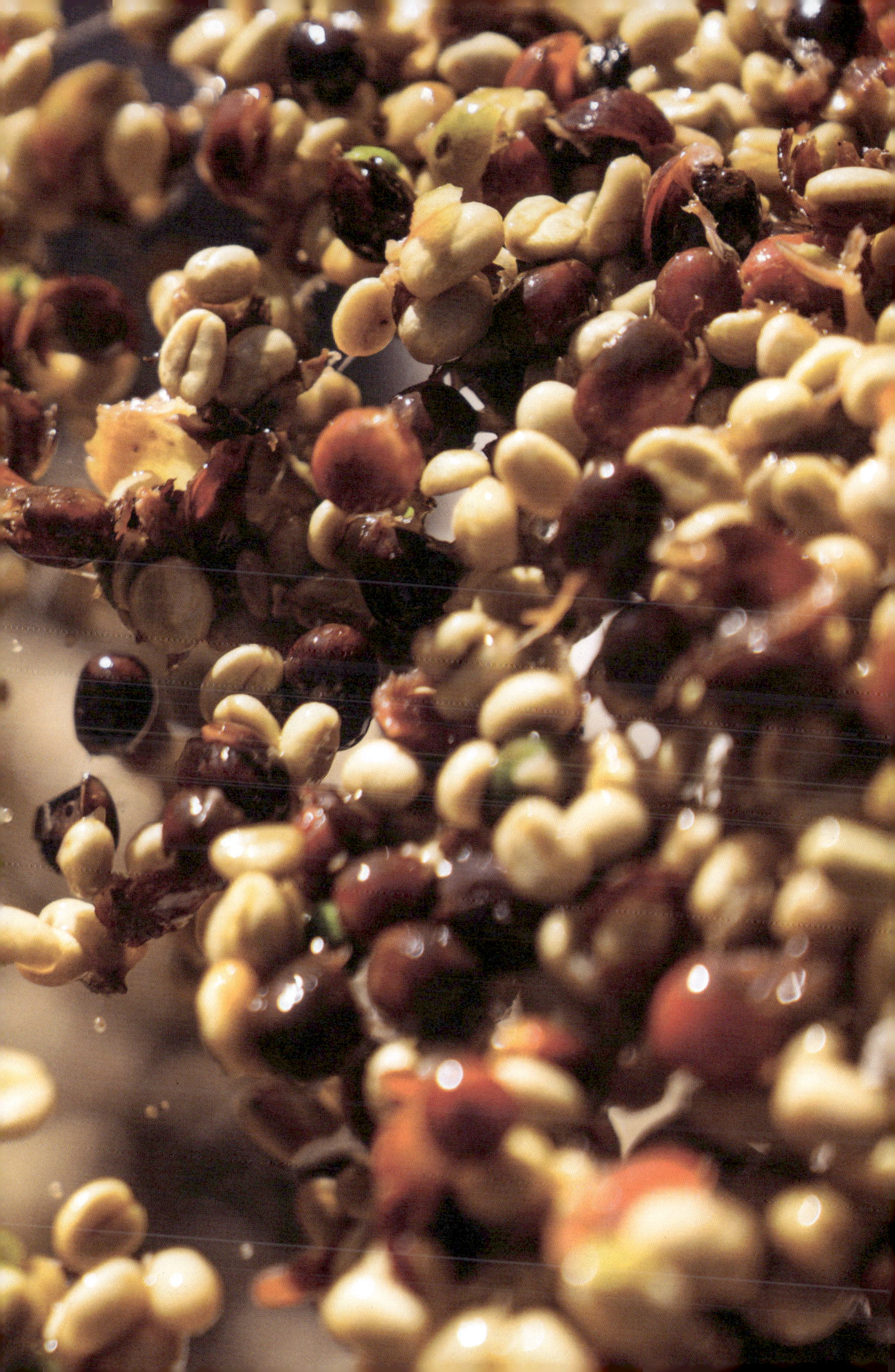

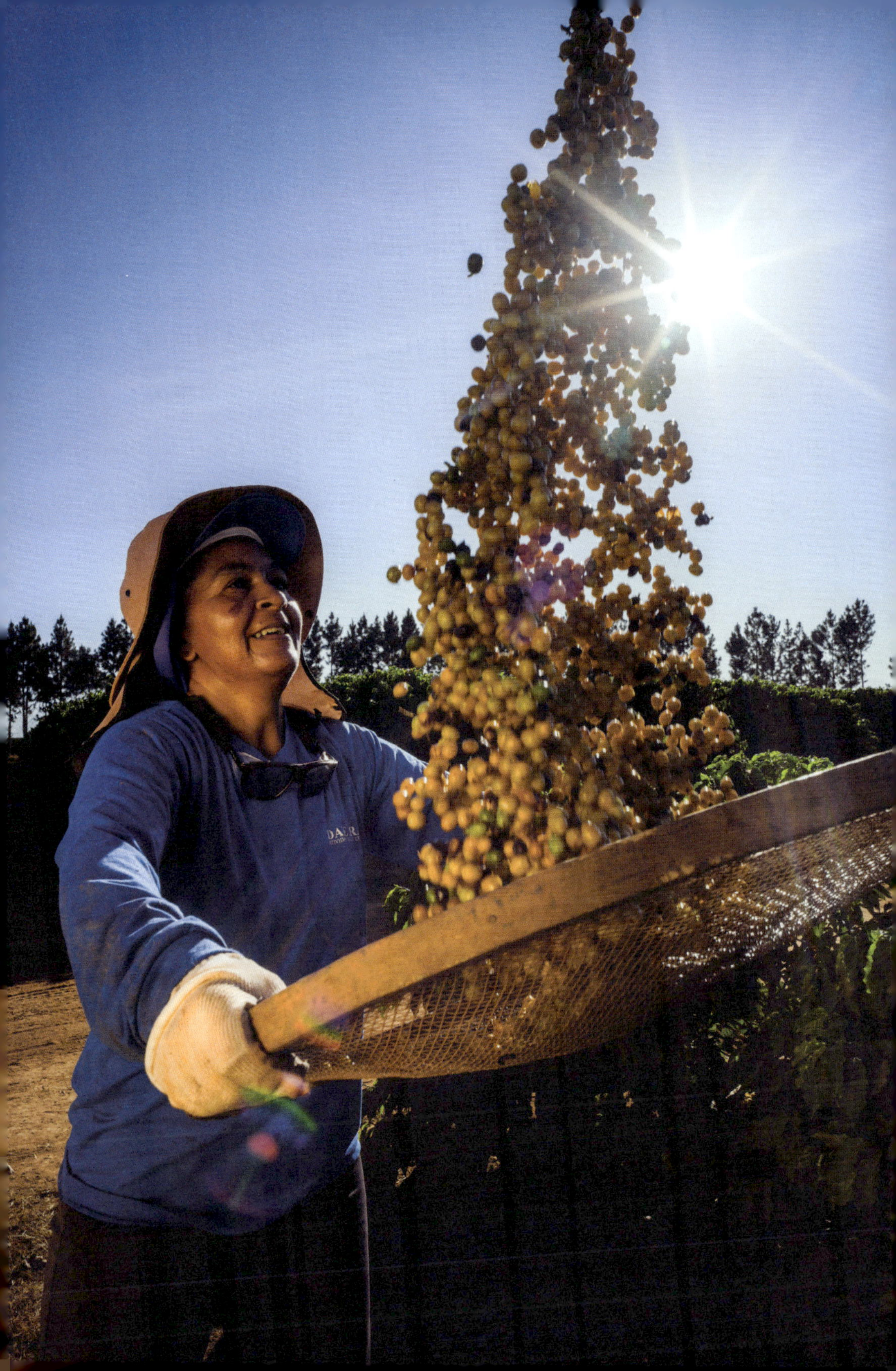

Single Origins

FROM CROP TO CUP

Coffee is grown in around 75 countries spanning five continents. Farmers and producers operate in a wide range of environmental, social, political and economic contexts. An entrepreneurial spirit and pragmatism recur among the people who grow coffee.

Farmers carry the risk of each year's production and must navigate consumer trends, changes in agronomic best practice, new varieties, the impacts of climate change and changes to trade agreements. When tasting coffee, it is always courteous to remember that making and drinking coffee are easy; growing tasty coffee is hard work. That said, the coffee farmers I've met are passionate about their crop and have a deep affection for coffee.

There are thousands of coffee farmers and producers worthy of inclusion in this section, but these four examples showcase a range of geographies, approaches, ages, process methods and philosophies.

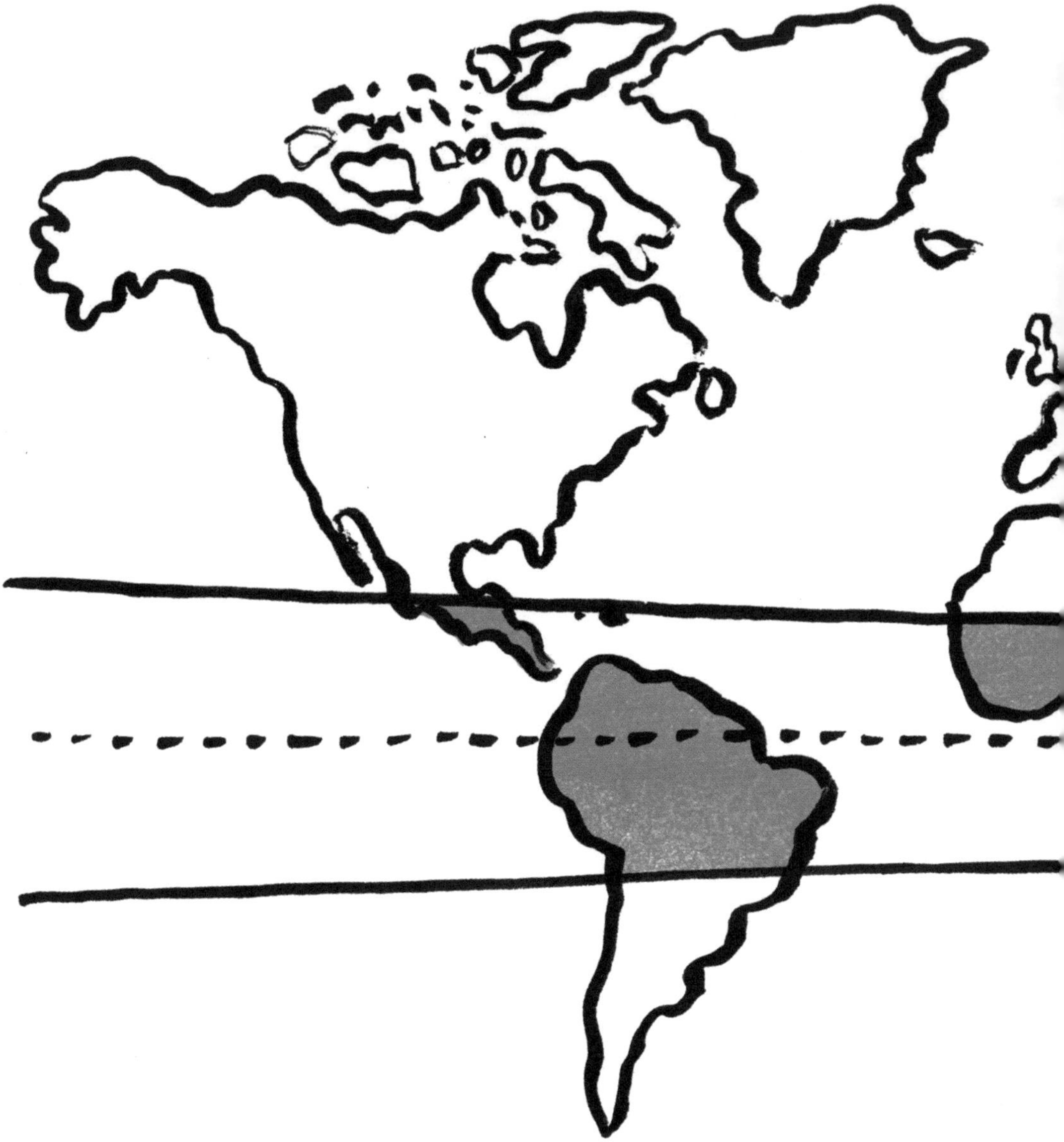

The Global Coffee

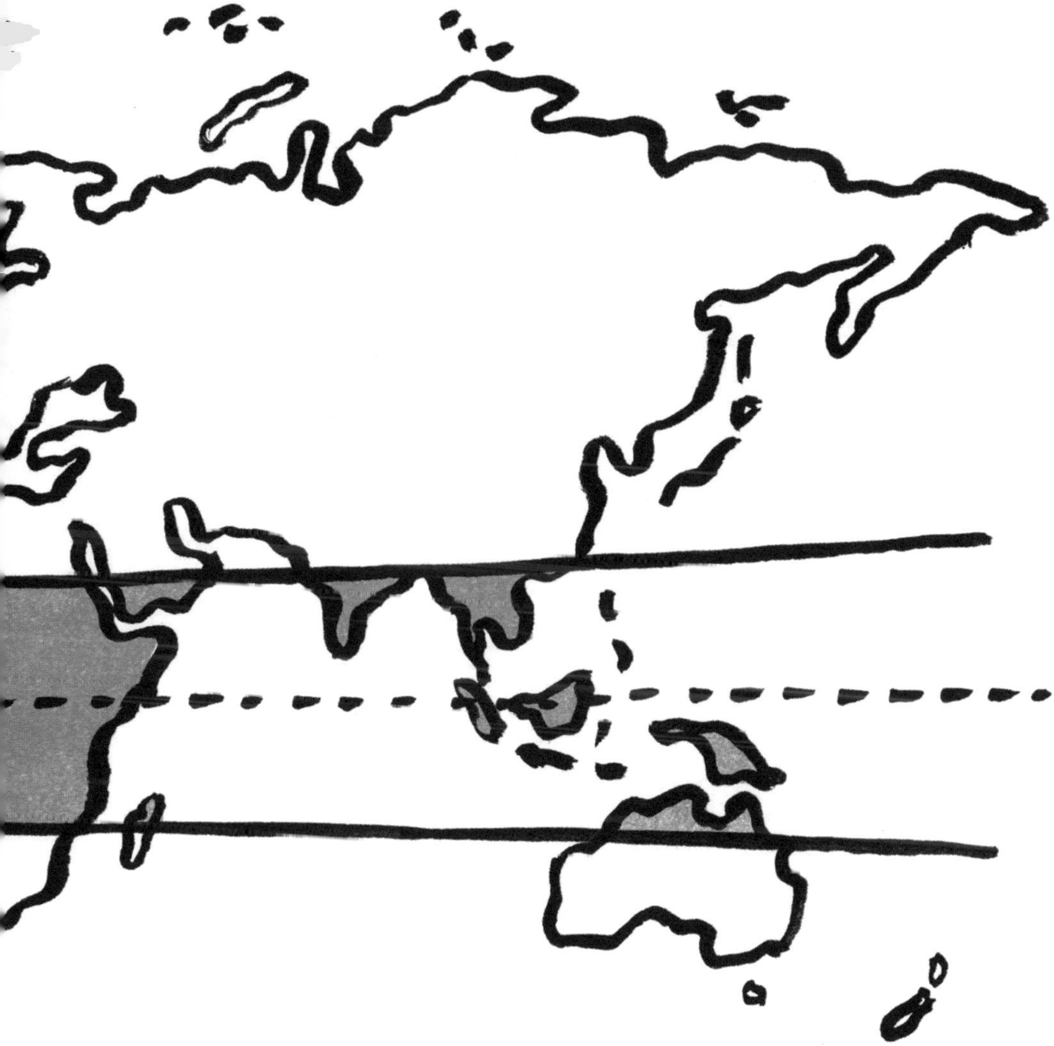

Producing Regions

BRAZIL – MECHANIZED HARVESTING AND NATURAL PROCESSING

Daterra Coffee, Minas Gerais, Brazil and the Cerrado savanna

Brazil is both the world's largest coffee exporter and the main producer of arabica. The Daterra coffee farm, owned by the Pascoal family, is located on the plains of Minas Gerais and sits within the eastern edge of the massive Cerrado savanna. Daterra is a large-scale coffee operation. The estate covers 6,400 hectares (15,800 acres), of which 2,800 hectares (7,000 acres) is planted with coffee. With the farm annually producing about 85,000 60kg (132lb) bags, its coffees are available worldwide. The combination of the landscape, size of the farm and the region's limited water supply in the dry season lends itself to mechanical harvesting and natural processing.

To ensure ripeness, cherries are allowed to start drying on the shrubs before harvesting. From the start of the harvest season in mid-May onwards, samples are taken from across the farm so the ripeness of the cherries can be inspected. When a plot has less than 15 per cent underripe cherries, a sample of cherries is picked, rapidly dried overnight and roasted for tasting the next day. The process is repeated until the crop is adequately sweet and ready for harvest. By this time the ripest of the cherries will be shrunken and dark purple while other cherries on the branch may still be underripe. Despite attempts to predict the coffee's sweetness using meters, the farm has found tasting to be the most reliable way to judge the optimal moment for harvesting.

Picking machines progress along rows, which are planted in concentric circles. Unripe and overripe cherries are discarded and the remaining cherries are separated into four streams for drying on patios based on the level of ripeness. The ripest cherries are sweeter and more chocolatey while the just-ripe cherries are fruitier, have more acidity and often have a flavour of plums. The higher-quality lots are sold as specialty coffee, with lower grades being sold into the commodity market.

Climate change is impacting the harvest and creates numerous challenges. For example, the farm has faced five consecutive years of hot temperatures. The hot, dry weather speeds up ripening and increases pestilence. Until the most recent harvest Daterra had been able to maintain total production volumes through irrigation and careful farm management, but the culminating strain on the shrubs has resulted in a recent harvest being down by one-third. The shrubs are producing cherries with smaller seeds, plus there has been an outbreak of coffee berry borer insects which has resulted in a higher-than-normal occurrence of defects.

Daterra is an interesting example of a large-scale coffee farm because of its advanced agronomy and long-term focus on wider environmental issues. Today over half the land on the farm is dedicated to restoring the ecosystem of the Cerrado. These efforts have led to Daterra being acknowledged as among the most sustainable Brazilian coffee farms as well as being certified as a low-carbon coffee farm.

Plots are progressively replaced with new, more drought-tolerant varieties. The incremental approach, combined with the time it takes for a coffee shrub to mature, means that it can take over a decade for a variety to be scaled to the point where it is a significant part of the farm's total production. Farm management has to plan decades ahead as well as manage annual coffee production.

Water is one of the most pressing pressing concerns. There is a deep appreciation at Daterra that the water crisis has been brought about by global climate change as well as the degradation of the savanna. It has recently built three massive 5-hectare (just over 12-acre) water tanks, which allows the farm to collect rainwater during the wet season and irrigate the shrubs during the dry season. Simultaneously, the family is actively rewilding other parts of the Cerrado savanna, and the Daterra team is encouraging neighbouring farms to collaborate on efforts to restore the local habitat. The hope is that, by restoring local ecology, the savanna will better store water during the wet season, helping to protect the future of the farms as well as restore the natural biome.

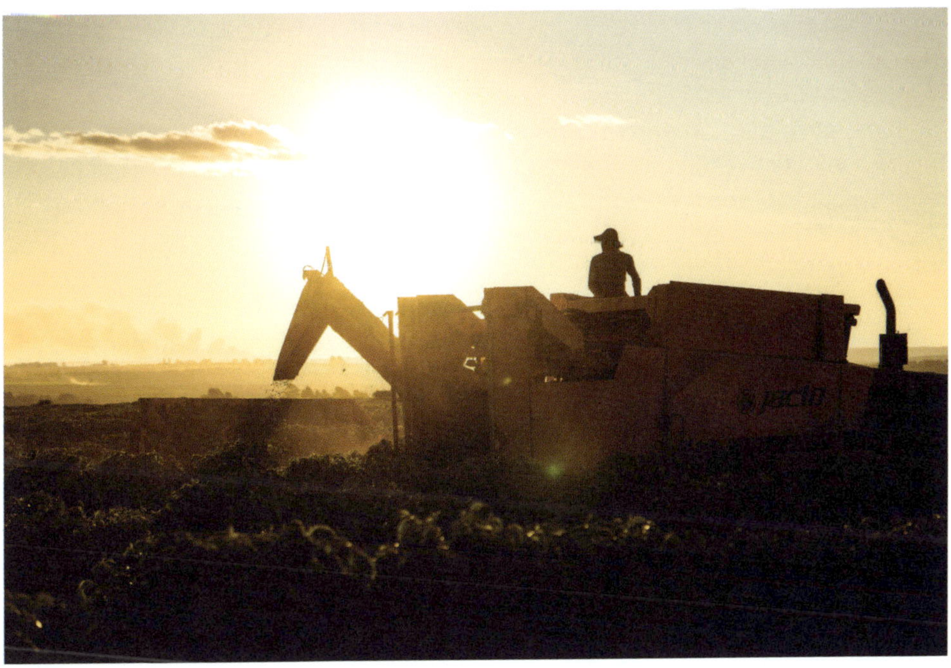

THE GODFATHER OF HONEY PROCESSING

Antonio Barrantes Zuñiga and the micro-mills of Costa Rica

As the eldest son, Antonio, known as Toño, was taken out of school in 1979, at the age of 14, to start full-time work on the family farm. The bargain young Toño struck with his father was to pursue coffee farming. His grandfather, Leoncio Barrantes, had founded a dairy farm, and his father, Manuel Barrantes, had invested in about a hectare of the Villa Sarchí coffee shrubs to diversify the farm's income. The variety is still grown on the family farm today.

Converting to coffee farming requires significant upfront capital, and the investment required for Toño to commence coffee farming was beyond the farm's financial resources. In a committed move, Manuel Barrantes arranged finance from one of Costa Rica's coffee baron families, essentially contracting future harvests to their mill. But the responsibility for the tending of the shrubs and harvesting was to be with the teenaged Toño. 'My father gave me the responsibility that comes with trust,' explains Toño. 'In these circumstances you have to grow up very fast.'

At the time, Costa Rican coffee farmers grew and harvested their cherries before selling them for cash to a large mill that would wet-process the cherries. Toño's commitment to building a commercially viable coffee farm simultaneously upended

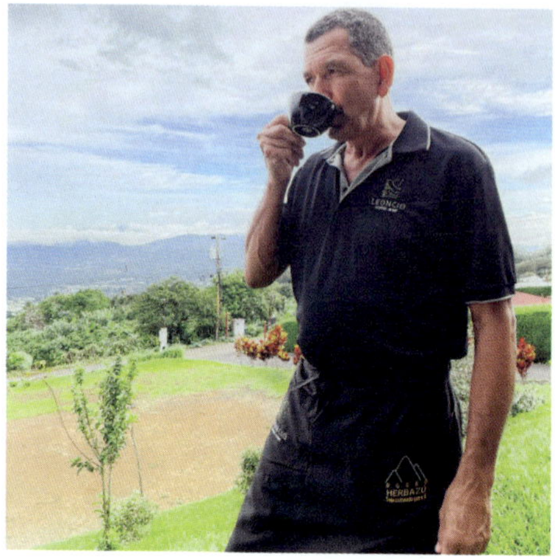

this convention and established the popularity of micro-mills and honey processing across Costa Rica.

Despite initial financial strains, the switch to coffee farming was to pay off over the coming decade. In the initial years Manuel strongly disliked the financial obligation and considered selling off a parcel of land to settle the debt. However, Toño got lucky on two fronts. First, Costa Rican coffee was gaining global appeal and coffee prices were rising across the 1980s. Second, Barrantes's land was fertile after years of the soil being enriched with cow manure. By 1990 Toño's annual coffee production had increased from just 50 bags a decade earlier to more than 1,800 bags.

Even as coffee production become the farm's main source of income, Manuel continued to run the farm and would pay each of the family members a weekly wage. The arrangement was stable throughout much of the 1990s. The farm supported the entire family, with many of Toño's younger siblings able to further their education as well as assisting with farmwork and the annual coffee harvest.

A transformative moment arrived in 1998 and was triggered by a crisis. After almost two decades of rising or stable coffee prices, global prices decreased, leaving the farm increasingly under financial pressure just as Manuel was reaching retirement. Toño's father took the decision to split the farm into 13 three-hectare (7½-acre) plots, one for each of his children.

The siblings banded together and continued to operate the farm as they previously had. There was never any discussion about dividing the land into individual plots: 'We never sat to talk about it; there was too much to do to manage the land.' But the economic reality was that, with the lower coffee prices, three hectares produced an insufficient income to live on. Kattia, the youngest Barrantes sibling, suggested during the 1999–2000 harvest that they investigate milling their own coffee. She was preparing for her final university exams and had been studying the larger Costa Rican coffee mills. The hope was that by vertically integrating the business they could get a larger portion of the coffee's selling price.

Toño identified a Costa Rican engineering business that constructed large coffee mills but that had also been exporting small milling equipment across Central America. Building their own mill and processing their own coffee was to be another calculated gamble. The family had sufficient savings to pay only for the construction of the concrete terraces required for drying, not the cost of the machinery. Furthermore, the farm had insufficient water resources to soak the cherries in tanks after milling.

The money for the machinery was found through a mixture of personal loans and a commitment of bank finance. But their plan required them to harvest the coffee, mill off much of the cherries' flesh, and then immediately dry the cherries on terraces. They would be unable to soak the cherries to remove the remaining flesh. If you know Toño's story, you know that this ends well. But it's hard to overstate the commitment displayed and risk taken by Toño and his siblings at this point. They had secured short-term finance to fund an untried process that demanded they take on additional risk without the certainty of either the outcome or a buyer for their coffee.

The 2000/2001 harvest ended in March, and the coffee they processed remained unsold across April, May and June. A local buyer who sampled their coffee told them it was good, and that they should be hopeful. But word got back to Toño that the buyer had subsequently told their neighbours that he couldn't bear to break the bad news to them: their coffee was, in fact, unpleasant and unsellable.

As the months passed, money started running short and suppliers ceased extending further credit. Compounding the situation, their coffee-growing neighbours petitioned Manuel to intervene and bring Toño's adventure to an end. From their perspective, growers had no business in milling their own cherries, let alone the expertise.

Things finally changed in July. A forward-thinking American coffee buyer was excited by the wine-like acidity, smooth body and fruit-forward flavours the farm's unusual process created. In Spanish, a cherry's flesh is called *miel*, which also means 'honey'. Since some of the *miel* was retained on the bean as there was no subsequent soaking process, the process method is now widely called 'honey processed' and is widespread across Costa Rica, El Salvador and Nicaragua. It is similar to the pulped-natural process, which is common in Brazil.

The first sale freed up the money to pay down the farm's debts and to prepare for the forthcoming harvest. It also triggered a wave of excitement in the United States. The next crop would be sold to Starbucks, and that enduring relationship would facilitate a series of encounters that would enable successive innovations across the farm.

Toño planted out new varieties, including San Roque, a mutation of the SL-28 variety. In Kenya, the variety is prized for its crisp blackberry flavour. The San Roque shrubs took several years to adapt to the local climate and establish themselves but when they did finally produce fruit, the coffees showed flavours of red grape and stone fruits such as nectarine. They were aromatic with wafts of vanilla and benefited from a balance between a lime-like acidity and a sugarcane sweetness.

In 2015 Toño won first place in Costa Rica's Cup of Excellence with this San Roque crop. The shrubs grew on the plot of land his father had considered selling 35 years earlier. This plot is now named Finca Leoncio, after his grandfather, while the mill was named Herbazú, a contraction of Hermanos Barrantes Zuñiga – the 'siblings Barrantes Zuñiga'. The coffees processed at the Herbazú mill are among the most sought after in the world. Today, all Toño's coffee-growing neighbours have their own micro-mills and use the honey-process method.

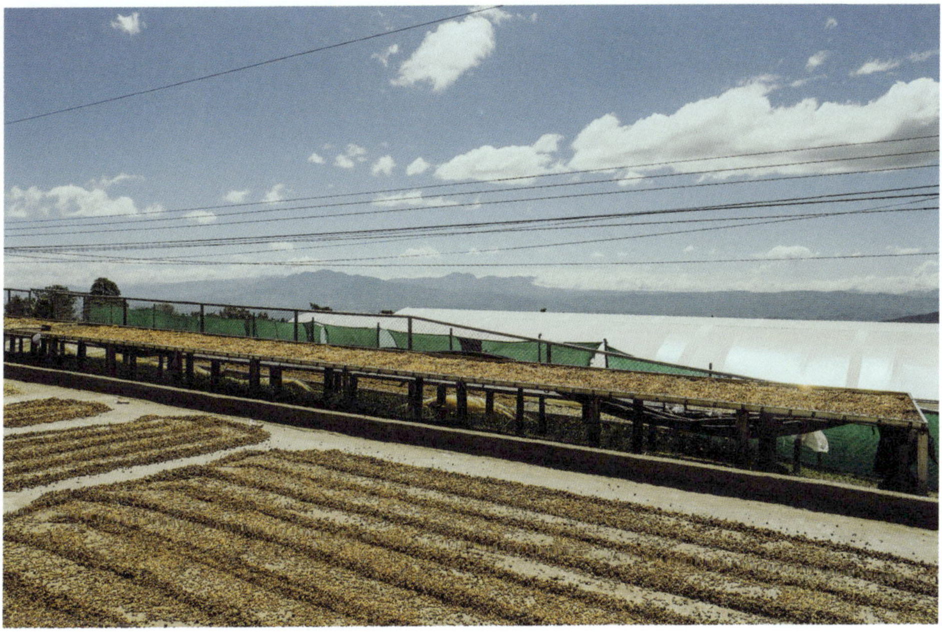

Toño's sense of purpose and curiosity are charming. He radiates the type of pragmatic and reassuring confidence that fosters loyalty. And like all passionate business owners, he can readily recall business and economic information, including the yield, farm output and prices in various years as well as the people he's connected with and been supported by along the way. With his mastery of the numbers and recollections of the farm's business operations, it's only when reviewing my notes that I remember he didn't have the opportunity to complete secondary school.

To date, Toño has won ten Cup of Excellence awards and was recognized in 2025 as a 'Legend of Excellence'. The vertical integration of the business has continued. The opportunity to plant various varieties led Toño to establish of a coffee shrub nursery, with seedlings now sold across the region. Plus, the family has opened a roasting business to sell its own coffee direct to local coffee drinkers. Its success led it to open a coffee shop that looks out over the farm's coffee shrubs and into the valley below. As Toño, who is now in his sixties, explains: 'In coffee, you can never stay still.'

INDONESIA, WET-HULLED – A COFFEE-GROWING COOPERATIVE

Rama Aulia Saputra of Sumatra Permata Gayo

Rama is an Indonesian coffee entrepreneur who operates Sumatera Permata Gayo (SPG), which translates as 'Gems of Gayo [Province]'. The collective encompasses more than 500 smallholders, organized by village groups, who grow coffee on domestic holdings across the region. An SPG representative is responsible for each group as well as for buying the coffee cherries. Growers are paid for their cherries, and the system enables each coffee lot to be defined by the village.

Indonesia's wet, humid climate has necessitated a unique coffee processing method called *giling basah*, or wet-hulled. Once harvested, cherries are mechanically pulped locally to remove part of the flesh from the cherry. The cherries are left to start drying under cover. However, the high local humidity slows drying and the beans can swell in size and take on a bluish-green colour. While damp, the remaining flesh is then removed using a mechanical process.

Each coffee lot is then transported to the low, flat, hot climate of Medan, where the coffees are further dried and prepared for export. Indonesian wet-hulled coffees are predominantly bitter with the best versions having some sweetness. They have low acidity and are identifiable by their earthy and spicy flavours, such as cinnamon, nutmeg and dark chocolate. The inclusion of Indonesian wet-hulled coffees into

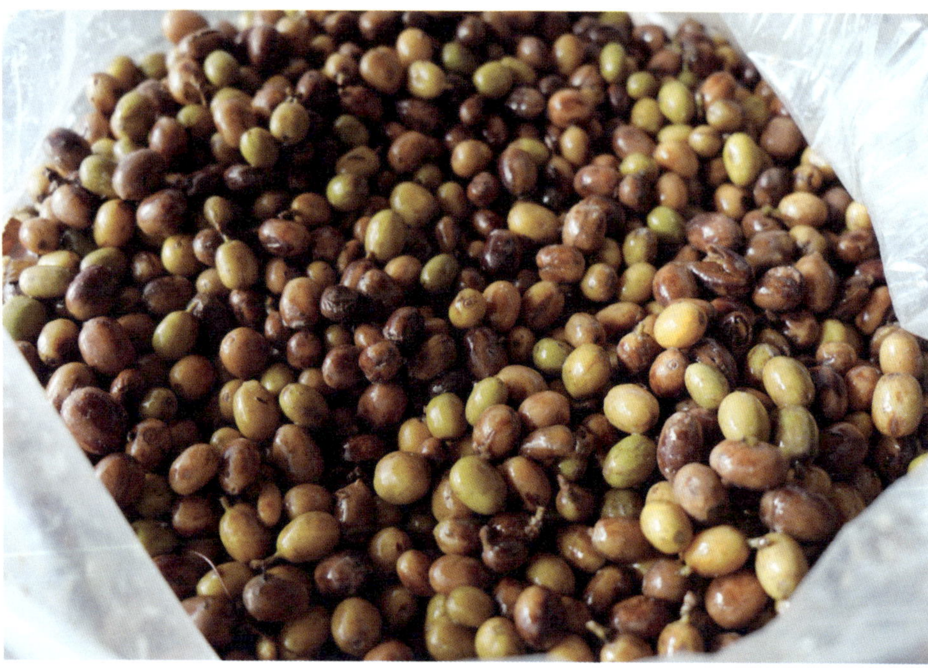

roasters' Christmas blends can add a hint of festive spice.

Rama describes the experience of coffee farming as an epiphany and finds his new work meaningful. Rama has obtained his Q Grader qualifications and regularly attends international coffee events to both build relationships with coffee buyers and appreciate market trends. Under his leadership, SPG now selects lots for either high-quality processing or experimental fermentation processing techniques. Now 10 per cent of the collective's total output is specialty grade. The mixture of high-quality and experimental lots creates export opportunities as well as fetching a higher price for the green coffee.

SPG is able to see these lots getting around twice the price of their standard offer. But, critically, these small lots also drive total sales. International coffee buyers may purchase just several hundred kilograms of these specialist lots but will also purchase a large volume of standard wet-hulled coffees to fill an entire container. A standard 20ft-long (6m) container can hold as much as 19,000–24,000kg (roughly 42,000–53,000lb).

Indonesian wet-hulled coffees are available globally, but are especially popular in the United States and Antipodean coffee markets. SPG exports around half of its total volume to the United States and Europe.

There are significant challenges ahead for the collective. Climate change is impacting coffee production in several ways. Indonesia sits upon the equator and has two harvests each year, a main crop and a fly crop. Until relatively recently, the main harvest occurred May–October with a smaller harvest in November–December. Warmer, wetter conditions are changing the local conditions, and the main harvest is now in October–November. The conditions also make coffee growing more difficult. Before 2023 the defect rate was less than 8 per cent; it is now over 9 per cent, and Rama is aware it may continue to rise. 'The collective will continue to invest in sorting, grading and experimentation to maximize the quality and price received,' explains Rama. The future of the collective has to be based on maintaining quality as well as on increased volumes.

SPG is an interesting case study because it is an example of how experimentation, updating processes and intentional relationships are necessary to build a viable coffee export business. It is also notable because across the world the coffee industry is struggling to attract a new generation of growers. Now only in his thirties, Rama will be able to make a contribution to the global coffee industry for decades to come.

ETHIOPIA, SMALLHOLDER PRODUCTION AND THE ROLE OF STATIONS

Atrie Weno of Coffee Legends

As cherries ripen between October and February, growers pick and deliver their crop to a local station in return for payment and a paper receipt. The majority of cherries in Ethiopia are grown on smallholdings but processed at local stations, which are scattered in a patchwork across Ethiopia's coffee-growing regions, serving as hubs to connect rural coffee growers with transport networks. Many growers walk several kilometres to deliver their cherries on foot, but some remote farmers must travel over a dozen kilometres.

For many growers across the Sidama region in the south of the country, coffee is their primary source of income. And with the cherries ripe, farmers are eager to receive payment. The Rumudamo station is just one of more than 80 that Daye Bensa, an Ethiopian coffee-producing company, operate across the Bensa, Aroressa, and Chere districts of Sidama.

Once delivered, the cherries are visually inspected and sorted into lots based on the grower's local village and the delivery date. The cherries are further graded in flotation tanks and the resultant micro-lots are processed separately. Typically, these micro-lots are mixed together to create lots for export. Cherries from growers that are of potentially excellent quality are processed distinctly as smaller nano-lots. These exclusive lots command high prices and can enhance the international reputation of the station.

Most stations process both washed and natural-processed lots. In general, the better quality lots are reserved for washing, although processing is largely determined in response to export demand. Forecasts are generated from each of their global customers' previous purchases – as well as customers' forecasts – to generate production targets. Each station receives a quota based on quality, village, process method and bean size. It is not uncommon for lots to be pre-sold or already allocated to customers around the world.

The task of the station manager and the quality control team is to ensure that the station's output fits the forecasts as closely as possible. It can be a challenging task. For example, a recent harvest has ripened later than is normal and the yields are also significantly reduced, resulting in a tough season for growers. This has led to an ongoing dialogue between headquarters and the stations to ensure the crop's commercial value is maximized and enough lots are assembled to meet Daye Bensa's contractual obligations.

I'm drinking coffee with Atrie Weno from Coffee Legends, an Ethiopian coffee importer in London. It's a cold winter's afternoon and he has just returned from a much warmer Addis Ababa where he has been buying coffee for the year ahead. He's been sampling what I'll be drinking six months from now. He clearly

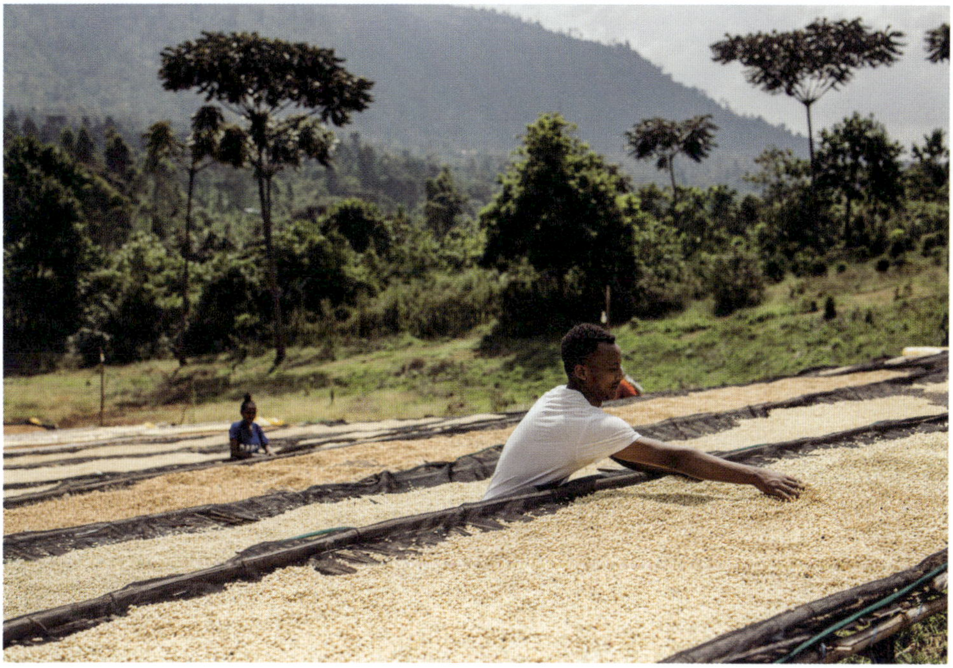

enjoys sharing stories of Ethiopian coffee farmers and patiently clarifies my understanding of Ethiopian production processes.

It's an important season for Atrie. In 2023, after a decade working at Daye Bensa Coffee, he started his own business importing Ethiopian coffee into the United Kingdom. His import volumes have grown quickly and Coffee Legends is now expanding into other European markets. Each season he buys a selection of lots from various stations and sells them to specialist roasters.

His business strategy has been to target the small, high-quality coffee roasters scattered across the country. In his first year he imported just one container comprising four lots: two washed and two natural. None of the coffees were pre-sold and he criss-crossed the UK throughout the year meeting roasters face-to-face to communicate the coffee range, its provenance, and to build relationships.

As the importer, he is invoiced for the coffee once it is exported from Ethiopia, but he only gets paid once he has dispatched an order to a roaster. Brokers can carry significant supply chain risk. As well as channels for selling coffee, brokers are a conduit for market information to be passed back to the country of origin.

Atrie's first order was for a single 60kg (130lb) bag to a micro-roaster, from a container of over 300 bags. He recounts his experience with a warm nostalgia, but it sounds like a challenging situation. He laughs, drawing on an Ethiopian saying, 'Once

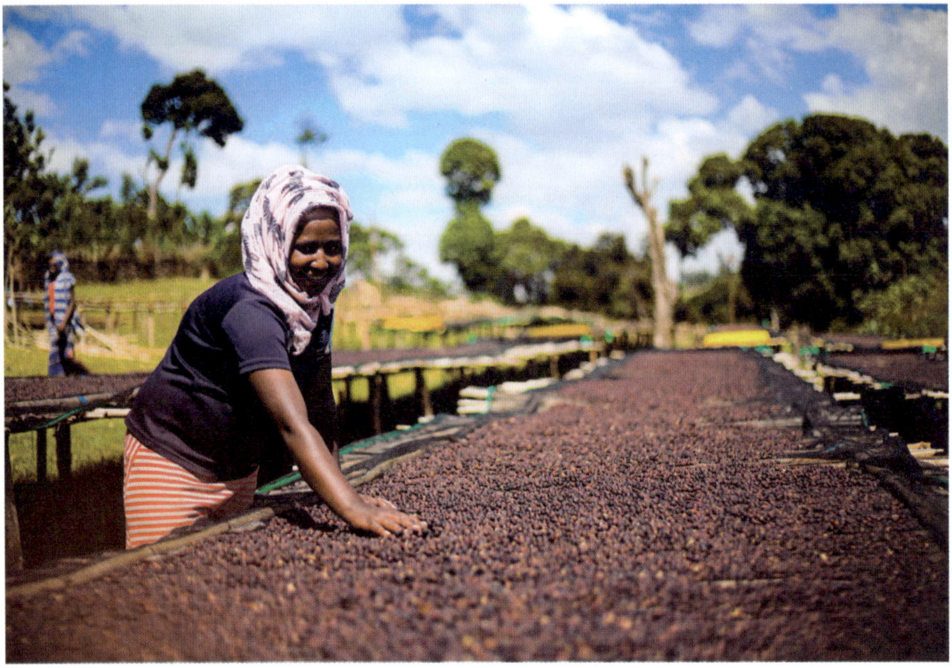

you are in the water, you shouldn't say that it is cold'.

This year, key roasters have already purchased from the current harvest based on pre-shipment samples. The trend in Europe is for more natural-processed coffees. Washed coffees remain popular and there are also some lots processed using experimental fermentation techniques. Coffees from Daye Bensa are available worldwide and you have quite possibly have drunk one of their coffees if you have purchased a Sidama coffee from a reputable roaster. They have also recently won the contract to supply another key international coffee brand. Contracts of that size are measured in containers and tonnes, not bags.

Atrie spends a significant portion of the year in Ethiopia and is an engaged member of the British Ethiopian community. He generously invites me to the next feast day celebration at the community centre, just a short walk from our meeting spot. Most brokers import coffees from all key origins so that they can offer a full range to roasters. Coffee Legends is remarkable because of their African focus and Atrie spends months of the year in Ethiopia sourcing coffee, checking samples and facilitating export as well as spending time with his extended family. He is able to offer a unique perspective that extends from the latest growing conditions to current consumer trends.

As well as selling greater volumes of Ethiopian coffee into Europe, Atrie wishes for coffee drinkers to better understand the challenges faced by coffee growers. Farmers in Sidama only receive cherry prices that barely cover the cost of growing. Additionally, they must often feed and pay itinerant labour during the harvest season as the region does not have a sufficiently local workforce to pick all the cherries by hand. Even in rural Ethiopia, cherry prices are tied to the international commodity coffee price (the c-market), which is established by futures traders on the New York Stock Exchange. This index is a world apart from the working reality of the farmers, managers and graders that Atrie liaises with, but all their livelihoods are impacted by its fluctuations.

Growing high-quality coffee continues to be a key route for farmers to receive greater income. Later in the season farmers will return to the station with their receipt. Proceeds from lots that have received an above-average export prices because of their quality are shared among the farmers that contributed to the lot. This second payment is just one of a number of the initiatives to encourage farmers to invest in their shrubs and to continue growing coffee instead of farming other cash crops.

Artie's objective is to untether the specialty-grade coffees he imports from the c-market price. His strategy is to better tell the stories of coffee growers. He named his company Coffee Legends to draw attention to the people that grow the coffee as well as demystify their work and chronicle their endeavour. He hopes that if roasters and coffee drinkers can better appreciate the work that goes into growing and processing coffee, they'll be more willing to pay a price that reflects its worth.

If roasters and coffee drinkers can better appreciate the work that goes into growing and processing coffee, they'll be more willing to pay a price that reflects its worth

COUNTRY	ARCHETYPICAL FLAVOUR PROFILE
Bolivia	Predominantly sweet with gentle acidity. Flavours are often delicate, lightly floral and subtly fruity, with occasional tea-like or cocoa mouthfeel and astringency.
Brazil	Low acidity often with some sweetness and a heavier body. Nutty–chocolate flavours are common. Some coffees have pronounced bitterness like burnt caramel. There can be stone-fruit flavours in coffees grown at higher elevations.
Burundi	Crisp acidity with berry flavours. Can be floral and may show light bitterness and a soft astringency, especially in washed lots.
Yunnan, China	Low acidity with mild sweetness. Can be lightly fruity or floral, but often slightly astringent when woody or earthy flavours are present.
Colombia	Classically fruit-forward with red berries, plums and pronounce sweetness supported by balanced acidity. A wide range of experimental ferments means flavour profiles vary considerabl
Costa Rica	Citrus and tropical fruit flavours with pronounced acidity underpinned by sweetness. Often lighter-bodied. Honey-processed coffees can be particularly fruity and sweet.
Dominican Republic	Low-to-medium acidity with some fruit and occasional herbaceous traits. Can present a cocoa-like mouthfeel and light bitterness.
Ecuador	Aromatic coffees with floral and tropical notes balanced by sufficient acidity to complement their sweetness.
El Salvador	Sweet with low acidity and often complemented by a pleasant, viscous mouthfeel.
Ethiopia	Floral, citrus, and berry-driven aromas and flavours. Washed lots tend to have pronounced acidity with sweetness and light bitterness; natural lots are typically fruitier and sweeter.

COUNTRY	ARCHETYPICAL FLAVOUR PROFILE
Guatemala	Chocolatey and sweet profiles are common, alongside citrus-led lots with brighter acidity. Both styles often have a smooth, rounded mouthfeel.
Honduras	Sweet with gentle acidity that supports caramel and tree-fruit flavours.
India	Arabica lots often have low acidity with spice and herbal traits, plus cocoa-like astringency. Monsooned coffees are earthy with enhanced bitterness.
Kenya	Aromatically complex and intense. Washed coffees are characterized by their high acidity and often show blackcurrant and citrus flavours as well as lighter body.
Mexico	Often sweet with caramel and chocolate flavours and a heavier mouthfeel. Higher-elevation lots are typically lighter-bodied and more citrus-led.
Nicaragua	Sweet with some fruit expression and sufficient acidity to create balance. Mouthfeel is often smooth and rounded.
Panama	Gesha lots are renowned for jasmine florals and vivid tropical fruit flavours.
Peru	Predominantly sweet with a heavier body. The best lots can be chocolatey with enough acidity to provide balance.
Rwanda	Acidic and sweet with red fruit and citrus flavours, and can be floral. Often have a silky mouthfeel.
Tanzania	Sweetness underpinned by both sourness and bitterness. Berry flavours are typical, and a black-tea-like astringency is common.
Yemen	Intensely aromatic with dried fruit and spice flavours and wine-like acidity. Often sweet yet tangy.

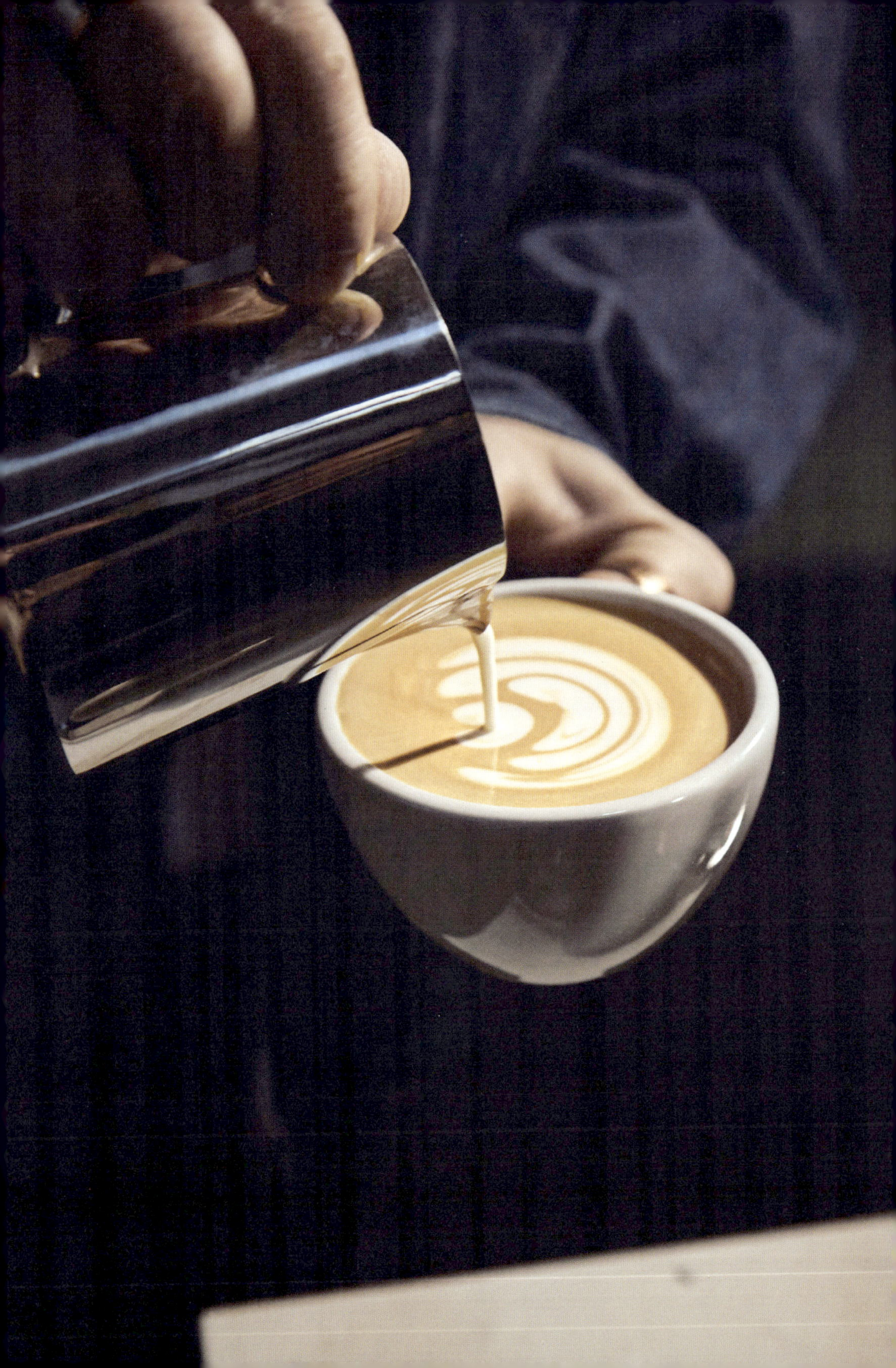

Augmenting Coffee

CUSTOMIZING COFFEE

We have assessed black filter coffee because it offers the greatest clarity on each coffee's defining characteristics. However, most coffee drinkers opt for a milk coffee. Iced drinks are also popular, especially in the summer, and many people also add a spoonful of sugar. Do these habits defile coffee? The answer is a resounding no. People are simply following a universal rule as they seek to create a balance of tastes.

MILK

The most popular coffee serve in London, where I live, is the flat white. It is typically five or six parts of milk to a shot of espresso. This is, in fact, a traditional serve disguised under a contemporary name. The original Italian cappuccino was roughly the same size and proportions.

Milk has been a popular addition to coffee since the heyday of the Vienna coffeehouses because the milk balances coffee's bitterness. The city's urban dairies enabled farm-fresh milk to be supplied to the city's coffee establishments within hours of the cows being milked. This just-in-time supply chain was critical for the milk not to sour.

Two technologies have contributed to milk being the most popular coffee companion. Refrigerated supply chains and pasteurization introduced the necessary infrastructure for milk to have a shelf-life that can be measured in days. But demand for milky coffees was created as a by-product of a 20th-century technology, the espresso machine. Steam can be drawn off the hot-water boiler and used to heat the milk. This technique has the added benefit of incorporating air to create a mass of tiny bubbles, which baristas often call 'microfoam'.

Above 50°C (122°F) the proteins in the milk unfold, which traps the tiny air bubbles within the milk. Plus the fats start to melt, enhancing creaminess. Good training teaches baristas to stop heating the milk at about 70°C (158°F) so that the proteins don't fully relax, and well before the milk scalds. If you ask for an 'extra-hot' coffee, a good barista will preheat your cup with boiling water rather than burn your milk.

At these temperatures the lactose sugars in milk don't actually caramelize, but the combination of the texture and temperature changes the drinker's perception of its taste. It's perceived as sweeter.

Espresso blends often fall in the Classic and Comfort profiles, making sweet steamed milk an ideal companion. As well as being sweeter on the palate, the fats also further reduce the perception of bitterness. While hot milk was traditionally added to coffee to dilute it and act as a counterweight to unbalanced bitter coffee, many of today's espresso blends have greater balance. It is no coincidence that the more concentrated flat white has overtaken the once-popular more milky caffè latte. There are some espresso blends that fit Clarity and Curious profiles. If balanced, these are often acid led with sufficient sweetness and bitterness. In a coffee shop these are often presented as 'guest espressos', and you are encouraged to try them as an espresso or maybe a macchiato. This is largely because the tangy sourness of the espresso and milk typically don't pair nicely.

Since milk serves are very popular, a good espresso blend needs to be flavoursome enough and sufficiently well balanced to be drunk alone. A typical blend is slightly bitter and slightly sweet and often has a hint of acidity. When milk is added, the sweetness complements the bitterness and enhances the inherent sweetness.

To further enhance the mouthfeel there has been a global movement towards 'barista milks', which have a higher fat content. These milks are easier for baristas to stretch, and benefit from a heavier, silkier mouthfeel. The standard dairy milk in supermarkets in London, Rome, Bangkok and Atlanta are very different in weight and even flavour. But increasingly baristas milks in each of these countries are converging.

The most popular of the alternative milks is oat milk. It is the closest in mouthfeel, texture and weight to dairy milk. While there are various oat milks, each market-leading brand is relatively similar to the milk in their country of origin. For example, brands from northern Europe are heavier and creamier than oat milks from, say, France. If you have a favourite oat milk, your preference is likely to be based on your conception of the weight and texture of a good dairy milk.

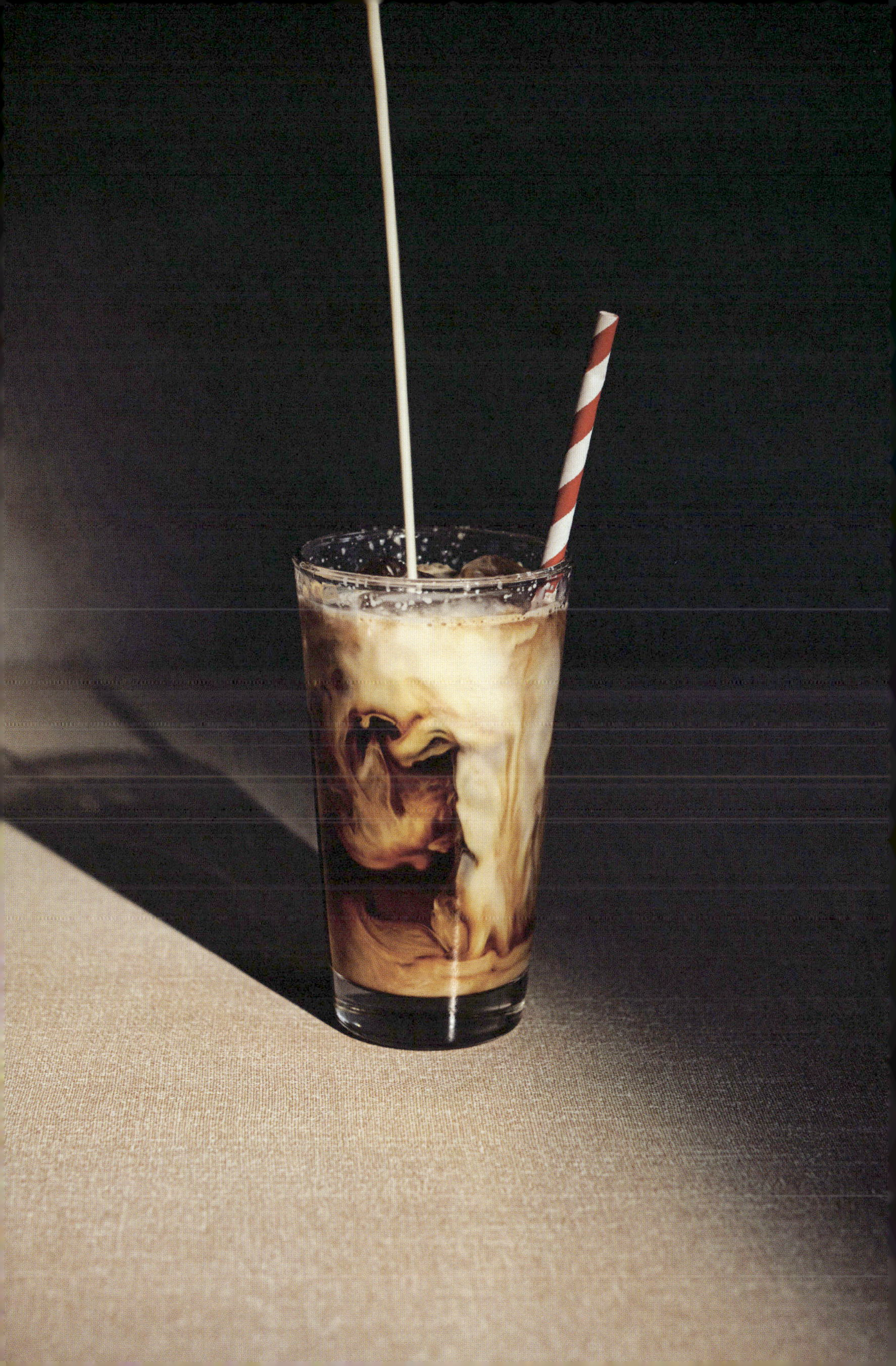

SUGAR

Sugar has been used to offset coffee's bitterness since it became comparatively affordable in the late 17th century. As coffee production techniques have developed and roasting technologies advanced, a typical coffee is now significantly less bitter than it was several decades ago. Correspondingly, granulated sugar has become a less popular additive to classic coffee serves such as espresso, macchiato, the flat white and caffè latte.

It remains commonplace, and necessary, to find sachets of sugar on tables in establishments that serve predominantly bitter espresso. In coffee shops where the espresso has greater balance, it's more typical for the sugar to be concealed in a corner or even to be unavailable. And the sugar that is available is typically the less sweet and more flavoursome demerara sugar – a crystallized golden-brown sugar that is created by blending cane molasses with white sugar.

While adding granulated sugar to hot coffee is in decline, the sugar content in a range of coffee serves can be very high. Cold serves are often particularly sugary.

ICE

Coldness significantly reduces the perception of sweetness. Interestingly, reducing the temperature masks sweetness more than bitterness or sourness. If you add a cube of ice to a shot of espresso that was previously broadly balanced, the coffee tastes more bitter.

There is a wide range of cold coffee drinks available, and many of these are served with ice. They can be grouped into three buckets.

Iced black coffees may be as simple as a shot of espresso poured over cold water and ice. Other options include cold-brewed coffee (which is actually steeped at ambient temperature), which is subsequently refrigerated and then served over ice. One of the selling points of cold-brewed coffee is that it is generally less bitter than black coffee subsequently iced, although both typically benefit from a little sugar syrup.

More popular are *iced milk drinks*. These are typically cold milk poured over ice with a shot of espresso poured over the top. With the milk unheated, it also has reduced ability to reduce the perception of bitterness in the espresso. And, of course, the perception of the bitterness is increased because of the ice. It's so common for a little sugar syrup to be added into an

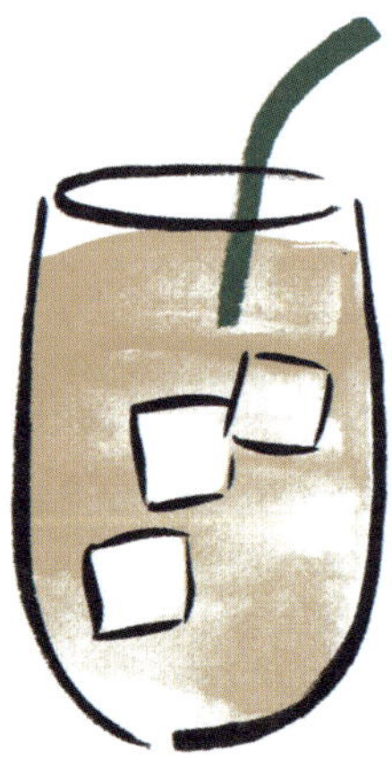

iced flat white or iced caffè latte that it is now more typical for a shop to add it as standard.

Some coffee establishments have a frappé option, which is a Greek technique of aerating cold milk in a spindle mixer. This adds some of the texture of stretched milk and has a similar effect of enhancing the perception of sweetness. However, many frappés have sugar syrup added and the name is used by coffee shop chains as the family of their sweetened iced coffee drinks.

The third category of iced drinks are predominantly sweet and the coffee's flavours are secondary to the range of *flavoured sugar syrups, sweetened creams and confectionery toppings*. These drinks are wildly unbalanced towards sweetness, but the perception of that sweetness is reduced because of the coldness. In this case, the purpose of the coffee is to add a trickle of bitterness. And, in fact, unbalanced, heavily roasted bitter coffee is more desirable in this case. These serves are more prevalent in high-street coffee chains, which typically use a robusta-based espresso blend that is predominantly bitter.

Because these coffees are both cold and milky they can be deceptively, and extraordinarily, sugary. For example, I have just checked a high-street coffee chain's drinks menu, and they have a signature drink that has more than 40g (1½oz) of sugar – that's about ten heaped teaspoons! While this drink is probably not best categorized as 'coffee', it's useful to note that coffee has long been used as a bitter foil to enhance the balance of sweet items.

Because these coffees are both cold and milky they can be deceptively, and extraordinarily, sugary

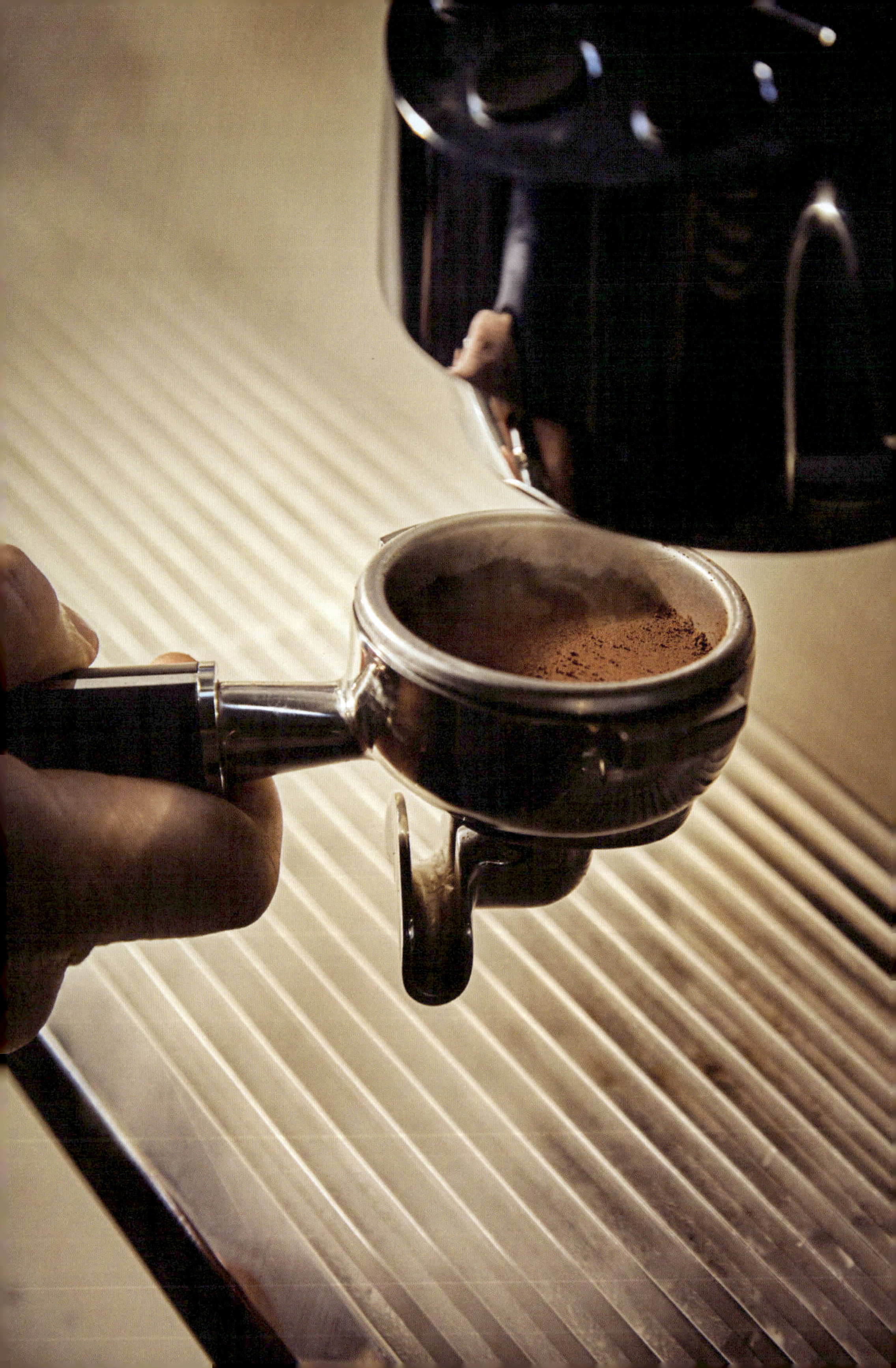

SIGNATURE DRINKS

Signature drinks can contain other ingredients to enhance or complement the coffee's flavours. They are often conceptualized as non-alcoholic coffee cocktails and can be either hot or cold. The name comes from a round in the annual barista championships where competitors serve a non-alcoholic, espresso-based beverage of their own creation.

Many competition serves are fussy to prepare and seek to showcase a barista's skills rather than provide a balance of tastes. However, the most common signature drink – as well as the most enduring – is the mocha, which is a drinking chocolate mixed with a caffè latte. The sweetened bitter chocolate further leverages the sweetness of the hot milk and the bitterness of the coffee.

Signature drinks have become increasingly popular as seasonal serves. Maybe the most commercially successful is the Pumpkin Spice Latte (PSL), which combines the North American harvest festival with Italian espresso nostalgia.

Such has been the commercial success of the PSL that coffee companies, large and small, have sought to emulate the serve with their own ever-changing menu of seasonal drinks. The most recent focus has been on cold summer-seasonal drinks. There have been some weird and wacky flavour and texture combinations, presumably because the focus has been on presenting bright colours in a transparent takeout cup. Many of these serves don't deserve to endure, but the best ones always offer a balance of sweetness with bitterness, and sometimes a dash of acidity, regardless of the flavour combination.

CO-FERMENTATION

If signature drinks are the ultimate example of baristas punching up flavours, you can think of co-fermentation techniques as coffee farmers pursuing the same agenda. As part of the process to remove the flesh surrounding the coffee cherry's seed, fruit pulp, fruit juice, spices or yeast strains are added to the coffee cherries. The addition of external sugars and yeasts enables the development of new flavours thanks to fermentation processes that would otherwise not occur during coffee processing. The upshot is that co-fermentation methods can create sweeter, louder and more expressive flavour profiles. In many cases, farmers simply add what fruit they have readily available. Examples include orange peel, pineapple, passion fruit and grapes.

Co-fermentation has attracted controversy within the coffee community. Some fear that this obfuscation undermines coffee's transparency, which has been a key pillar of specialty coffee's proposition for the past 50 years. Equally, co-fermented coffees have been used at the highest levels of barista competitions. There is also a live debate on whether it should be mandatory to label co-fermentation coffees. You have quite possibly tried a co-fermented coffee without knowing it.

Solely assessing co-fermentation through the prism of taste, the technique creates new possibilities for balance and alignment. The method increases the sweetness of coffee from imperceptible levels (remember you actually taste the perception of sweetness) to demonstrably sweet. This change has the capacity to move bitter Classic coffees to sweeter Comfort coffee profiles, as well as enhancing the sweetness of Clarity coffee to offer balance with sourness and bitterness.

Second, the flavour of the fruit can carry through into the cup, boosting the alignment between taste and flavour. Despite all the controversy and discussion, it's clear that when coffee drinkers blind-taste a well-balanced, highly aligned co-fermentation coffee they generally like it.

There are also lots of funky, even crazy, co-fermented coffees available. Some are brilliant and enjoyable, especially if you are excited by Curious coffees. Many are very sweet, some are poorly aligned, and quite a few are challenging to drink.

There are likely to be two contradictory trends cascading forwards. There will be a set of coffee drinkers who happily buy and enjoy co-fermented coffee where the co-fermentation intervention is secondary to the coffee's terroir, processing and

For the first time in history it's possible to deploy coffee as a sweet foil to balance the acidity and bitterness of other ingredients

natural flavours. Within this group, co-fermentations that enhance a balance of tastes and alignment will be preferred. These are coffees that will be drunk, and they will largely fit into our Comfort and Clarity coffee profiles.

There will be another bucket where the co-fermentation process dominates the coffee's natural flavours. These coffees might be unnaturally sweet or have a single clear defining artificial flavour, say banana or pineapple, for example. Some coffee drinkers will deem these coffees adulterated. However, taking a sweet, flavoursome co-fermented coffee and serving it over ice or as an ingredient in a signature drink creates a whole new realm of possibility for baristas. For the first time in history it's possible to deploy coffee as a sweet foil to balance the acidity and bitterness of other ingredients.

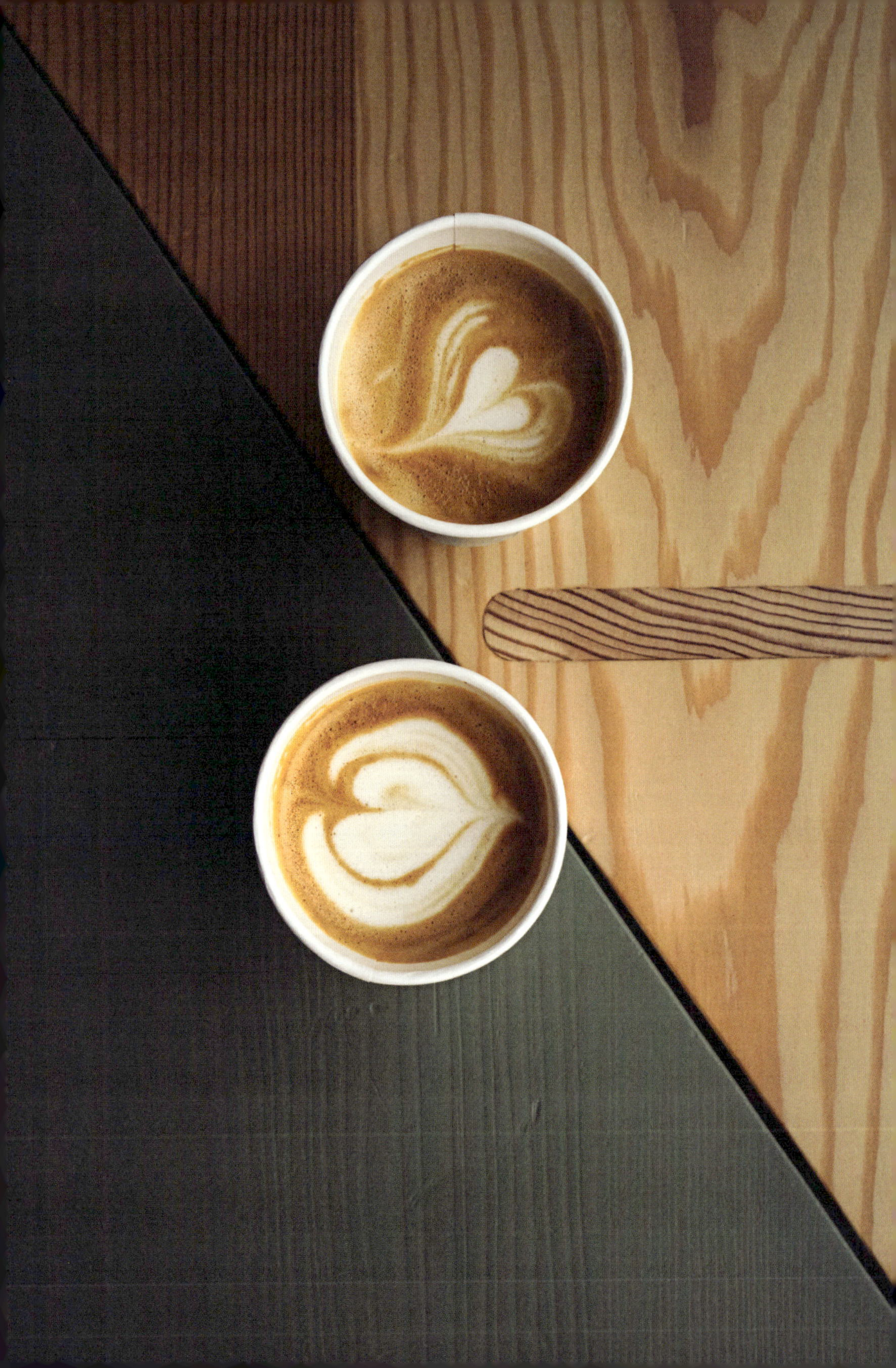

Choosing Coffees That You Like

HOW TO READ COFFEE BAG TASTING NOTES

Coffee drinkers are inundated with choice. Not only are there thousands upon thousands of coffees to choose from, but we are also bombarded with brands, celebrities, slick packaging designs and promotions, all seeking to guide our choices. Selecting coffees that you will enjoy requires your coffee-tasting skill as well as a foundational knowledge of coffee production, the supply chain and an awareness of your own preferences and expectations.

THE COFFEE BAG

Coffee beans are sold based either on their brand or their origin. Brands blend multiple lots to create a stable, signature house style. The components of the blend may change from year to year, or even within a year, but the objective is for the favour profile to remain constant.

Beans sold on the strength of the brand typically display little, or perhaps even no, origin information. The brand owner wishes to retain flexibility over the blend's mix and does not wish to

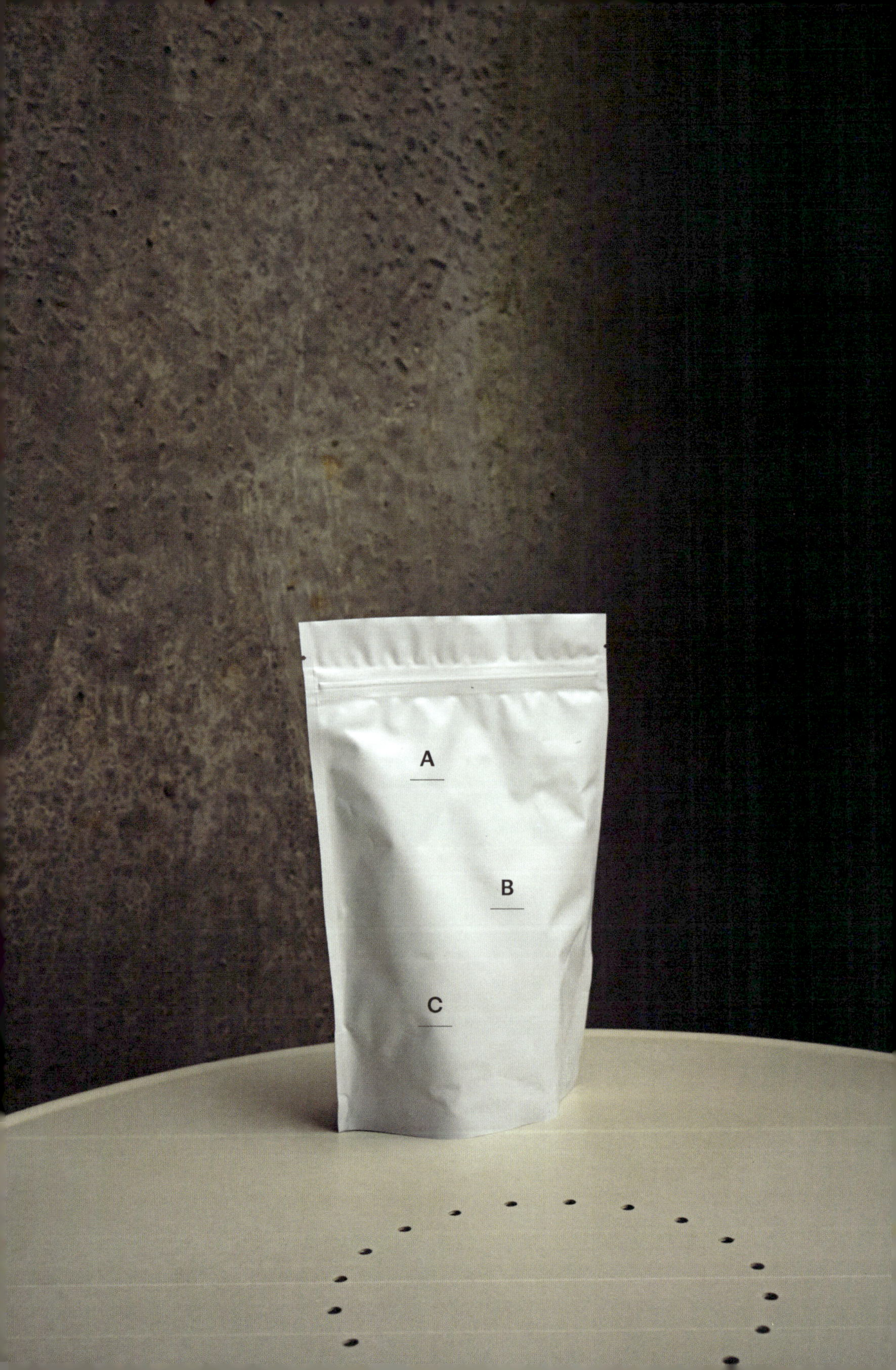
A
B
C

A Name of farm, producer or washing station, plus region and country

B Tasting notes

C Variety, elevation and processing information, plus roast date

dispose of printed bags every time the composition of their blend changes. These companies typically forward-contract green coffee to ensure consistency, but a range of circumstances, including a spike in sales, a challenging harvest or disruption to logistics networks, may necessitate changes to the coffee.

Such blends might be available as whole bean, ground or even instant, and typically fit a Classic coffee profile. Instead of specifying origin or flavour, the blend might be sold on the basis of its 'strength' or 'boldness'. These terms don't really make sense from a tasting perspective, but they usually refer to a combination of a heavy mouthfeel, a predominantly bitter taste and a high intensity of flavours in the lower half of the Flavour Wheel. These coffees are typically available through mainstream retailers such as supermarkets.

I have just navigated to the coffee section on a leading supermarket's website, and the first option is described as 'uncomplicated' with a 'rich intense' roast. The product's descriptor explains: 'Our signature blend combines smooth Colombian beans with a bold Vietnamese kick for a perfectly balanced cup...[I]t's strong, smooth and crafted for every occasion.' If you can identify a brand's blend that you enjoy, then you're in luck. You will be able to buy a coffee to your liking, year-round, with little risk or effort.

Many coffee drinkers, however, prefer coffees with more readily identifiable flavours and a harmonious balance of taste. To pick these coffees it is necessary to consider both the coffee's origin information and tasting notes. Coffees that are promoted on the basis of their origin typically have a label affixed to the bag that displays specific information about the coffee. This enables the roaster to cost-effectively use the same bag for multiple coffees and the label is readily updated with each coffee's information. These coffees are often collectively called 'single-origin' coffees.

UNDERSTANDING ORIGINS

Single-origin coffees may be named after the lot, farm, farmer, washing station, region or even country. The only constraint is that the beans are entirely from the stated geographic area. The rule of thumb is that that the more specific the geographic identifier the smaller the lot. And the smaller the lot, the more likely it is that there are clearly identifiable distinct flavours.

You need to be a master of languages to correctly pronounce all the locations. Plus, the political situation in several coffee-producing countries is dynamic. Consequently, roasters will often simplify the origin information for clarity and consistency but also compress information to fit the available wordcount on their label.

For example, on a broker's green coffee price list, the description 'Diima Bensa Shantawene #4 Organic Natural' includes the origin and production information as well as a producer's categorization. This is the fourth organic lot from Shantawene village in the Bensa district of the Sidama regional state in southern Ethiopia. The producer has also classified this coffee as part of their 'Diima', meaning 'red', range.

The Sidama regional state was created in 2020 following a local referendum. Sidama largely, but not exclusively, sits within what was the Sidamo province, which has been broken up into smaller administrative regions. Sidamo coffees have benefited from strong consumer awareness following years of promotion and remain recognized alongside other key Ethiopian regions, such as Yirgacheffe and Jima.

The roaster buying this lot might sell it as 'Shantawene Natural Organic', as it's quite probably the only lot from Shantawene that they purchased this year. Conversely, another roaster might embrace the producer's classification and title this coffee 'Diima Bensa Natural'. There is no standard, and things can get very murky very quickly. I search terms and places all the time to check that I have correctly identified people's names as well as understood the places, districts and classifications.

There is no obligation for a roaster to buy the entire lot. So it is not uncommon for several roasters to purchase the same coffee – although you might never know, especially if they opt to label it differently. It also possible that a roaster buying this lot might opt to label it generically as 'Sidama Organic', or even less accurately – to provide continuity with a segment of their customers – as 'Sidamo Organic'. However, since this entire lot consists of fewer than one hundred 60kg (132lb) bags, roasters are likely to use a more comprehensive name to communicate its scarcity and provenance. Such a coffee is likely to be both sweet and sour and is likely to be best classified as a Clarity coffee.

VARIETY, PROCESS AND ELEVATION

Coffees with distinct flavours often have the variety, process and elevation listed on the bag. The information is useful for two reasons. First, it's an indicator of lot size, and second it offers additional clues as to whether the flavour profile is likely to be archetypical of the origin, or something completely different.

When lots comprise multiple varieties or many farms, either the labelling becomes too complicated to be communicated succinctly or the traceability is lost. These larger, generically flavoured lots are not likely to have specific variety, process and elevation information.

Lots can still be quite large and fully traceable. For example, I am considering a washed coffee from the Nariño region of Colombia that is a Caturra variety and comprises 24 farms. Despite the lot's size, this variety is common to the region and the farms that comprise the lots are at high elevation. The coffee is likely to be sweet, exhibit red-fruit flavours such as plums or cherries, and have medium body. I would guess that the combination of the sweetness and the more generic fruit flavours would position this coffee within the Comfort profile. A smaller lot with more specific flavours and greater acidity would be more likely to be within the Clarity profile.

Coffees with distinct flavours often have the variety, process and elevation listed on the bag

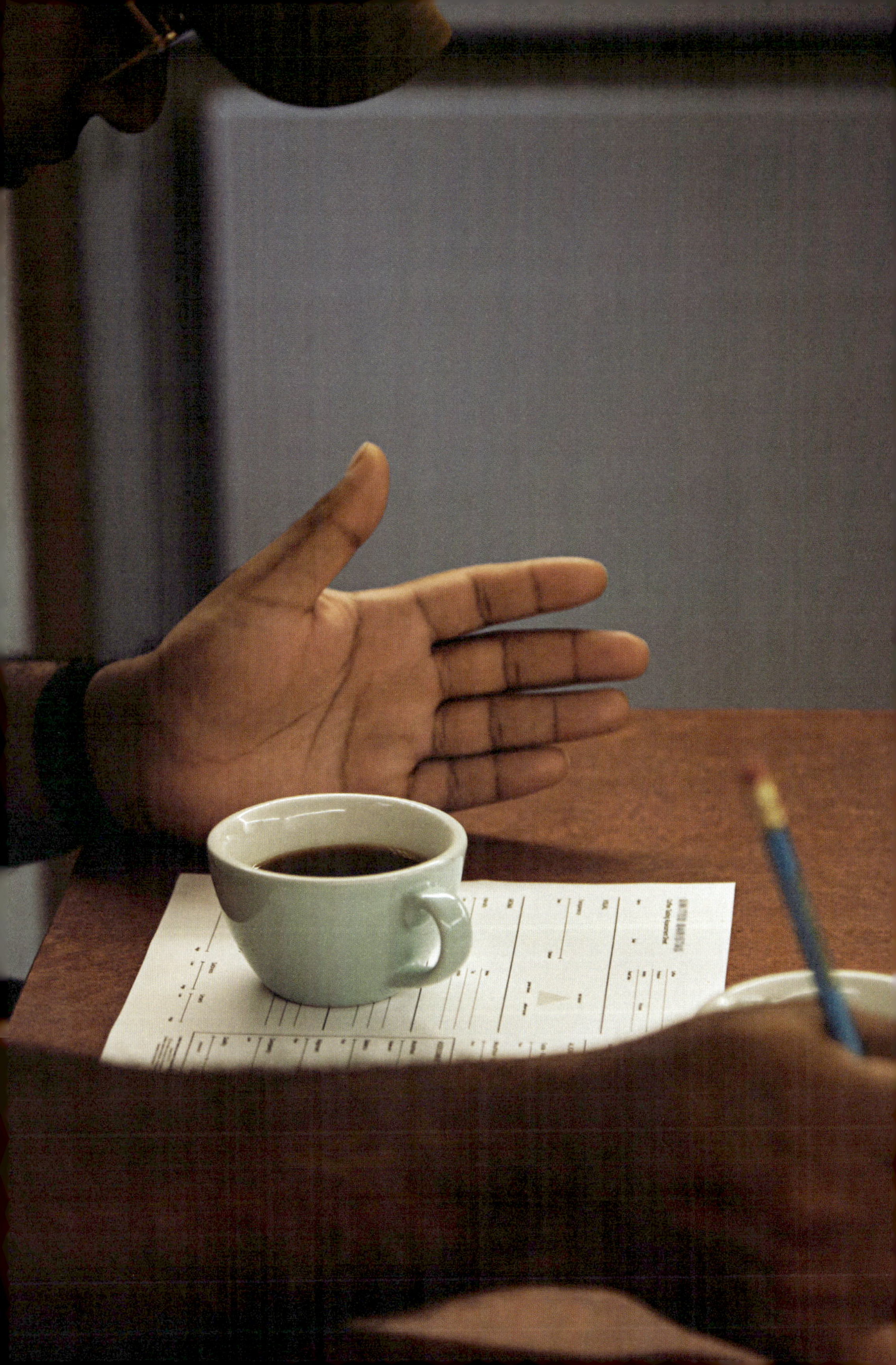

PARSING TASTING NOTES

Having scanned the origin information, I then consider the tasting notes. Many coffee drinkers have frustrations with tasting notes as there is frequently a disconnect between the expectations created by the flavour description and the actual flavour of the coffee. I find it easier to accept that for many roasters tasting notes are part flavour communication and 100 per cent marketing copy. So, it's necessary to parse their tasting notes for meaning.

Compounding the situation is that it has become commonplace for roasters to reduce tasting notes to a few words, often just three terms. For example, I've just grabbed four coffees from my sample cupboard and the various descriptors are 'Pink Champagne, Lychee, Watermelon'; 'Chocolate, Hazelnut, Raspberry'; 'Complex, Fruity, Tropical, Full Body, High Sweetness'; and 'Apricot, Champagne, Hibiscus'. You're not crazy to think that these flavours can't all be true.

Admittedly, I get sent some rather zany coffees. So here's a selection of descriptors from some of the world's most esteemed coffee roasters: 'Orange, Fudge, Caramel, Cherry', 'Mango, White Wine, Pear', 'Candied Chestnuts, Mangosteen, Butterscotch' and 'Plum, Vanilla, Lemon'. The point is that, at first glance, these descriptors aren't much better. One of the challenges to understanding such terse tasting notes is that it's often impossible to appreciate whether a descriptor refers to an aroma or flavour.

Complicating matters even further is that the descriptors are sometimes used to hint at a flavour–taste combination or even describe a mouthfeel texture. I think this current state of affairs is unacceptable. The coffee community can, and should, do better to communicate each coffee's distinctive flavours. As we have been exploring, when one systemically assesses a coffee's aromas, mouthfeel, taste and flavours, it isn't that hard to paint an accurate picture of its flavour profile.

To gain a insight into each coffee, I start by deconstructing the descriptors. If they are not specified, I assume that they are flavours with corresponding tastes. For example, in the example above, 'fudge' and 'caramel' are both references to sweetness, and 'orange' and 'cherry' are both sour and sweet fruits. Deconstructing tasting notes helps you place the coffee within the firmament of possibility.

I know this coffee well as it is regularly served at a local coffee shop and I have drunk it many times. This coffee is, in fact, tangy with some bitterness. It is pleasant to drink, primarily because of its balance between sourness and bitterness. It often has citrus flavours of lemon or lime. For me, this coffee is at its best when the citrus flavours are closer to grapefruit, which better aligns with the bitterness. There are a few other identifiable flavours, especially in the middle, but there is some earthiness at the base. If we consider the flavours as a vertical stack, it might be described as hollow. When prepared in a way that makes the brew balanced and aligned, this is a Clarity coffee, but it can easily be over- or under-extracted and then becomes too sour or too bitter. It is misleading to imply that this coffee is sweet. There are much sweeter coffees available, and this coffee's predominant taste is sourness.

Next, parse the deconstructed tasting notes against the origin. Taking the sample coffee described as 'Pink Champagne, Lychee, Watermelon', I can see that it is a natural-processed coffee from a larger farm in Kenya. There is no variety information. Honestly, I'm uncertain how to accurately deconstruct these tasting notes, as it reads more like a perfume than a coffee. However, I can immediately identify that it is not an archetypical Kenyan coffee – these are prized for their blackcurrant and blackberry flavours. The majority of Kenyan coffees with these flavours are of the wash-processed SL-28 variety.

I don't yet know whether this coffee is tasty or not, but I am suspicious because I can't imagine the flavours and because a pink sparkling wine from Champagne would more commonly be called a rosé champagne. My fear is that this roaster has overstretched themselves and that the coffee risks being both unbalanced and poorly aligned.

Next, let's consider a coffee described as 'Complex, Fruity, Tropical, Full Body, High Sweetness'. Reading the label I can see that it is a Typica variety from a known Colombian producer made using a process described as 'anaerobic washed'. Deconstructing the tasting notes point to there being many distinct aromas and flavours, many of which are fruit-led, but there are some funky flavours from the fermentation that are likely to push the overall flavours from cherries and plums into tropical fruit. Plus, the body is heavier and it is described as being predominantly sweet.

I associate most tropical fruits with being both sour and sweet, so I am unsure whether this coffee has enough sourness to balance the sweetness and whether there is sufficient flavour–taste alignment. I suspect it's quite heavily fermented and that the flavours will be intense. If it benefits from a harmonious balance of tastes and good alignment, it would probably be classified as a Clarity coffee; if it lacks sourness and is complex but with poor alignment, it would be better classified as a Curious coffee.

Finally, I write this as I'm drinking the coffee described as 'Chocolate, Hazelnut and Raspberry', which is a bit generous. I think it would have been more accurately described as cocoa (it's not that sweet), with hints of nuts and berries, the flavours being less distinct than the tasting notes imply. It is nonetheless delicious.

It's actually slightly bitter, which aligns nicely with the cocoa and the nuts, but there is just enough sweetness and sourness to create balance and align with the berry notes. The mouthfeel is silky and soft. This coffee is from an esteemed producer and roasted by a reputable roaster. This coffee would be best classified as a Comfort coffee, and I would go so far as to say that almost all coffee drinkers would find it pleasant. If you normally drink Classic coffees, you'd be surprised – but hopefully in an appreciative way – of the sweetness, flavours and mouthfeel. And even if you prefer Clarity or Curious coffees, you'd still recognize its balance, structure, sophistication and alignment.

Whether this coffee is good value is a slightly different question. This coffee is rather expensive, and I find myself considering whether I could wholeheartedly recommend it. This coffee is from Honduras, but it's possible to find coffees with a similar structure and profile from Guatemala, El Salvador, Costa Rica and even Peru.

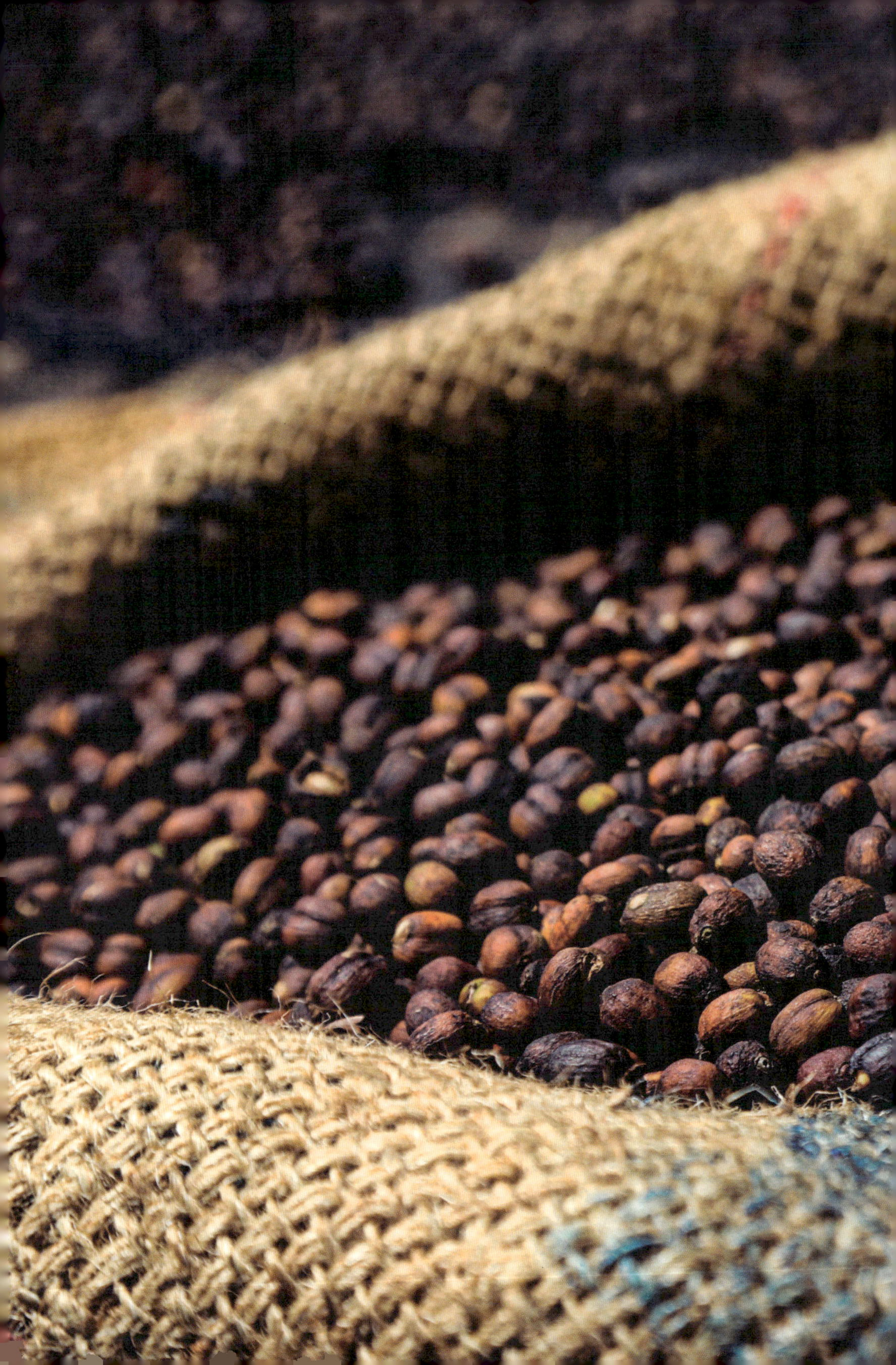

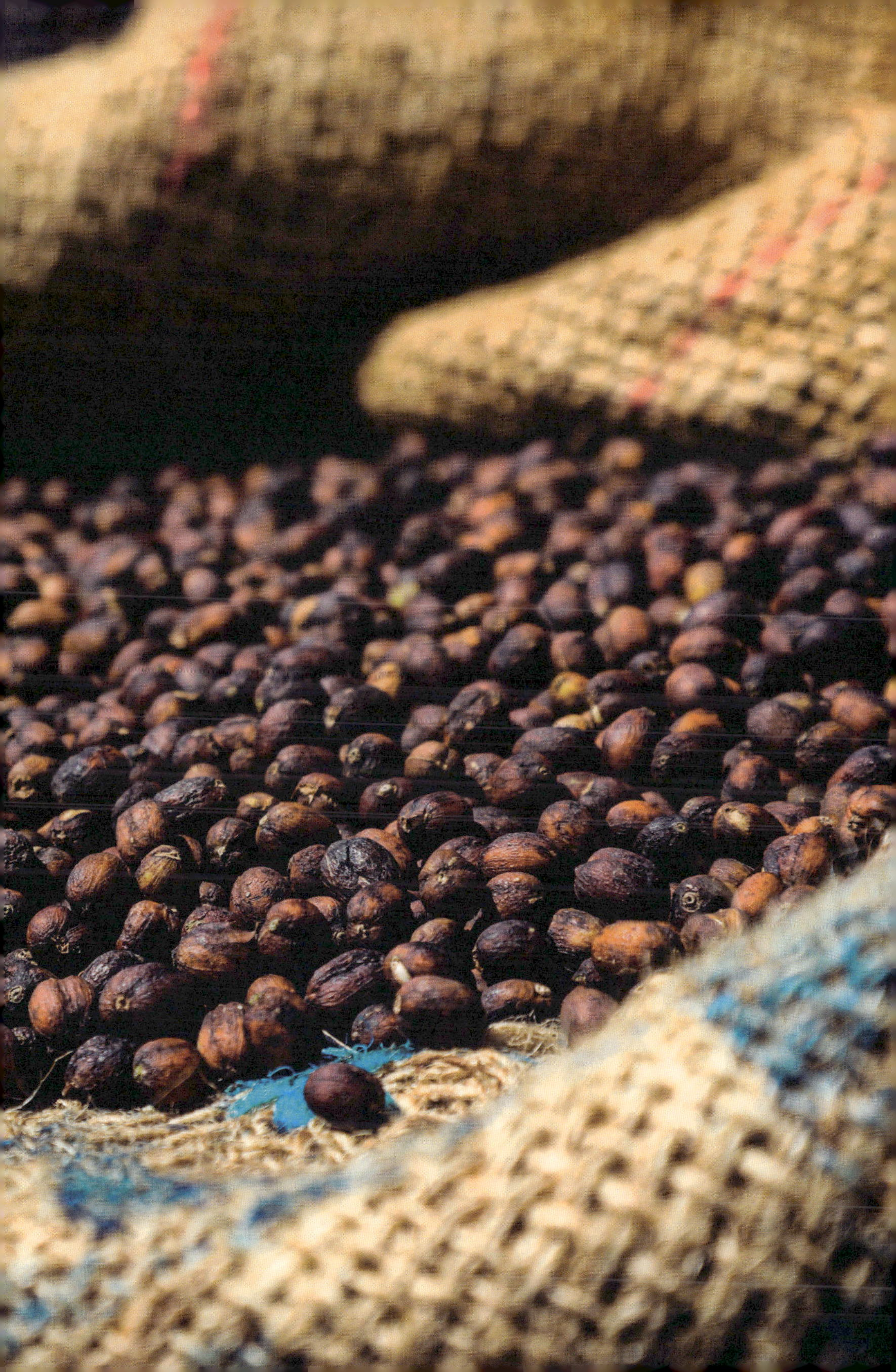

CONSIDERING ORIGINS, VARIETIES, PROCESS AND TASTING NOTES TOGETHER

It's necessary to consider the origin information and tasting notes in concert. The first thing I determine is whether the coffee is an archetypical example of its origin. If it is, you can then look for clues to indicate its quality. Check the tasting notes for information on complexity and alignment, but also consider whether the coffee is in the right price range for a coffee of its provenance.

If is significantly cheaper, then it is likely to be a lower-quality example of the archetype. There is often less value in buying a cheaper version of an exclusive origin. The coffee will still be comparatively expensive, and you are likely to be able to buy a better coffee for the same price from another origin. It's generally worth paying good money for good examples of prized origins.

An interesting example is the recent popularity of Gesha, a variety originating from south-western Ethiopia. By the 1950s it had been distributed through Central America where it was sold to farmers for its disease resistance. This has since shown to have been a sales tactic as Gesha shrubs have both a low yield and have since been proven to be fragile and management-intensive.

For decades Gesha was commonly intermingled with other arabica varieties and blended into lots. The perception of the variety changed in 2004 when Hacienda La Esmeralda in Panama won a coffee competition with a coffee lot that offered aromas of jasmine and bergamot and a balance between sweetness and sourness. The lot was 100 per cent Gesha, and the coffee quickly became one of the most prized and most expensive coffees.

Farmers around the world have been quick to adopt the variety. You can now buy Gesha from Costa Rica, Colombia, Guatemala, Ecuador, Peru, Taiwan, Thailand and China as well as Hawaii, Kenya and even Australia. Plus, Gesha coffees are now being exported again from Ethiopia. Many of these are expensive because of the variety's low yield and high desirability. Some are tasty, balanced and aligned, but many are not, and only some are worth their asking price. Few cheap Gesha beans have the flavour profile available from the best Panamanian producers.

It's been relayed to me that Gesha shrubs take up to a decade to produce cherries with their signature traits. Planting Gesha is a long-term investment, and it's possible the global quality of Gesha will continue to improve as shrubs mature. But even mature trees don't always produce the signature flavour profile. It's no wonder that some of these coffees are extraordinarily expensive.

If the tasting notes point towards the coffee being of a non-archetypical flavour profile, then you especially need to consider the lot size and roaster.

APPRECIATING LOT SIZES

Small coffee lots generally have more specific geographic and production information as well as benefiting from greater complexity. To create a larger lot, coffees from multiple parts of a farm or multiple farms are combined. If one small lot does have distinct flavours, these are likely to be subsumed as other lots are mingled.

Coffees from small lots are not available year-round. The typical cadence is for coffees to arrive in a roaster's warehouse about three to six months after harvest. It takes several weeks for the coffee to be processed. It must then be prepared for export, and it typically takes several weeks or even months for coffee to be transported by sea to your local port.

Green coffee prices are largely determined by two factors: lot size and quality. *The Specialty Coffee Transaction Guide*, an annual industry study, consistently shows that higher-scoring coffees command higher prices. It also shows that, on average, a larger lot size costs less per kilogram for coffees of the same quality than smaller ones. For example, for coffees assessed by quality control to be 85 to 86 points, lots larger than 40,000lbs (roughly 18,000kg) were over 20 per cent cheaper than lots under 1,000lbs (roughly 250kg).

It's tempting for coffee businesses to present this fact as supply and demand working with a premium paid for smaller, distinctive lots. But the reality is that each lot, regardless of its size, attracts a similar administrative and selling cost. In smaller lots, these costs must be apportioned over fewer kilograms, making the coffee more expensive on a per-kilogram basis.

While lots might be as small as 180kg (almost 400lb), the same quality control, forms and paperwork and cupping samples have had to be completed as with a multiple-container-sized lot. The lot size is typically not displayed on the bag. But with a quick internet search you can frequently find the lot information on the coffee broker's website, especially for smaller lots.

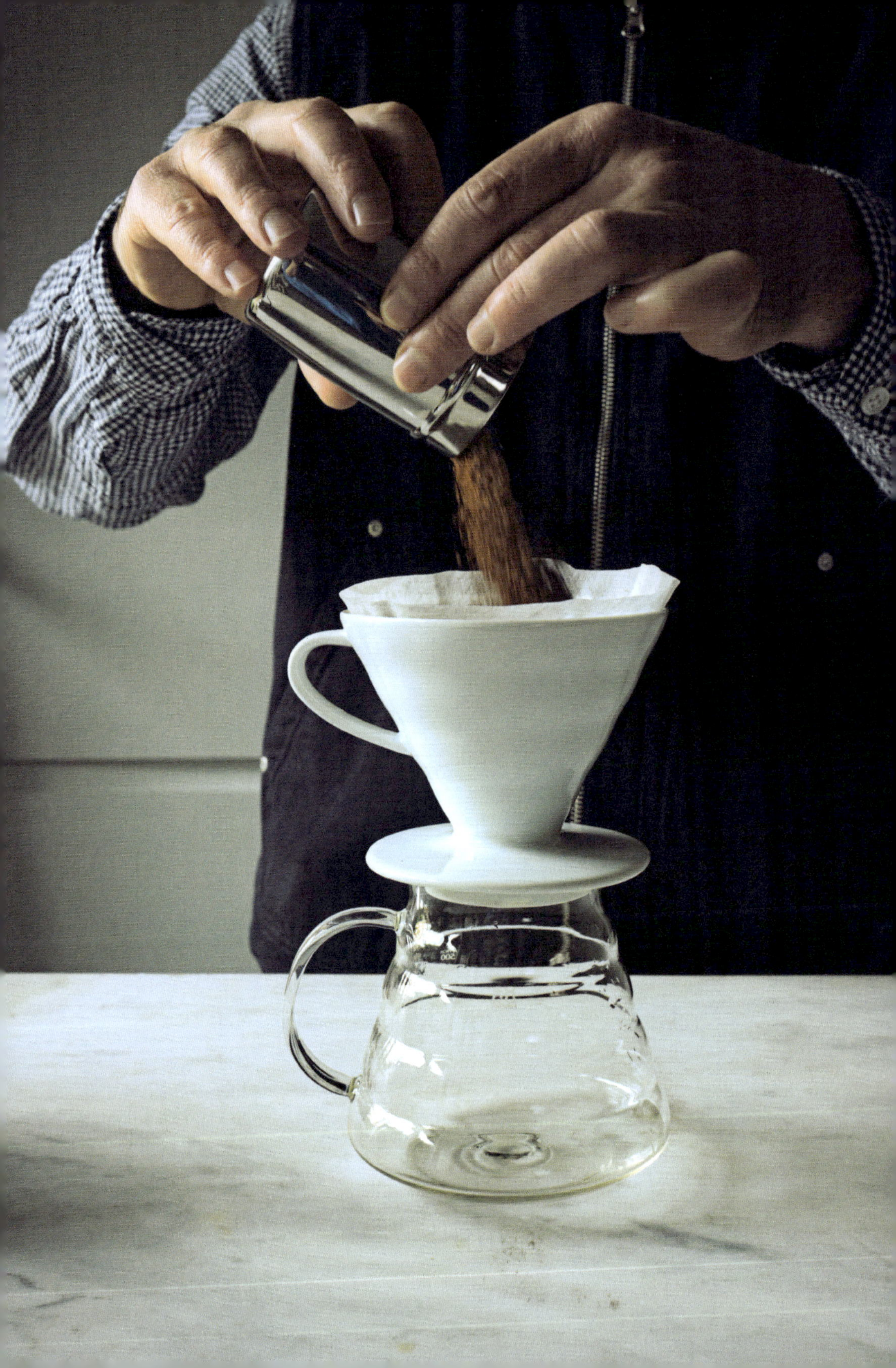

ROASTER PROFILES

Most roasters have a house style. This is seldom codified or publicly communicated but usually exists as an internal working hypothesis on why some coffees have been more commercially successful for them than others.

Buyers and roasters have long grappled with the reality that higher-scoring coffees often aren't more popular. In fact, many roasters privately bemoan the fact that their lower-graded coffees sell better. After a few drinks, roasters start to spill their trade secrets. And they have many different ideas.

For example, some roasters believe their customers prefer coffees with fruity notes, while others take a countervailing view. Often, their strategy is more nuanced. For example, some roasters buy coffees with flavours spread across the top, middle and base. Others purchase coffees that have flavours grouped in the middle or base. And I have already mentioned a buyer who believes their customers like coffees with similar aromas and flavours. It's not really worthwhile considering whether any of these ideas are right; rather, it's useful to recognize that each coffee roaster buys coffees with a target customer in mind. One of the wonderful things about coffee is that the industry is a big tent and there is room for multiple styles, approaches and philosophies. As a coffee drinker, it's useful to identify roasters who share your outlook and preferences.

While roasters have a house style, they also feel the need to cover all key origins. I recently surveyed coffee bean options from ten leading roasters in London. Between them they offered 151 coffees, excluding pods, sample packs and subscriptions. One roaster alone had offered 24 different coffees, including two blends, one decaf and a variety of single origins.

Most of these ten roasters are medium-sized coffee specialists, and there are many such businesses throughout the world. These are businesses that typically have their own roasting facility and are set up to roast tonnes of coffee each week. Many sell coffees to coffee shops, cafés and restaurants as well as directly to consumers through their online shop. Some also have their own coffee shops. But the working reality is that none of these roasters have an all-star coffee line-up. Each is equipped to source and roast some coffees better than others.

Coffee roasters of this size are typically viable because they have one or two coffees that make up the majority of their volume. This is most often an espresso blend that they can wholesale to hospitality businesses. Espresso blends from these companies typically fit a Comfort profile, with some roasters veering towards Clarity and others towards Classic.

These medium-sized roasters also often have good-value Comfort and Clarity coffees. They have economies of scale, efficient roasting processes

Coffee tasters must continually check themselves and ensure that they are appraising the liquid and not assessing the brand

and the deep industry connections required to cost-effectively source, roast and sell small flavoursome coffee lots.

The larger of the medium-sized roasters increasingly give up sourcing small lots because of the associated hassle and limited contribution to their bottom line. For me, the perfect-sized roaster is one that is large enough to be organized, have the financial resources to forward-contract the best coffees and the operational efficiency to cost-effectively roast them, but are not too large or too lazy to lose interest despite all this hard work.

Looping back to the sample coffees, I probably would not buy the coffee from Kenya described as 'Pink Champagne, Lychee and Watermelon'. As well as the origin, process and flavour descriptor raising some concerns, the roaster is one of the larger independent roasters that specializes in espresso blends, which it complements with a range of single-origin coffees for filter. The roaster is less well set up for sourcing and roasting delicate Kenyan coffees.

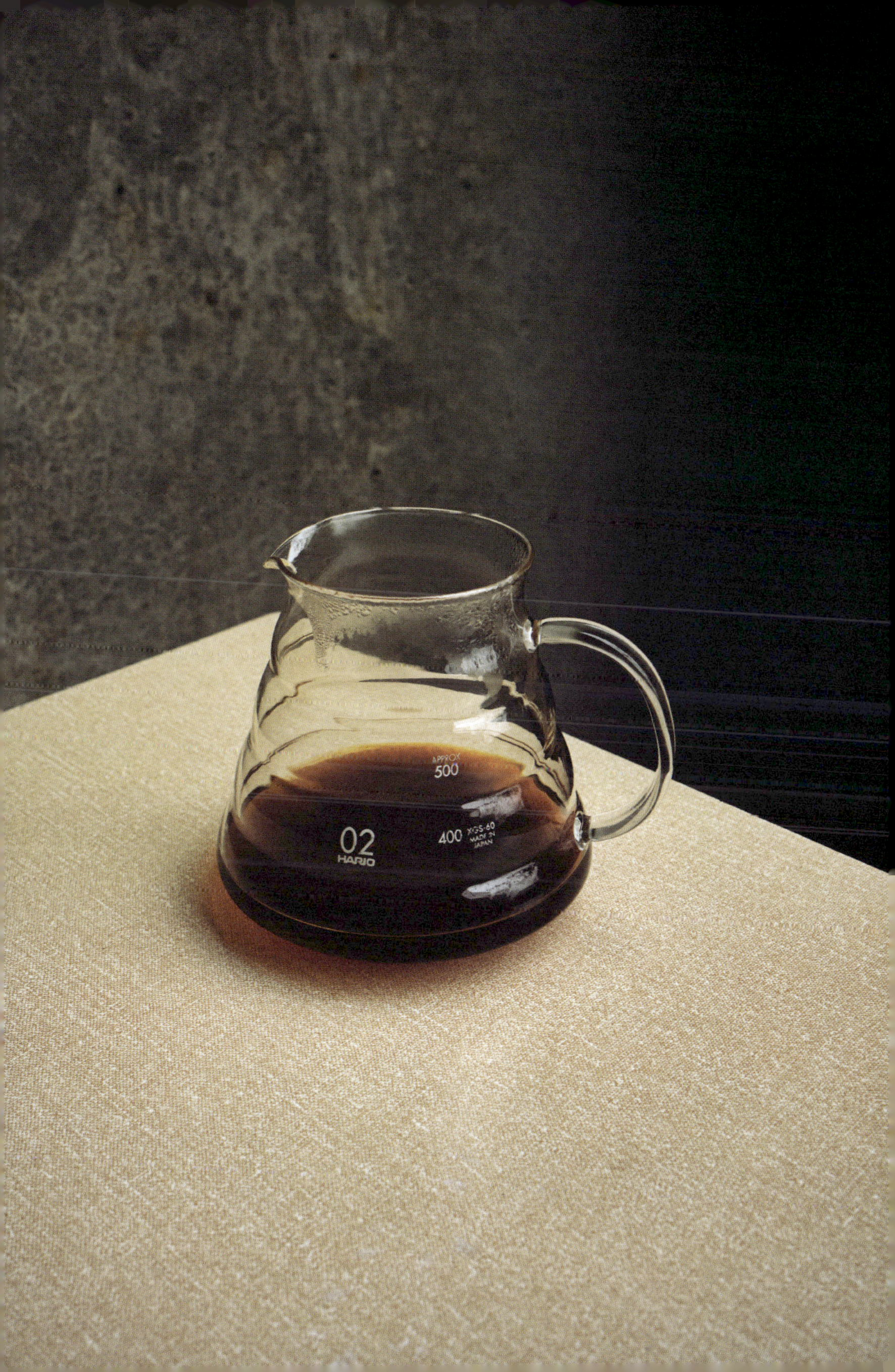
APPROX
500
02
HARIO
400
XGS-60
MADE IN JAPAN

My guess would be that this coffee stood out on a cupping table, was competitively priced and was purchased as a 'hero' filter coffee. For the same price, coffee drinkers can more safely buy better-tasting coffee elsewhere, and lovers of berry-led Kenyan coffees should turn their focus on other lots available from other roasters.

The same logic applies when considering the coffee with the descriptor of 'Apricot, Champagne and Hibiscus'. This is not a coffee that I would typically buy. It was marketed as a feature coffee from a larger independent roaster that also specializes in their espresso blend. It is a Yellow Catuai variety processed with a pulped-natural method from Brazil. When I saw the flavour descriptor I couldn't believe it. But if it was true, I wanted to experience this bizarre combination of flavours.

As it turns out, the tasting notes are, predictably, nonsense. It is sour without any identifiable aligned flavours and has a unpleasantly astringent mouthfeel. My curiosity was sated for the price of a bag of coffee, and my prejudices about this coffee roaster's respective strengths remain intact. That said, I think it's important to approach coffees with an open mind and update your ideas and working assumptions whenever they are challenged by the facts – that is, by what you actually taste.

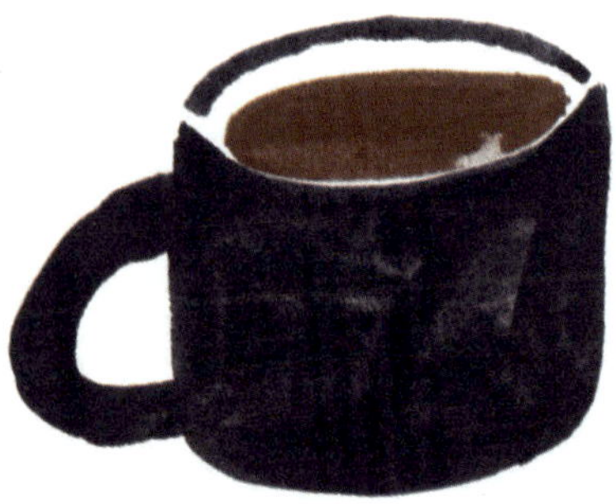

Coffee tasters must continually check themselves and ensure that they are appraising the liquid and not assessing the brand, marketing, variety, origin or reputation of the producer. I frequently try coffees I suspect I won't like. Do I regret the misadventures? Not at all. For a relatively small sum of money I get to explore a world of flavour from the comfort of home or work. And no one is compelling me to buy, or try, these same coffees again.

Most of the successful medium-sized businesses have become profitable by taking market share from the larger coffee companies, which typically source and roast coffees with a Classic profile. If you like the bitterness that comes from roasting, then you want to stick to large roasters. They have large, efficient roasting facilities and specialize in sourcing coffees that suit their commercial focus. Many of these coffees are sold on the basis of their brand, not their origin. But high-quality Classic coffees are often best sourced from the larger of the medium-sized roasters. These coffees have the familiar pronounced bitterness, but it's from the bean and not the roasting.

Almost all medium-sized coffee roasters started out as small, quirky

Coffee roasting is a competitive business, and things can move quickly

businesses roasting in a small industrial unit using a tiny roaster, or even their garage. As the cost of buying small roasters had decreased, and green coffee has become more readily available, numerous start-up coffee roasters are springing up. They have to make a name for themselves in a competitive market so they often choose coffees with punchy flavour profiles. Unless they are unusually well financed or connected, these roasters only get the option of choosing lots that have been passed on by the medium and large roasters. Sometimes these roasters are able to buy Clarity lots that are too small, or arrive too late, for a medium-sized roaster. If the roaster is skillful, they can be very tasty. Also, if the roastery is keen to build a customer base, they can be very well priced. However, more commonly, very small roasters' ranges are filled with Curious coffees because it helps them stand out.

Coffees from esteemed growers and producers are often best purchased from medium-sized roasters. They typically add them to their range at reasonable prices. Many medium-sized roasters need to offer a steady stream of quality coffees to burnish their reputation. In most cases I recommend that you avoid purchasing esteemed coffees from the large international brands, despite the fact they are often very competitively priced. For example, one roaster I am thinking of builds an annual marketing campaign around an expensive lot they have purchased at auction. Even though they have all that sourcing and roasting infrastructure, they often don't taste quite right because the roast profile they apply to the coffee is better suited to their core coffee range.

It's easier to find the right roasters for you if you can identify the coffee profile you want and appreciate the comparative strengths of each roaster. In fact, the economics of coffee roasting is a more reliable way to source tasty coffees at good prices than a roaster's reputation. At coffee tastings we assess each coffee blind – that is, without the participants knowing either the roaster or the origin. Time and again, people are blown away when the coffee they have just tried doesn't fit with their perception of the roaster's reputation. Coffee roasting is a competitive business, and things can move quickly. If a roaster you like is no longer offering as many tasty coffees as they once did, it's a signal that they've shifted strategy and are targeting a new segment of consumers. This means it's time for you to explore other options.

SPECIALTY ROASTER BLENDS

An increasing number of independent roasters create their own blends comprised of traceable, single-origin coffees. These retail products seek to retain the vibrancy of small lots combined with the convenience of year-round availability.

Sometimes roasters give these blends novel names they can trademark and build a consumer following around. Other roasters simply label these options as 'espresso blend' or 'filter blend'. They typically fit into Classic, Comfort or Clarity profiles.

BUYING BEANS

Start by considering your coffee preferences and requirements, and then identify roasters that are financially and operationally set up to deliver these coffees. Every viable roastery business has a specialism, and it is useful to understand their respective strategies and philosophies so you can build a shortlist of roasters you buy from.

I have about 20 roasters I purchase from. About a dozen are on near-permanent rotation, which leaves space for a wide rota of roasters from which I buy unique, specific or unusual lots. I frequently buy coffee online. Many roasters offer free shipment if you purchase two or three bags. All too frequently I buy two coffees that play to the roaster's strengths and then throw in a wildcard coffee, just to see what happens. A positive take is that I have tried very many wild, wacky and peculiar coffees. Some of these were interesting, but few were pleasant. In general, it's better to stick to the roaster's comparative strengths.

Many coffee shops have an ever-changing edit of coffees from a range of roasters, and retail them at reasonable prices. However, few baristas have the necessary understanding of coffee's tastes and flavours to help you pick a coffee that you might enjoy. While many baristas are proficient at making coffee and have drunk an extraordinary number of coffees, few have well-developed tasting skills. Some struggle to distinguish sour from bitter, and most are unaware of the distinctions between aroma, taste and flavour. This can make buying beans from a shop quite tricky.

It is my dream that all coffee drinkers will one day be able to walk into their local coffee shop and have an accurate and meaningful conversation with the barista about the range of coffees available. In fact, this is why I started work on this coffee-tasting framework.

The ultimate expression of this would be a barista who can recommend a coffee that you might enjoy at breakfast or to complement, say, a cheesecake. They would be the barista performing the function of a sommelier. But while we wait for this day to come, let's explore how to pair coffee with food so you can pop into your local coffee shop and impress your barista with your coffee-tasting knowledge.

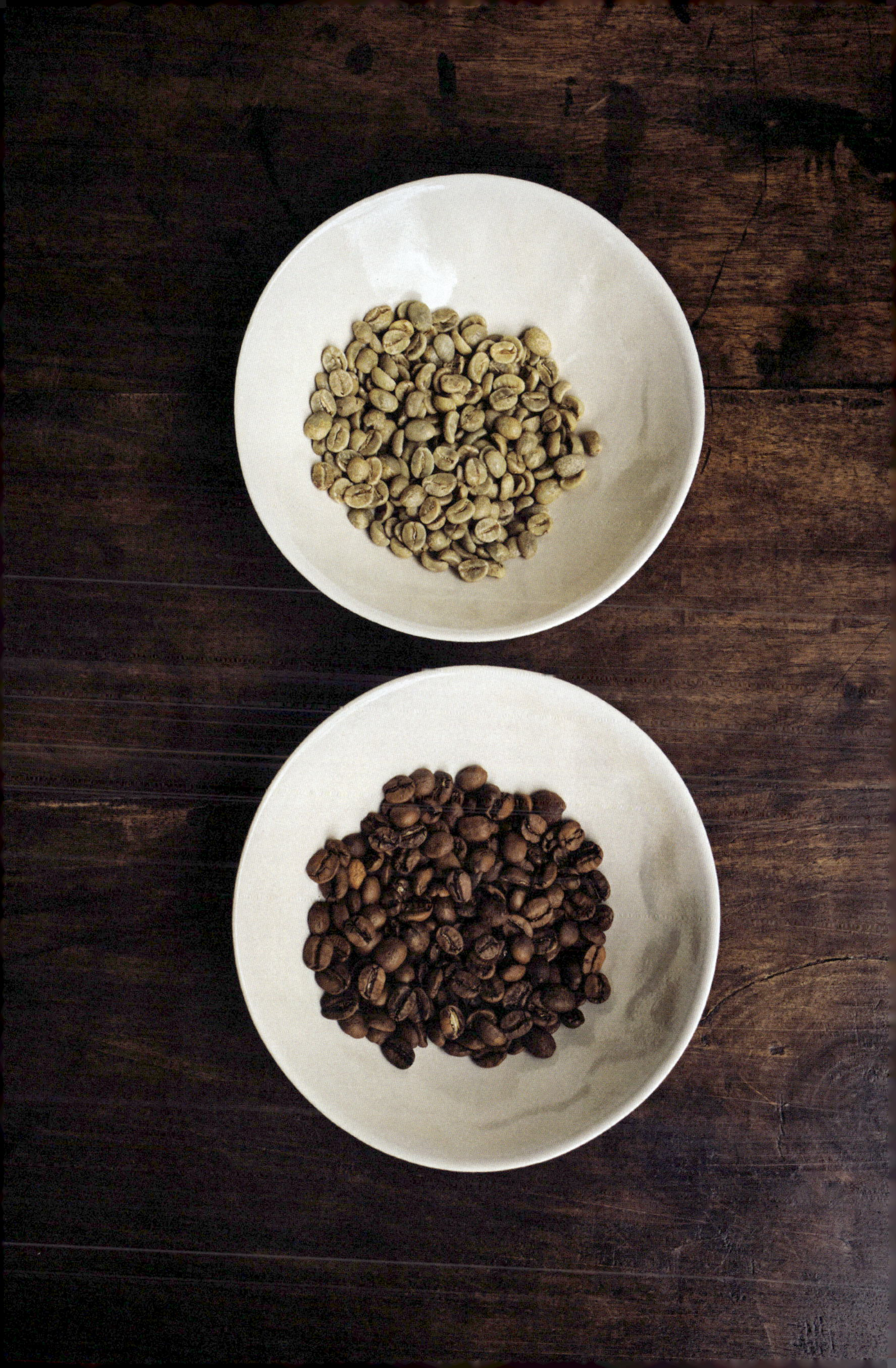

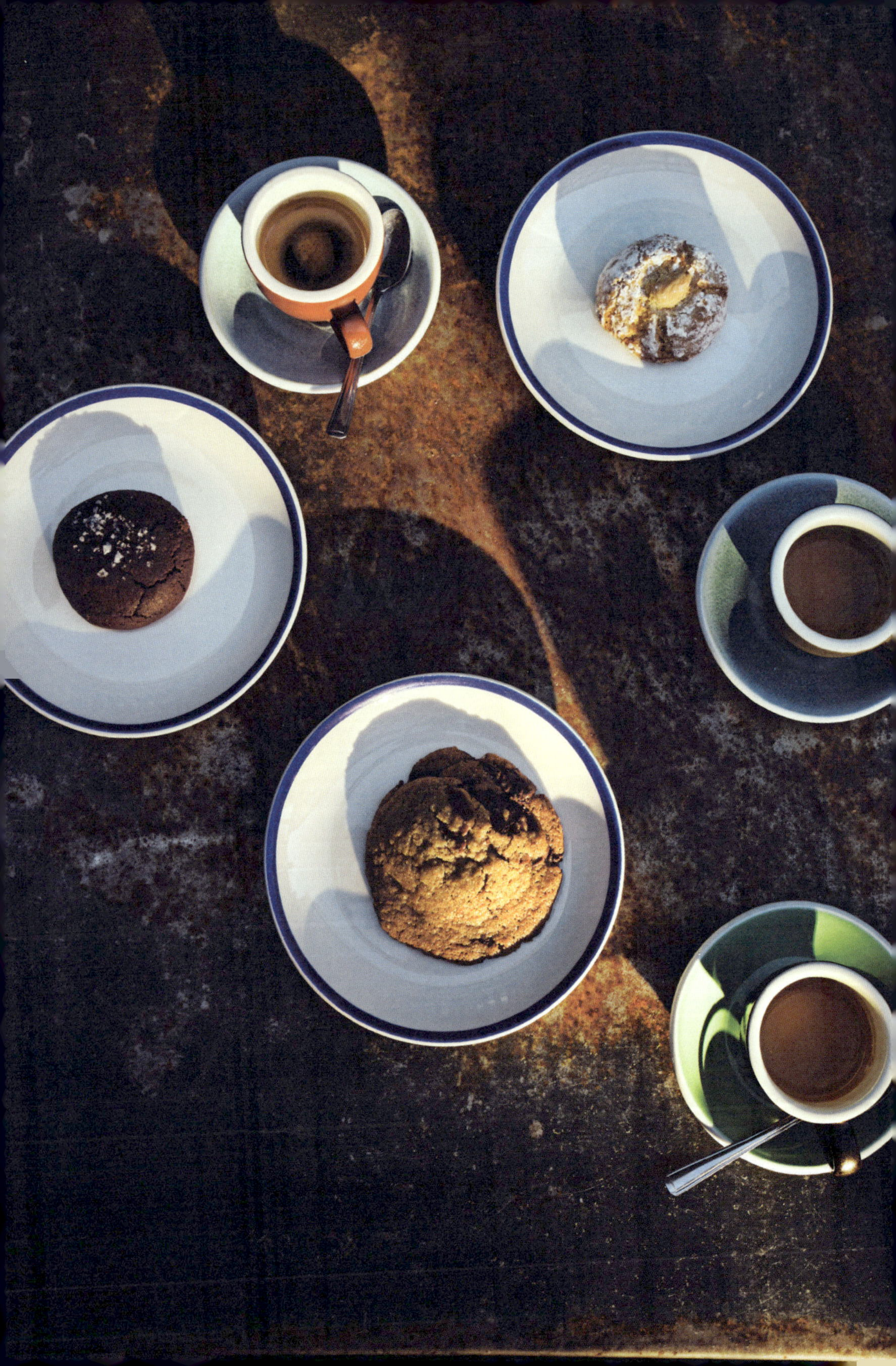

Magical Moments

MAGIC MOMENTS CREATED

Sometimes serendipity plays her hand and you find yourself enjoying a coffee that matches the food, conversation and location. In these moments, everything feels perfect.

There are two routes to creating a special coffee-drinking moment. The first is to leave it to luck. The other is to create this moment for someone else – and share it with them. This is the essence of hospitality and the never-ending work of a good barista. It's why I think Kaldi brought coffee cherries to share with his family and friends. Youthful shirking aside, he was fundamentally a generous character.

ORCHESTRATING AN EXPERIENCE

The tricky thing about constructing 'magical moments' is that they are ephemeral. There is no set formula; everything depends on everything else, including the fickleness of people.

First, don't give people what they think they want; rather, give them things you know they will appreciate. I seldom give guests choices; instead, I plan ahead to prepare food and drink pairings I think they will appreciate. I believe this approach to be fundamentally more generous, and it often leads to a much better time.

You can help them transition into a new frame of mind

Second, set the context and pacing so they are on your terms. You can guess their mood and needs on arrival, plus you can help them transition into a new frame of mind, if necessary. You are under no obligation to meet them where they are at. In fact, you will probably have a much better time if you encourage them to adopt your plan. Most people will be willing to do this if they feel safe. So, to do this well, you have to anticipate their needs, which requires both a generous spirit and planning.

Third, keep your workings and the structure concealed. The purpose of entertaining is to converse, gossip, entertain and be entertained. These are the top priorities. Everything else, including your effort, your planning, your work, the coffee and the pairings, is of secondary import. As a general rule, never volunteer this information and provide only a high-level answer to a question. You never want your guest to know, or even guess, the extent of your consideration, planning and preparation.

If you can achieve these three things, you can make your guests feel seen, cared for and nurtured.

ANTICIPATING YOUR GUESTS' NEEDS

Aim to anticipate your guests' needs, even before they have identified or maybe even understood them. If you can anticipate their next step, you can gently invite them to do the very thing they want to do.

For example, on arrival and after the initial greeting, tell your guests you need a couple of minutes to finish preparing things and invite them to freshen up while you do so. Five minutes later, you can be sitting down, with coffee, maybe with cake, comfortable and relaxed. This is a much better context in which to start a conversation. Plus, they are now on your timeline. In about 60–90 minutes, there's going to be a natural break as they excuse themselves for a bathroom break. You can now control the speed with which you serve and the number of items you serve, and you can predict the ebb and flow of the conversation.

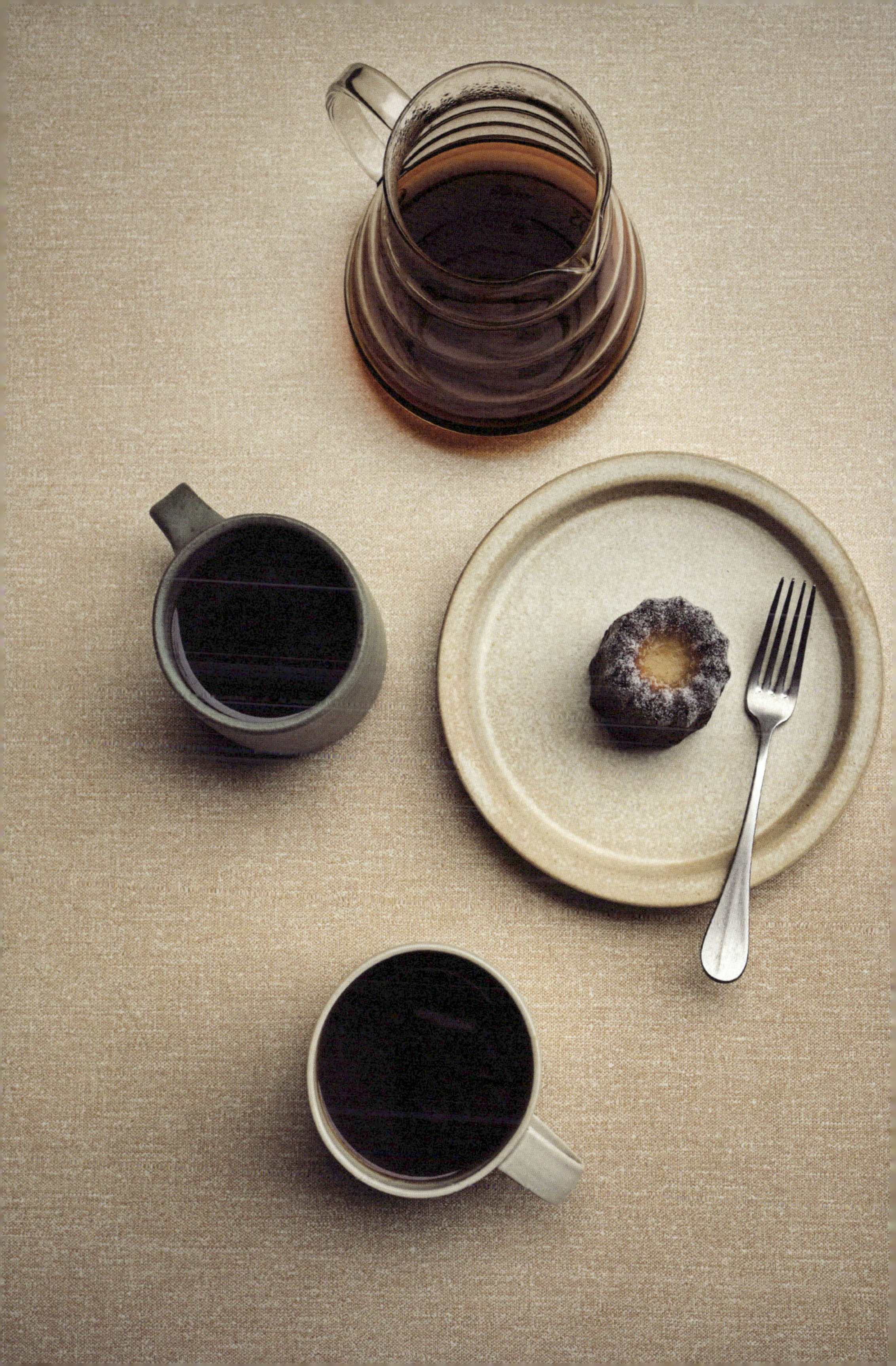

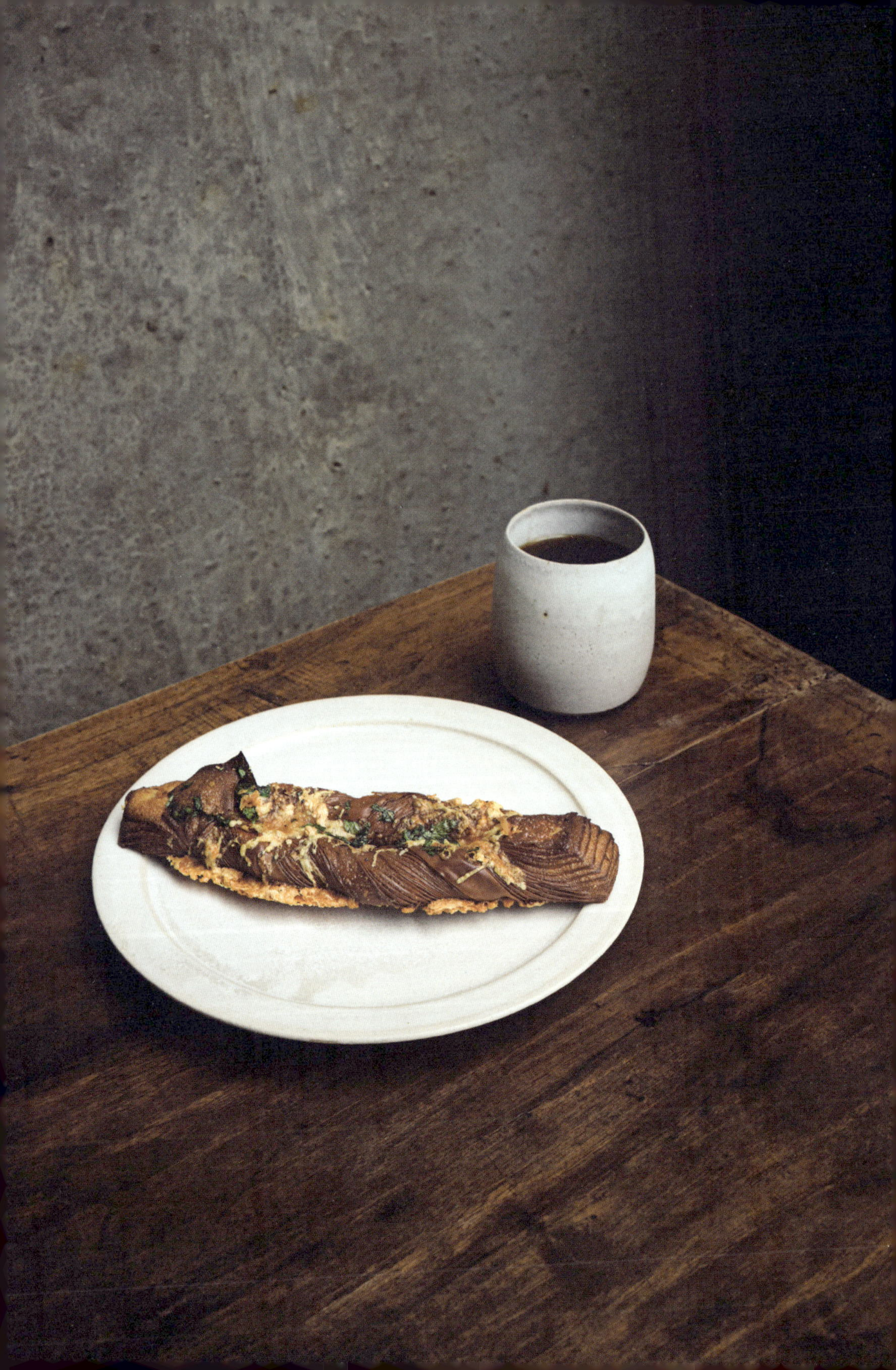

PAIRINGS

When planning a coffee–food pairing I often think about the context, including what's in season, the time of day, the duration of our catch-up and my guests' preferences and dietary requirements.

For example, I have a friend who delights in Clarity coffees, so I might settle on an Ethiopian Yirgacheffe that is natural processed so it's a little fruitier alongside the archetypical jasmine, bergamot aromas and tea-like astringency. I've picked this example as it can be quite tricky to pair floral coffees. They don't complement chocolate, the body and flavours are too light to stand up to dense baking such as a cake, yet the sourness and bitterness of the coffee would ideally be balanced with sweetness.

There are two pairing routes I foresee. Option A is to go for a dry sweet biscuit, such as shortbread, which is a traditional Scottish biscuit made from one part white sugar, two parts butter and three parts plain flour. For this pairing, I would definitely want a bake sprinkled with a little sugar. The objective of the pairing is to create a balance of tastes and textures between the items, so you want to take a sip of coffee and then a small bite of shortbread. The acid in the coffee will cause one's mouth to salivate, which will be counterbalanced by the dry crumb of the shortbread; the sugar will help balance the sourness and bitterness. Shortbread is quite bland, which allows the coffee's delicate flavours to shine through. You can take things a step further and add a little lemon zest to the shortbread to match the coffee's acidity.

Never explain the strategy to your guest: good pairings should work without explanation.

An alternative, and more adventurous, pairing would be a Parmesan cheese twist. This pairing also uses dryness to sit alongside the coffee's acidity, but this time the balance of tastes is created with the introduction of umami and salt, which reduce the perception of bitterness and enhance flavour.

The pairing of coffee and biscuits is nice and contained; it would be ideal for an afternoon tea. But with Parmesan cheese twists I have the option of seamlessly slipping from coffee to cocktails. We could transition straight from coffee to a lemon-garnished martini, a dirty martini or even a classic negroni.

Finally, it would be possible to merge these options. Parmesan shortbread tastes surprisingly good and is a delicious complement to some coffees. With an understanding of sour, bitter, sweet, umami and salty, you can appreciate why the combination is lip-smacking.

FOOD-FIRST PAIRINGS

It's often better to build a pairing by first considering the food. Let's take the example of a friend who likes dark, rich chocolate cake. The cake will taste predominantly sweet, especially with chocolate icing, so a pairing needs to introduce acid and bitterness. Moist cake can be heavy and sticky in the mouth, so the coffee also has to either cut though the crumb or be sufficiently heavy to compete with it.

Let's start with what I would avoid. Chocolate and lemon can be a weird combination, despite the balance of bitterness and sourness, because we intuit that citrus acidity can curdle milk. Citrus flavours in coffee work better with chocolate that has cocoa solids. So in this instance it's usually better to avoid predominantly tangy coffees, especially those with lemon or lime flavours. Chocolate often pairs better with berries, drupes and nuts.

If your friend enjoys Clarity coffee, you can consider a fruity coffee with bold flavours such as dried fruits, blackcurrants, cherries, nectarine or pear. You typically find these flavour in some Central American coffees as well as some from Colombia. Blackcurrant is a key tasting note for some coffees from Kenya, but they are probably going to be too light and too acidic for this purpose.

If they prefer Classic or Comfort coffees, you'll need to construct the balance of tastes in a different way. There are numerous possibilities, but my approach would be to identify a coffee with either a bold nutty or spicy flavour. The mouthfeel will need to be sufficiently heavy to compete with the cake. As the cake is sweet, the coffee could be predominantly bitter, though it could have a little sweetness. These types of coffees typically have low levels of sourness. So, to create a harmonious balance of tastes, serve your chocolate cake topped with raspberries or strawberries to add a sour edge. You could choose other fruit options, but make sure that the fruit is easy to eat and not too wet and pairs with both chocolate and coffee. Diced pear could be another option, especially if poached in sugar syrup and a spice such as cinnamon or clove.

The coffee also has to either cut though the crumb or be sufficiently heavy to compete with it

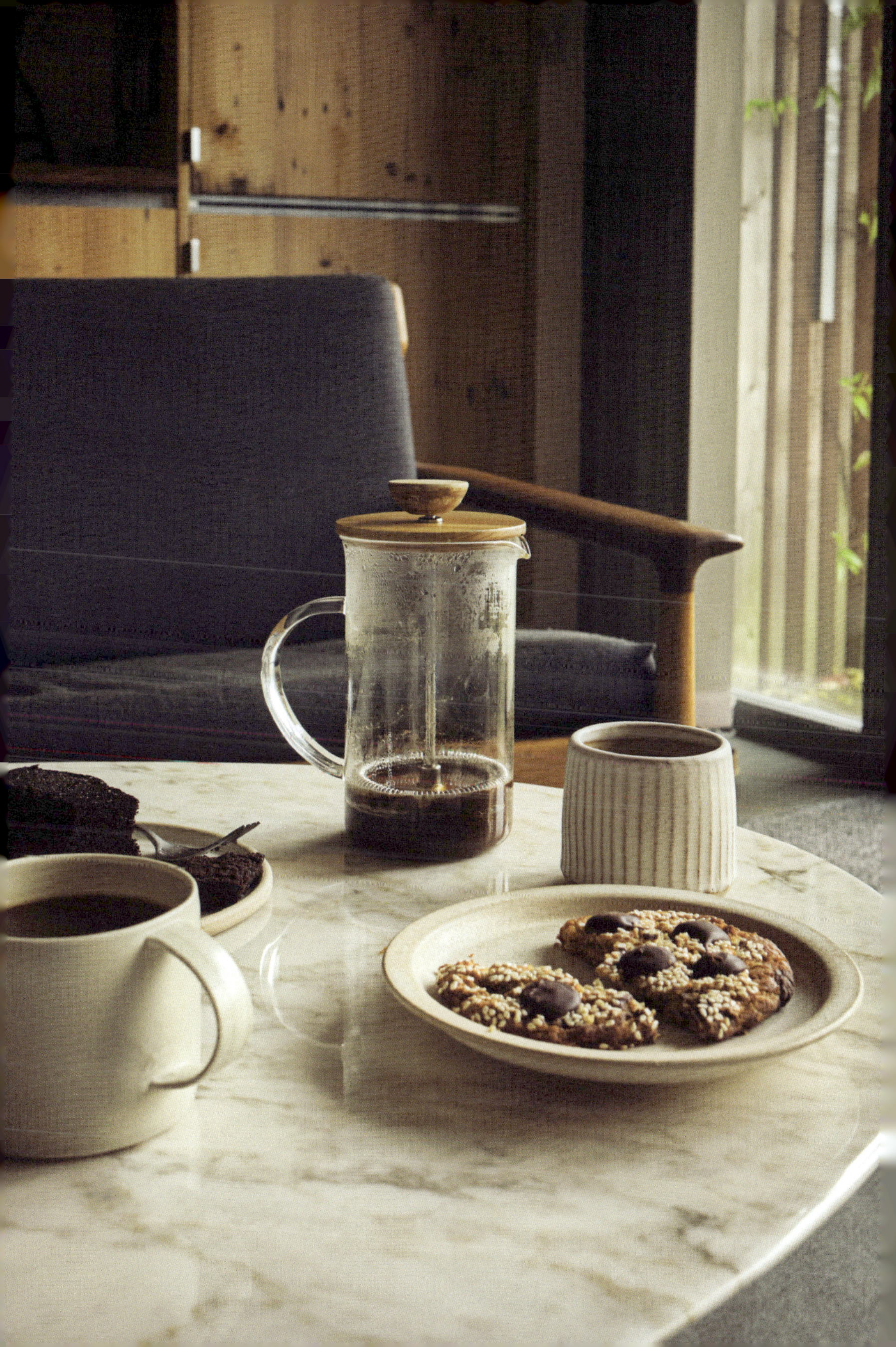

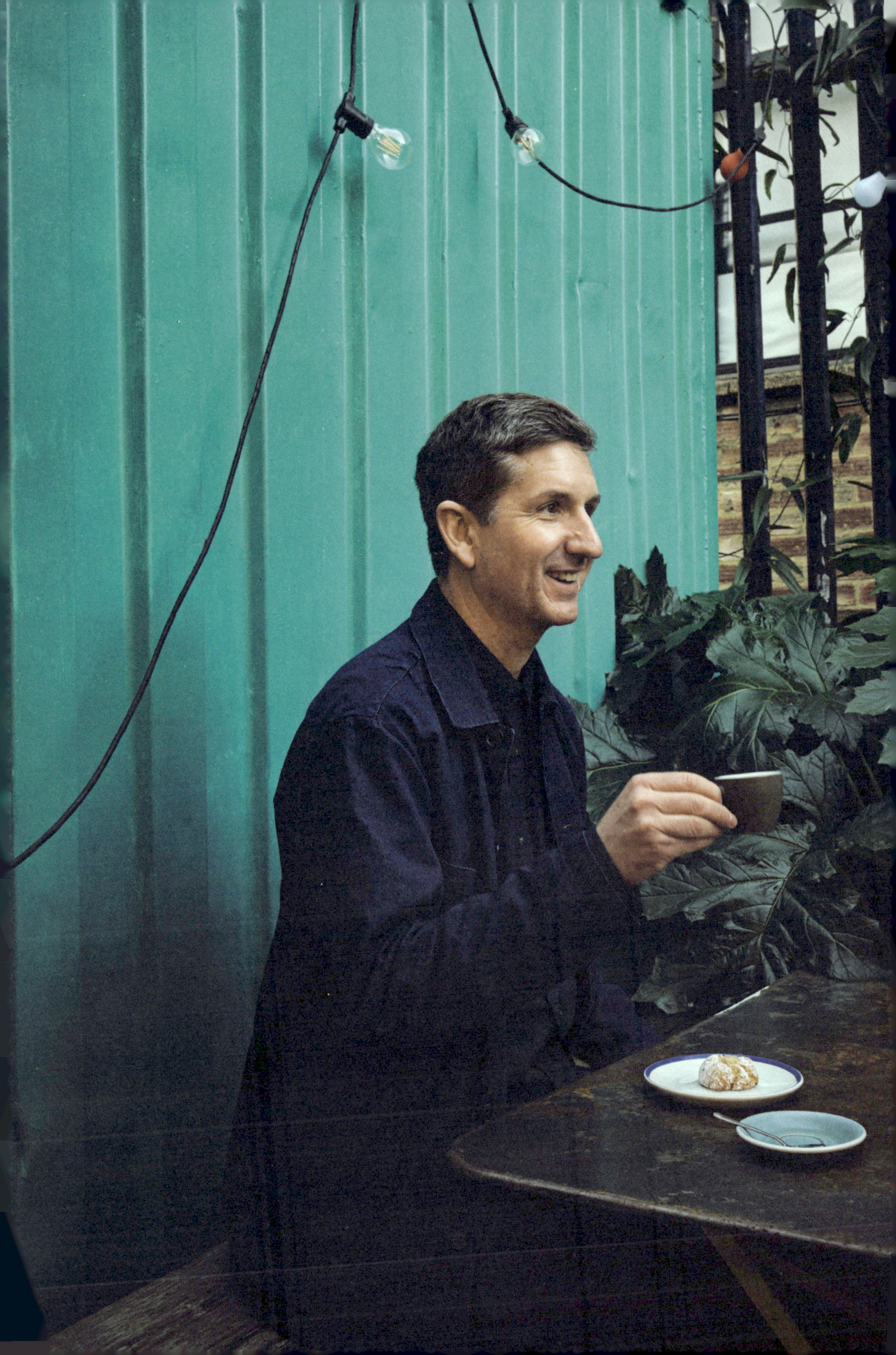

My personal take is that a good pairing should speak for itself

CURIOUS COFFEES

The most intriguing pairing possibilities exist with Curious coffees. Their lack of balance can make them a useful counterweight, but the lack of alignment requires close attention to flavours. The challenge is to create a balance of tastes across the pairing and simultaneously enhance the pairing's alignment.

Many Curious coffees have pronounced acidity, but not all have aligned flavours despite their complexity. A tangy sour coffee with some bitterness that has stone fruit and vegetal flavours can be quite challenging to drink by itself. But when paired with an item, let's say a citrus tart, that meets the intensity of the acid, and benefits from a little bitterness, the results can be lip-smackingly tasty. To create balance, the guest will eat a little tart and then drink a little coffee. They will happily bounce back and forth enjoying the combination, but few people will appreciate why.

CONVERSATION FIRST, COFFEE SECOND

Not all will appreciate such precise pairings, so it's essential to keep your guest's default preferences front of mind when planning and not let your own preferences dominate. Nor should you let your desire for recognition for your excellent pairings get in the way of the conversation.

Coffee geeks often struggle with this. Having sourced and brewed a specific coffee, they want to tell you all about it. My personal take is that a good pairing should speak for itself. A useful rule that baristas have followed is only to comment on the coffee if your guest enquires about it.

BALANCE

Exquisite, perfectly balanced coffees are best avoided at times like these. While making for delicious drinking, almost anything you serve with these coffees is likely to undermine the harmonious balance of tastes.

I largely reserve coffees with perfect balance for drinking on their own. They are ideal for an afternoon cup or a 15-minute catch-up with a colleague. But I seldom select these coffees for consumption at breakfast or as a complement to afternoon tea, which are the two key times in the day when I drink coffee.

As coffee production techniques have advanced to create coffees that are better tasting and more complex, some traditional pairings are unravelling. For example, the classic pairing of coffee and croissants tastes less good with high-quality, flavoursome coffees. Clarity or Curious coffees paired with croissants can be outright weird and unpleasant. The sweet-and-salty pastry demands a bitter counterweight. Similarly, you need to ensure that a coffee has sufficient body to pair well with the iconic TV pairings of crispy bacon, pancakes or cherry pie.

New pairings are being created all the time. It's possible to amplify the acidic with combinations such as yuzu curds or rhubarb compote. A light, acidic coffee can be a delicious complement to the salinity and fat of smoked salmon and dill at breakfast. Or, it's possible to reinterpret the Ethiopian fireside classic and serve vibrant, floral, sour coffees with salty, buttery popcorn.

Other classics parings endure or can be updated. When looking to create a pairing, you can safely rely on options such as almonds, hazelnuts and walnuts; fruits such as blackcurrants, apricots, oranges and avocado; spices such as a cinnamon and cardamom; and floral scents like rose or vanilla. As long as you create a balance of tastes across the pairing, you're taking a solid first step to a magical moment.

TIM'S TASTING TIP

When in need of a quick but special pairing, macarons are my go-to option. Made from egg whites, sugar and almond meal, their texture and sweetness complement coffee, whether black or white, filter or espresso. They are readily available in a range of flavours, and filled with ganache, buttercream or jam. It's quick and easy to match them to Classic, Comfort, Clarity or even Curious coffees. I select two small complementary-flavoured macarons per person, if possible, but one larger macaron per person works almost as well.

THE WONDERFUL EVERYDAY

Your life, like mine, is probably too time-pressured to regularly bake biscuits and source coffee for long, leisurely, aimless conversations with friends. In practice, magic moments have to be squeezed into my routine, which is a filter coffee at breakfast and either a filter or espresso-based coffee after lunch.

I keep at least two different coffees at home and in the office. One is of a Comfort profile, and the other is typically Clarity or sometimes Curious. I default to the Comfort coffee at breakfast, but regularly pick the other as my mood or the pairing dictates. Having two coffees available is practical and cost-effective. You can then choose the coffee in the moment, plus you have options should you suddenly need to entertain. A good Comfort coffee pairs well with a standard breakfast of scrambled eggs, avocado on toast, or cereal.

I seldom drink coffee with lunch but afterwards I will brew a cup or prepare a macchiato. Most days, I'll make time to read or listen to a podcast; on a bad day I find myself back at my desk. I have never had a magical moment sitting at my computer. My recommendation is that you only drink coffee with a device when needs must; otherwise choose to take 10 minutes for yourself or to share with other people.

Alongside my coffee, I regularly have a plain biscuit with chocolate icing, but equally pear, nectarine

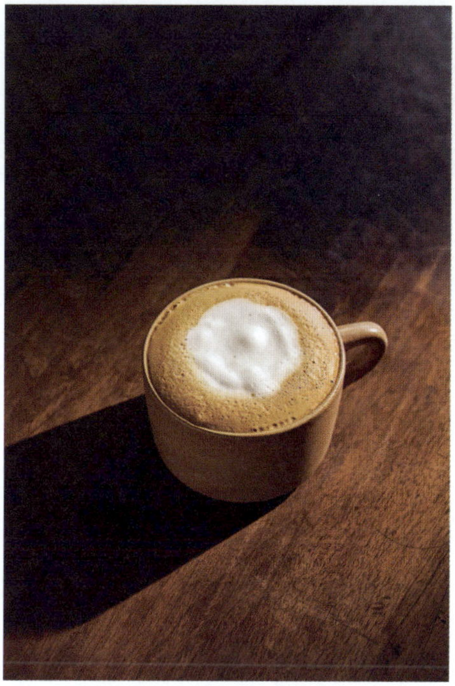

and peach are delicious coffee complements that I never grow tired of. I mix and match based on my mood, the weather, what's in season and the flavours in the coffee. In summer, a couple of strawberries, a chocolate biscuit and a cup of coffee are my idea of a mini magical moment. In the winter, pears, walnuts and coffee are also wonderful.

These are not so much recommendations as an insight into my preferences. There are an almost limitless number of possibilities, and you'll be able to identify pairings and moments that match your preferences, routine, diet and what's available in your supermarket. This only rule is to respect the importance of a harmonious balance of taste.

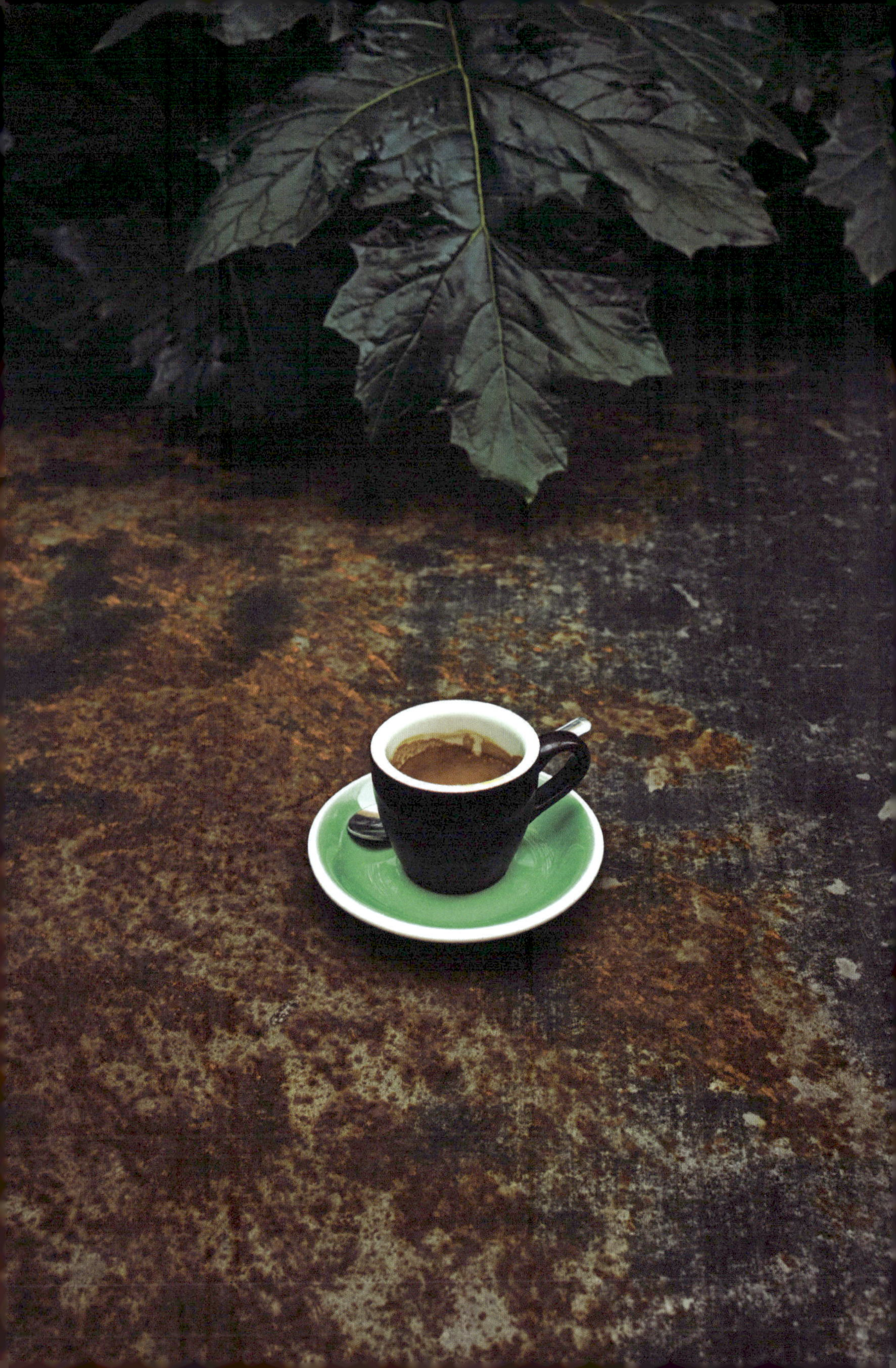

The Joy of Drinking Coffee

THE BEST COFFEE IS THE ONE THAT YOU LIKE

You probably have friends that enjoy visiting their favourite coffee shop, but have little interest in understanding why they like it. Coffee has, for hundreds of years, offered the benefits of mental acuity, prolonging energy and the fission of excitement that comes with casual social interaction. These aspects of coffee drinking have been integral to coffee becoming the world's favourite beverage.

But, if you have made it this far, you probably also have an appreciation of coffee's complexity and the curiosity to wonder why you like particular coffees. I believe that an understanding of coffee's aromas, mouthfeel, tastes and flavours only adds to the joy of drinking coffee.

It has always intrigued me that coffee tasting requires an interconnected set of skills. It greatly helps to have a basic knowledge of human physiology and an insight into how our brains process the various signals. It's also useful to have an understanding of coffee production, the supply chain and brewing techniques. Additionally, it's necessary to know common terms so that we can communicate what we are tasting and appreciate others' experiences. Then, and only then, do we have a chance to impartially assess each cup.

The coffee industry has rapidly developed in recent decades. It was in 1974 that the term 'specialty coffee' was coined to denote the emergence of small lots of coffees that reflected their terroir. Just over 50 years later, it's hard to think of a beverage trend that has been more enduring or impactful. This approach to coffee drinking has transformed the coffee landscape for producers, business and consumers. I think the world is a better place because of the existence of these smaller, tastier lots. But there are challenges ahead.

One of the most pressing is climate change. Over the coming 50 years coffee production will have to develop rapidly if it is to remain viable in a warmer, wetter and more changeable environment. There are changes under way and mitigations being implemented. Key coffee-growing regions will shift as plantations open at higher, cooler altitudes. New varieties are being bred to cope with higher temperatures, drought and disease. Old naturally evolved varieties are being tracked down for use in cropping and breeding programmes. Farmers are already prioritizing mixed planting and, if they have the land, reforestation to cool their local climate. Plus, they are experimenting with different varieties and innovative processing techniques to protect their revenues and to enable their farms to survive for future generations.

Consumers' preferences will also continue to change. There is a generational swing from simple black coffee to elaborate signature drinks, and back again. Every new intake of coffee drinkers redefines the desirability of various coffee serves as a socially acceptable way to rebel against their elders.

Despite all these forthcoming changes, I want to propose that at least three things will remain the foundations of coffee tasting. First, the hardware with which you and I taste – our nose, palate, olfactory nerves and brain – will continue to evolve much more slowly than the world around us. The basics of how we perceive and process aroma, mouthfeel, taste and flavour will remain unchanged for generations to come. Second, our deeply held preferences for sweet brews with a pleasant mouthfeel will continue to be the main gateway through which people start drinking coffee. Previously, salt and sugar made bitter brews agreeable, then it was the development of sweet, signature beverages and, more recently, it has been enhancements in coffee production that reduce bitterness.

Within each new generation of coffee drinkers, a proportion never move past the serve that initially got them drinking coffee. However, a significant number do. People like you and I will continue to want to understand why some coffees are tastier than others and how coffee production methods shape characteristics, especially as coffee these methods continue to advance and adapt.

And third, coffee will continue to be a social drink. While technological advancement will enable consumers to make café-like quality at home, people will continue to congregate, like the villagers in the Kaldi fable, in coffee shops and cafés. These establishments are likely to continue to be some of the best places to drink coffee thanks to their expertise, equipment and economies of scale – as well as their hospitality and atmosphere.

There will likely be changes to coffee tasting, too. The scientific understanding of how we taste and perceive aromas will continue to develop. In my lifetime umami has moved from being perceived as a marketing gimmick manufactured to promote MSG to being part of the tasting lexicon. It has now ascended

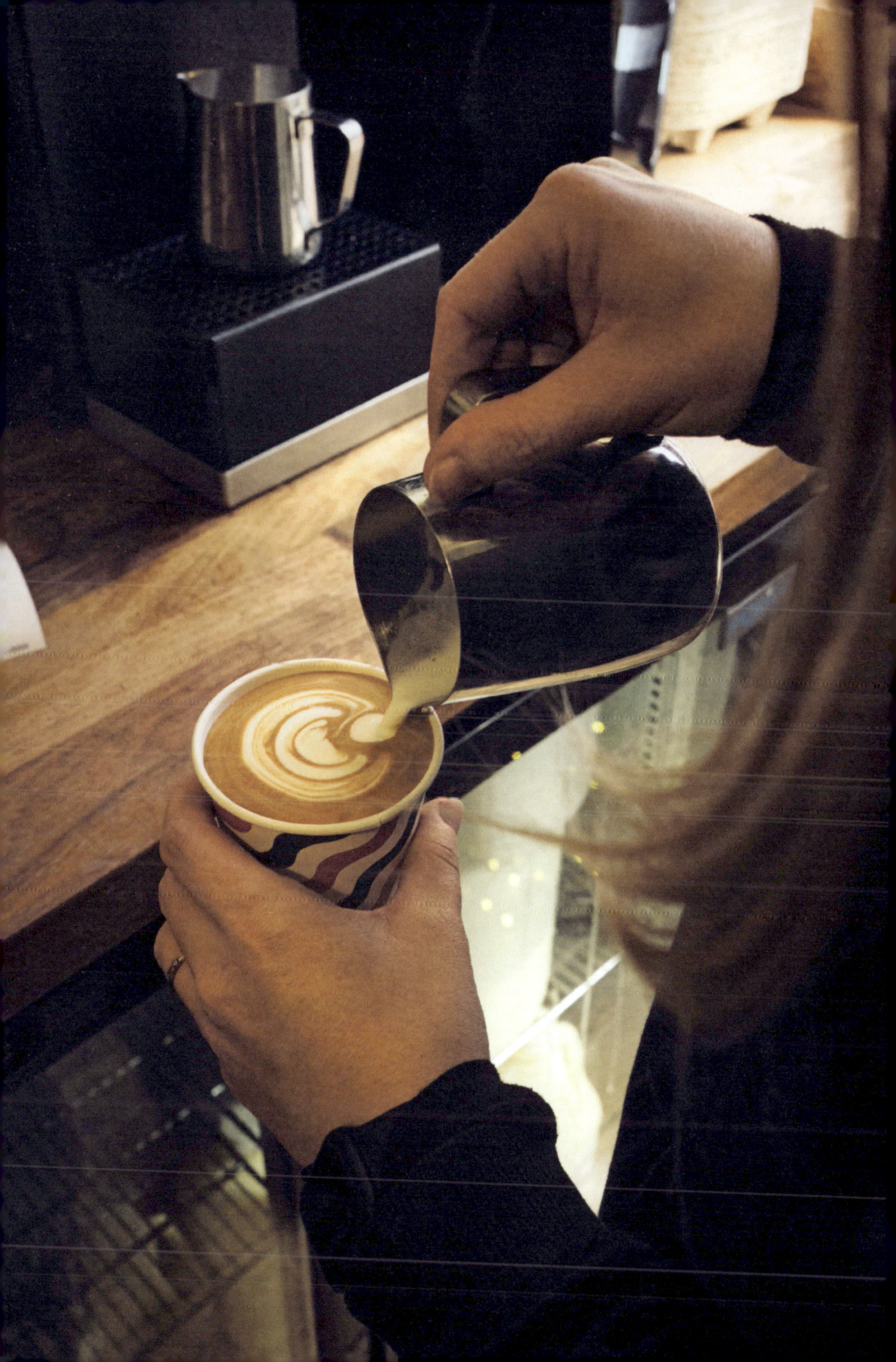

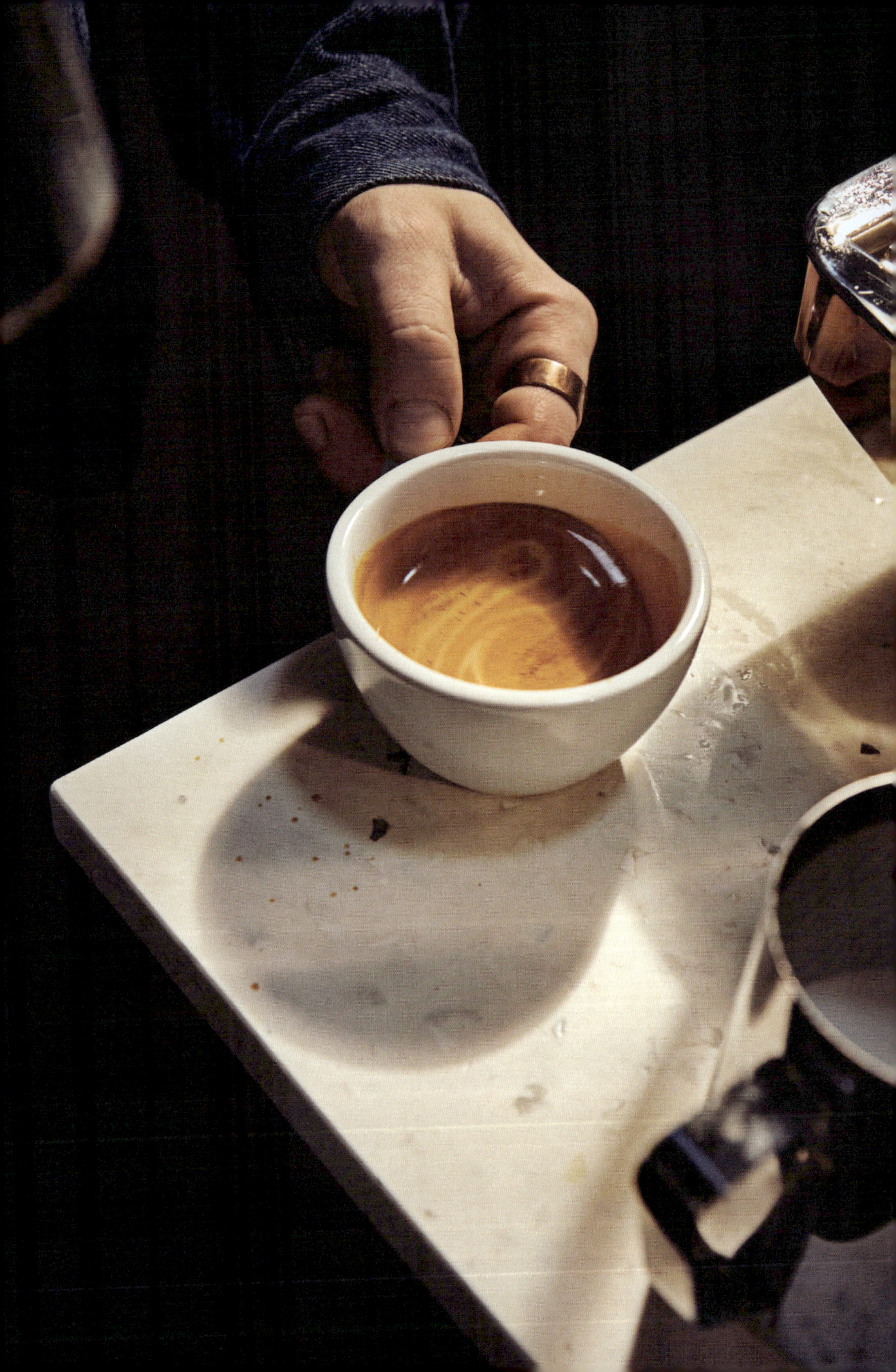

to the highest status possible, considered one of the primary tastes. The tipping point was the scientific consensus that humans distinctly detect umami on their tongue. There are other taste contenders, and it would be foolish to rule out further developments in our understanding. Coffee tasters may one day need to consider the balance of six, seven or even eight primary tastes.

Changes in coffee production will lead to new aromas and flavours in coffee. And changes in consumer preferences always shape the commercial opportunities for coffee farmers and producers. It's notable that new fermentation methods can add notes that previously tasters might have deemed to be faults. I think that this is exciting. Instead of there being a narrowly prescribed definition of quality, farmers and producers can be at liberty to create coffees they believe possible to sell for a profit.

These changes mean that this coffee-tasting method needs to continue to evolve and adapt, especially as the science of tasting continues to advance. But can I be so bold to suggest that there is a fourth aspect that is unlikely to change any time soon, despite all these challenges and changes. Since the day Kaldi first ate those cherries right up to the present, people have enjoyed coffees that balance sweetness, sourness and bitterness.

Intuitively, the villagers of the Ethiopian Highlands, the Yemeni merchants and Ottoman warriors, the English bankers and the Austrian socialites, all used salt and sugar to enhance the mouthfeel and create balance. The baristas of today are engaged with the same timeless endeavour. Weighing doses, timing shots and measuring TDS are all methods to create a harmonious balance of taste.

I hope that you feel that understanding coffee's aromas, tastes and flavours helps you to navigate the extraordinary range of coffees available and that it enables you to appreciate your personal preferences in a broader context. This knowledge empowers us to move past the tautology that the best coffee is the one that you like. Now you can appreciate why.

And here lies the mystic's greatest contribution to coffee tasting. A deeper understanding of coffee is also an examination of ourselves and the experiences that have shaped us. Drinking, tasting and enjoying coffee will continue to capture our imaginations for generations to come because it as much a discovery of ourselves as it is a journey into the world around us.

Index

PICTURE CREDITS

Photography by Laura Edwards (except Framalicious/Shutterstock 10; Bridgeman Images 12; © Daye Bensa Coffee 2023 130, 163, 164, 188–9; Daterra 134, 141, 149, 150, 155; Coffee Legends 139; Manuel Barrantes 156, 159; Rama Aulia Saputra 160)

ACKNOWLEDGEMENTS

It takes many people to make a single cup of coffee and – as it turns out – even more to make a book about drinking coffee. This book, and the ideas within it, are much improved by the countless conversations I have had with farmers, brokers, roasters, baristas, customers and other beverage professionals, only a few of whom are mentioned in the text. Many of the better ideas are also shamelessly borrowed from wine and whisky tasters and applied to coffee. Across beverages, tasters share a generosity of spirit, a common language and a curiosity about what makes some things taste better than others.

Specific thanks to Anna Ridley, who both encouraged me to write this book and guided me through the process. Making a book is far more involved than I had previously appreciated. Much credit is due for the work of Alison Starling, Jeannie Stanley, Ben Gardiner, and others at Octopus, who both grasped my vision and then toiled to realize it. Several individuals stand out for their contributions to my understanding of food and drink tasting, including Jim Gore, Joel Harrison, Laura Brousset, John Farrand, Daniel Primack, Frederic Grappe, Nate Brown, Billy Abbott, Ian Millar, Brian Kinsman and Neil Edwards.

My coffee knowledge has been shaped by many people over the years. I am especially grateful for the specific contributions and feedback on draft text from Flori Marin, Guy Bosley, Dale Harris, Mike Nunn, Alec Oyhenart as well as Nicole Ferris, Danny Davies, Jamie Treby, Natasha Yeo and Alexandra Dalton. Throughout my work and writing, I have frequently drawn on the research and writings of Professor Richard Stevenson, although I have not had the opportunity to meet him. Laura Edwards took the images and managed to set me at ease. Thank you. We were kindly hosted by Nola, Victoria Arduino, and Climpson & Sons for locations, as well as a number of other venues. Thank you for your hospitality and patience. I am going to single out Ephraim Jacobsen for buying me that coffee early one morning whilst we were travelling. That moment quite possibly changed my life.

Drinking coffee is the final step in a supply chain that begins at the farm. Coffee farmers are both the foundation and the future of the industry. Their contribution is less visible than the roastery and consumer brands that adorn coffee packaging, despite involving greater work and risk. My hope is that, by educating coffee drinkers about the fundamentals of tasting, consumers will be better equipped to select coffees they enjoy, and that farmers will receive greater recognition and financial return. A handful of farmers and producers are mentioned in this book; many more deserve our continuing gratitude.

Finishing writing this book coincides with the closing of a chapter in my life. My deepest thanks to my parents, who have always supported my various endeavours, whether or not they fully understood them. It is especially timely to make special mention of Meryl, my mother, who not only gave me my first sip of coffee but has long encouraged me to be a better writer. She has proofread a countless number of my essays and articles and, even now, has been raising queries and submitting last minute corrections. I will greatly miss drinking coffee with her.

ABOUT THE AUTHOR

Tim Ridley is a London-based coffee professional and the founder of United Baristas, a global network of over 10,000 baristas. He previously founded one of London's first quality-focused coffee chains, helping introduce flat whites and cold brew to a wider audience. The ideas behind *The Coffee Tasting Handbook* were germinated during this period, as he worked to align coffee selection with customer taste preferences. He is the owner of Ensemble, a coffee shop in King's Cross.

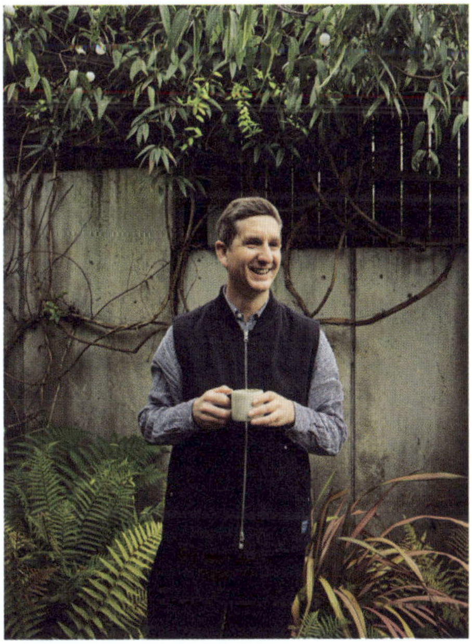

First published in Great Britain in 2026
by Mitchell Beazley, an imprint of
Octopus Publishing Group Ltd
Carmelite House
50 Victoria Embankment
London EC4Y 0DZ
www.octopusbooks.co.uk

An Hachette UK Company
www.hachette.co.uk

The authorized representative in the EEA is Hachette Ireland, 8 Castlecourt Centre, Dublin 15, D15 XTP3, Ireland (email: info@hbgi.ie)

Distributed in the US by Hachette Book Group
1290 Avenue of the Americas, 4th and 5th Floors, New York, NY 10104

Distributed in Canada by Canadian Manda Group, 664 Annette St., Toronto, Ontario, Canada M6S 2C8

ISBN: 978-1-84601-688-2
eISBN: 978-1-84601-689-9

A CIP catalogue record for this book is available from the British Library.

Printed and bound in Malaysia.

10 9 8 7 6 5 4 3 2 1

Commissioning Editor: Jeannie Stanley
Art Director: Ben Gardiner
Senior Developmental Editor: Pauline Bache
Editor: Scarlet Furness
Copyeditor: Robert Anderson
Prop Stylist: Rachel Vere
Picture Research Manager: Jen Veall
Senior Production Manager: Peter Hunt

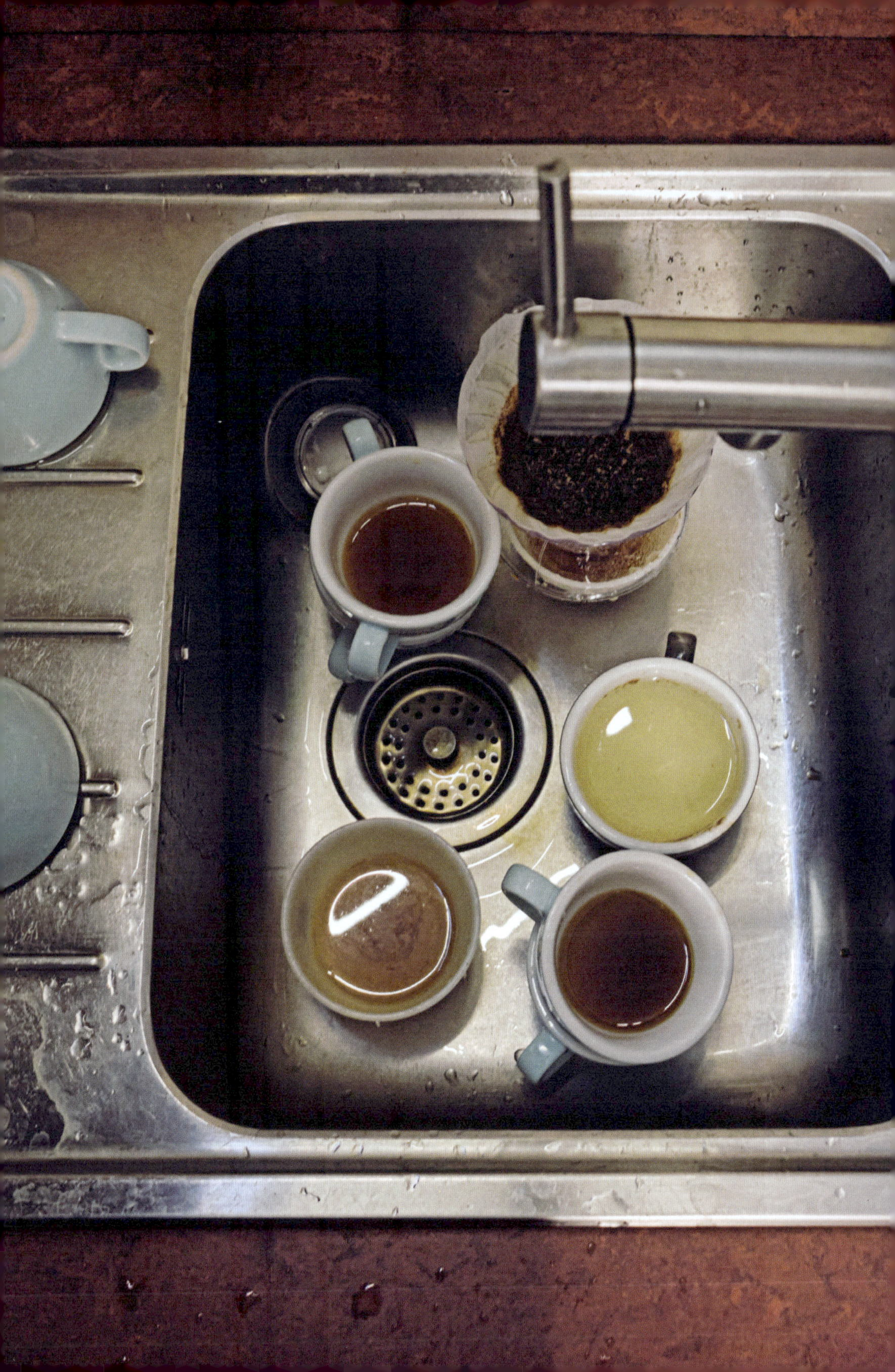